HOME NETWORKING
DEMYSTIFIED

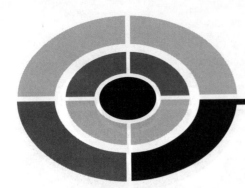

ABOUT THE AUTHOR

Dr. Larry Long set up a network in his home many years before the term "home network" was introduced into our lexicon. He wrote his first book on his first PC in 1978. The first edition of *Computers: Information Technology in Perspective*, which is now in its twelfth edition, was written with wife Nancy on their first home network in 1985. Two decades of home network upgrades and 50-plus books later, he is still writing computer books, which are widely distributed throughout the world.

Larry's goal is the same for every book: say something that will be of value to the reader and say it in an interesting, succinct, and easily understood manner. His words are crafted from many years of experience with personal computers, networks, and the people who use them.

Larry has served as a strategic-level consultant in over 100 organizations in the United States and abroad. He was a pioneer in the development of computer-based multimedia and Internet-based educational resources. He has over two decades of experience as a professor at the University of Oklahoma and Lehigh University. Larry's Ph.D. is in Industrial Engineering from the University of Oklahoma.

Larry lives in Arkansas with his wife, Nancy, and teenage sons, Troy and Brady, where they enjoy exploring the great outdoors. Larry plays tournament tennis, coaches the high school tennis team, and is an NCAA tennis umpire.

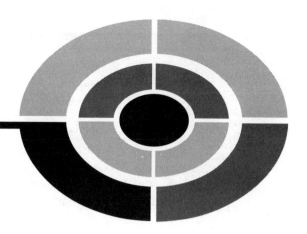

HOME NETWORKING DEMYSTIFIED

LARRY LONG

McGraw-Hill/Osborne

New York Chicago San Francisco
Lisbon London Madrid Mexico City
Milan New Delhi San Juan
Seoul Singapore Sydney Toronto

The *McGraw-Hill* Companies

McGraw-Hill/Osborne
2100 Powell Street, 10th Floor
Emeryville, California 94608
U.S.A.

To arrange bulk purchase discounts for sales promotions, premiums, or fund-raisers, please contact **McGraw-Hill/**Osborne at the above address. For information on translations or book distributors outside the U.S.A., please see the International Contact Information page immediately following the index of this book.

Home Networking Demystified

1234567890 FGR FGR 0198765

ISBN 0-07-225878-0

Acquisitions Editor
Wendy Rinaldi

Project Editor
Carolyn Welch

Acquisitions Coordinator
Alex McDonald

Technical Editor
Craig Zacker

Copy Editor
Bob Campbell

Proofreader
Susie Elkind

Indexer
Nancy Long

Composition
Apollo Publishing Services

Illustrators
Sue Albert, Melinda Lytle

Cover Series Design
Margaret Webster-Shapiro

Cover Illustration
Lance Lekander

This book was composed with Adobe InDesign.

To my wife Nancy—
partner, best friend, and the love of my life

CONTENTS AT A GLANCE

CONTENTS

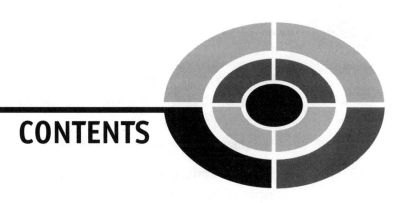

PART FOUR   PROTECTING AND OPERATING A HOME NETWORK

ACKNOWLEDGMENTS

I would like to thank my friends and colleagues at McGraw-Hill/Osborne for their significant contributions to *Home Networking Demystified*. Acquisitions editor Wendy Rinaldi committed herself and the considerable resources of McGraw-Hill/Osborne to this project. A quality editorial team, including acquisitions coordinator Alex McDonald and project editor Carolyn Welch, wove hundreds of threads into a meaningful tapestry on home networking. Technical editor and networking author Craig Zacker's creative insights are evident throughout the book. Copy editor Robert Campbell and proofreader Susie Elkind are the best in the business.

Special appreciation is in order for all the other nodes on our home network, the Longnet. My wife Nancy edits the draft manuscript and is always there with encouragement. My technically savvy teenage sons, Troy and Brady, stretch the limits of the Longnet, giving me loads of examples for the book.

PREFACE

The migration of PCs into the home was inevitable. And so it is with the home network. Home networking evolves in four phases. In Phase I you purchase the first PC for the home and, in Phase II, you add a second PC, and, possibly, a third. Phase III begins the moment you recognize you can make life a little easier and save a lot of time and money by sharing computing resources. During Phase III you build a home network so you can share files, printers, storage, and Internet access. In Phase IV the home network takes on a new perspective and you begin to see it as the tool that will transform your home into an electronic home. Since you're reading this book, chances are that you're already at Phase III and, possibly, Phase IV. This book prepares you for Phases III and IV and leads you through the steps to building a home network and to creating an e-home with a wealth of applications that can change the way you and your family live, work, and play.

If you're ready to move from stand-alone personal computing to home networking, hang on because it's quite a ride. Home networks enable incredibly helpful file and Internet access sharing, but they can do much more. The home network can spread digital home entertainment throughout the home. In an e-home, the family can view the photo album, videos, live TV, or recorded TV from any PC, any audio/video center, or the home theater. Music and radio can be piped to any PC or audio system, as well. Parents can work at home and enjoy the same level of connectivity that they would in the office. The home network creates a new cyberworld for gamers.

As the infrastructure for the e-home, the home network is dynamic and must be continually updated and upgraded to meet changing family needs and the requirements for innovative new applications. For example, the home network can also support a home security system, Internet telephone, video surveillance, an environmental control system, and a host of other applications.

Home networks are wonderfully flexible and can grow with your connectivity needs. The channels for communication in a home network can be wired or wireless. Having high-speed wireless capability means you can connect PCs, PDAs, and other wireless devices to the network from anywhere in and around your homes.

Fortunately, home networking technologies are affordable and increasingly user-friendly. A straightforward home network can be installed by anyone with a little technical savvy. However, the most successful home networks and those with the greatest potential are built and maintained by people who understand the options and have a clear vision of where they want to go with their network. The information in this book should give novices the confidence they need to create their first home network and give those people who already have a home network a new perspective on how they can leverage their networking investment to do much more.

People with a broad spectrum of personal computing/home networking expertise will use this book. The book flows so that the networking novice can read it from cover to cover, but it's written so the more advanced user can bounce around the book to home in on needed information. In either case, I recommend you begin with the "Step-by-Step Guide to Building a Home Network" in the Introduction to this book. The guide walks you through the entire book within the context of a 13-step approach to building and growing a home network.

Home Networking Demystified is divided into five parts and an appendix.

- *PART ONE—Home Networking: The Basics*. In this part, the home network is defined, its applications are summarized, and networking concepts are introduced.

- *PART TWO—Home Networking Technologies and Equipment*. This part describes the various strategies for wired and/or wireless connectivity and explains the functions and uses of the hardware needed for home networking.

- *PART THREE—Building a Home Network*. The focus of this part is the design and installation of a home network and the procedures for sharing computing resources.

- *PART FOUR—Protecting and Operating a Home Network*. This part presents the principles of network security and shows you how to maintain and troubleshoot your home network.

- *PART FIVE—The Internet, Entertainment, and Telework on a Home Network.* This part covers a wide range of applications for home networking, including those on the Internet, digital home entertainment, file backup, IP telephone, and the virtual private network for the teleworker.

- *Appendix: Home Networking Buyer's Guide.* The guidelines, considerations, and recommendations in this appendix can help you avoid purchasing pitfalls and get the network devices you need at the best price.

For a number of years my wife and I worked together at our home and communicated electronically with one another via walk net, passing floppies back and forth to each other. In the early 1980s we decided to install a network so we could enjoy the advantages of connectivity. It would be 15 years before we would hear the term *home network*, so we called it the *Longnet*. The Longnet still exists, but it has morphed many times to meet our family's ever-changing needs. Most recently we integrated the home theater and all phases of digital home entertainment into the network. The Longnet has enriched our lives in so many ways that it is now an integral part of our lives and what we do. I'm confident that your home network and the advantages of connectivity will have a similar impact on your family.

Larry Long, Ph.D.

INTRODUCTION

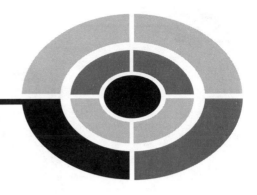

Step-by-Step Guide to Building a Home Network

Home networking has the potential to change homes and the way we live in ways we haven't seen since homes were outfitted with running water and electricity. This step-by-step guide provides an overview of this emerging technology and places the task of building a home network into sequential perspective. The guide includes cross-references to applicable subject matter in the book for each step.

STEP 1: Learn about Home Networking Concepts, Technologies, and Applications

With multi-PC homes now commonplace and an accelerated movement to digital convergence, the home network is emerging as a necessary component of the domestic infrastructure. The home network connects PCs for Internet connection, printer, and file sharing. Eventually, it will be the basis for connecting much of what we do and use around the house. Already, home networks are major players in digital home entertainment, home security, and Internet telephony. In the future, the home network will incorporate a wide variety of household systems, including environmental control systems.

Figure I-1   In Chapter 1, you trace home networking from its beginnings in the late 1990s to its potential today. It also answers the most frequently asked questions, including "What is a home network?" (any group of PCs or network devices linked via wired or wireless media in and around the home).

The first step in your home networking journey is to get a good grasp of home networking concepts, strategies, and technologies. The more you know about the principles of home networking, the easier it will be to build one, and then maintain and grow your network in the future. Most of your basic home networking questions are answered in these chapters.

- Chapter 1: "What Is a Home Network?" (see Figure I-1)
- Chapter 2: "Applications of Home Networking" (see Figure I-2)

Figure I-2   In Chapter 2, you learn that home networks enable sharing of Internet access, printers, files, and other resources. They also permit the integration of digital home entertainment with personal computing (shown here), including multiplayer gaming. The home network has emerged as the infrastructure for the e-home (electronic home) of the future.

- Chapter 3: "Network Concepts and Strategies" (see Figure I-3)
- Chapter 4: "Connectivity: Wired and Wireless" (see Figure I-4)
- Chapter 5: "Net Gear: Gateways, Modems, and More" (see Figure I-5)

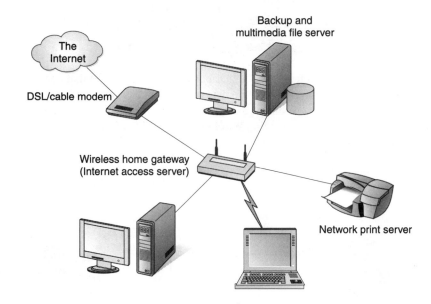

Figure I-3   In Chapter 3, you learn how home networks, which are local area networks (LANs), can be linked to wide area networks (WANs), such as the Internet. PCs in home networks are connected to a common hub called a home (or residential) gateway via a wired or wireless link.

Figure I-4   In Chapter 4, you learn about various transmission media that connect
network devices or nodes to form the home network. Home networks can be totally
wireless or wired, or they can be mixed-mode with a little of both. There are lots of
choices for each, the most popular being Wireless-G at 54 Mbps (shown here) and Fast
Ethernet at 100 Mbps.

Wireless CardBus
network adapter for
a notebook PC

Wireless home gateway

Ethernet PCI network
adapter for a desktop PC

Figure I-5   In Chapter 5, you learn about the hardware that enables connectivity between
PCs and other devices in a home network. A central hub, the home gateway, and the
internal or external network adapters work together to permit wired and/or wireless links
between PCs and network devices. The home gateway is a multifunction device that can
serve as a router to bridge the home network to the Internet, a wireless access point (AP),
and a switch for wired connections.

STEP 2: Design the Home Network

Once you have a good grasp of the principles of home networking, you are ready to create a network design. The result is a network diagram that graphically illustrates the physical locations and connectivity of all PCs, networked devices, and communications equipment in the network. Chapter 6, "Designing a Home Network," presents strategies and hints for preparing a network design. Also included are sample diagrams of wired, wireless, and mixed-mode (see Figure I-6) networks. Design considerations for having a home office for telework are included in Chapter 14, "The Home Office and Home Networking."

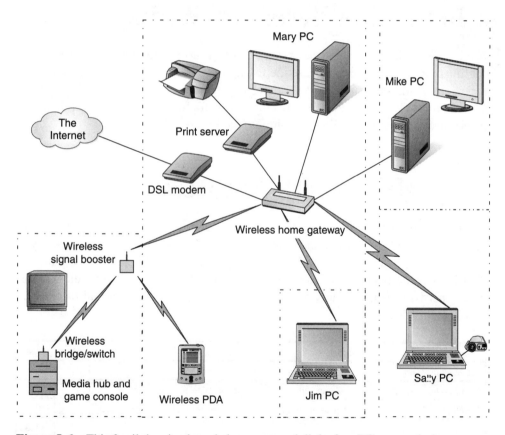

Figure I-6   This family's mixed-mode home network links four PCs—two desktop PCs via wired Ethernet and two notebook PCs via high-speed wireless. A wireless link to a media hub enables integration of the entertainment center into the home network. A wireless-enabled PDA is on the network anywhere in or about the house.

STEP 3: Purchase Network Gear

The shopping list, which is a by-product of the design process, identifies everything you need to purchase in order to build the home network designed in Step 2. Chapter 6 includes a home networking planner to facilitate documenting hardware and net gear needs and to create a shopping list (see Table I-1). The appendix, "Home Networking Buyer's Guide," includes guidelines, considerations, and recommendations to help you avoid purchasing pitfalls and get the network devices you need at a good price.

STEP 4: Install the Necessary Wiring

If the network design calls for a wired or mixed-mode network, you have several cabling options. You can either use the wiring in the home's existing telephone, use the electrical infrastructure, or you can install Ethernet cabling. Chapter 7, "Cabling a Home for an Ethernet LAN," details the trade-offs for the three wired options and demonstrates Ethernet cabling techniques (see Figure I-7).

STEP 5: Install Network Adapters

Most modern desktop PCs and all notebook PCs are sold with Ethernet network adapters for the local area connection (see Figure I-8). If you have older PCs, you may need to install Ethernet adapters or upgrade the old ones (see Chapter 8, "Setting Up and Installing a Home Network"). For PCs that will be wireless nodes on the network, you probably will need to retrofit them with internal or external wireless network adapters.

Item	Model	Pertinent Specs	Qty	Cost
Ethernet PC Card	DigLink 100 Card	Fast Ethernet	1	60
Wireless home gateway	SysComp 1000	All-in-one Wireless-G gateway	1	150
Patch cable	Category 5e cabling	Cat 5e snagless UTP Ethernet (3 feet)	2	10
Total				$220

Table I-1 This is one of a series of worksheets that aid in the preparation of a shopping list for a particular network design.

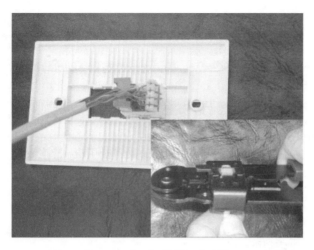

Figure I-7   You can purchase inexpensive bulk Cat 5e Ethernet cabling and make your own Ethernet cables by connecting individual wires to modular RJ-45 jacks and attaching connectors with a crimping tool.

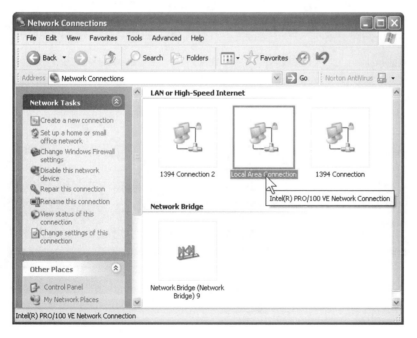

Figure I-8   Network adapters for a PC appear in the Windows XP Network Connections display, which shows net connection options for a particular PC.

STEP 6: Establish an Internet Connection

Networks are about sharing resources. Home networks enable the sharing of a single Internet connection among all PC users. The router, a home gateway function, provides a bridge between the Internet and your home network. A DSL or cable modem permits Internet access via an Internet service provider (ISP). Chapter 8, "Setting Up and Installing a Home Network," outlines the process for establishing a shared Internet connection. Chapter 12, "Internet Applications: Cruising the Internet," provides a survey of Internet applications (see Figure I-9).

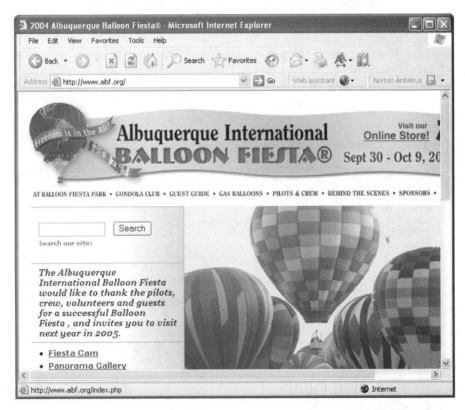

Figure I-9 Users on a home network can share a single broadband Internet connection. Parents can use the resources of the Web to plan a vacation while the kids send instant messages.

STEP 7: Set Up the Home Gateway

Once the network adapters are in place and an Internet connection has been established, it's time to set up the router or router/AP (for a wireless LAN). Although they can be separate devices, the router and the access point (AP) normally are functions of a multifunction home gateway. The gateway can have a variety of built-in functions, including broadband modem, firewall, and printer server. Chapter 8 describes what to do to configure and personalize the gateway functions for your home networking environment (see Figure I-10).

Figure I-10   Home gateways have a browser-based interface for entering and changing network settings. This screen includes entries for the basic settings for a wireless network.

STEP 8: Connect the PCs to the Network

If the network design calls for wired or mixed-mode operation, now is the time to connect the cables to all Ethernet PCs or to PCs linked through the home telephone or electrical systems. Chapter 8 provides details on how to complete the wired and/or wireless connections so that all PCs can communicate with each other and the Internet through the home gateway (see Figure I-11). The connection of Ethernet PCs may involve an Ethernet switch that can link several PCs to a single cable.

STEP 9: Set Up Network and PC Security

Cyberspace is filled with malicious people who target PCs on vulnerable Internet-ready home networks. Chapter 10, "Privacy and Security," discusses the use and implementation of firewalls, antivirus software (see Figure I-12), and other

Figure I-11   Run the Windows XP Network Setup Wizard or the Wireless Network Setup Wizard on each PC to create a LAN.

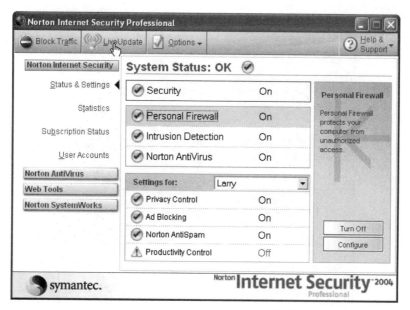

Figure I-12 Antivirus software is installed on each networked PC so that all incoming files and e-mails are scanned for viruses.

technologies that must be implemented to protect the home network from hacker attacks, computer viruses, spyware, adware, and other unwanted intrusions. Chapter 10 also presents procedural strategies you can adopt to make your network safer and to minimize annoyances, such as spam.

STEP 10: Share Printer(s)

Any printer on the home network can be shared by all users; however, the typical home network will need only one shared printer. Printers can be connected directly to the network via a print server or to any networked PC. Chapter 9, "Sharing Printers, Files, and an Internet Connection" details how printers and other resources are shared (see Figure I-13).

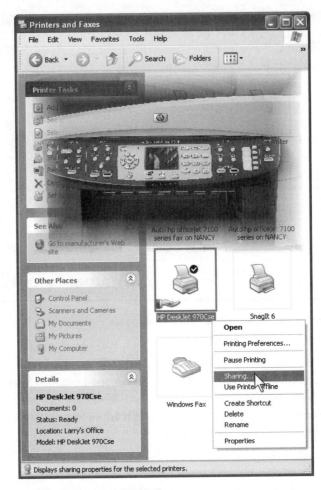

Figure I-13 Printers on any networked PC, such as the all-in-one printer superimposed over the Printer and Fax window, are easily shared among home network users.

STEP 11: Share Files and Folders

The network file/folder sharing feature built into Windows XP enables network users to share and use files stored on other PCs (see Figure I-14). Popular applications for file sharing include backing up files to other PCs, wireless mobile computing, and streaming files to a media hub in a home theater.

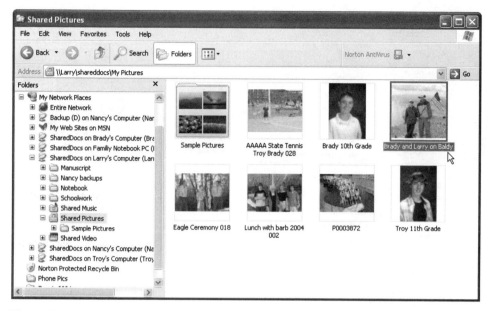

Figure I-14 Use Windows Explorer to access and manipulate shared files on a home network, such as the shared family photo album shown here, in the same way you would access files on your PC.

STEP 12: Set Up Multimedia, VPN, VoIP, and Other Applications

Chapter 13, "Growing the Network: Entertainment and Beyond," describes the state of the art for digital home entertainment and how you can leverage your home network to pipe music, pictures, and video (including TV) throughout the house via wired and wireless links. Chapter 14 includes sections that discuss how to integrate a home office PC into a corporate LAN via VPN (virtual private network) technology (see Figure I-15) and to convert a home to an Internet-based VoIP (voice over IP) telephone system.

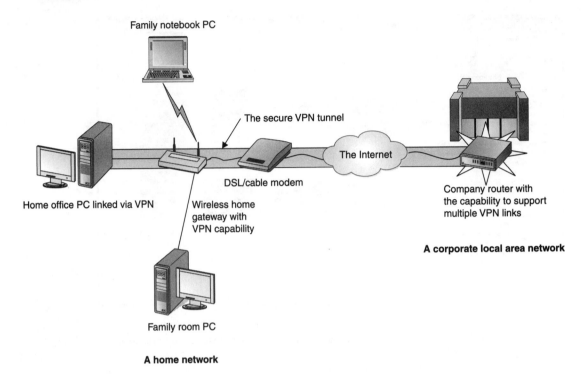

Figure I-15 Virtual private network technology enables a PC in a home office to be a part of a corporate LAN.

STEP 13: Maintain, Troubleshoot, and Grow the Network

Home networks are like most things around the house in that they must be maintained and, when something goes wrong, troubleshooting may be required. Chapter 11, "Maintenance and Troubleshooting," contains tips and hints that can help make your network administration duties go smoothly. It may be inevitable that your home network grows in scope and sophistication, perhaps from entertainment into security, VoIP, and other areas. Figure I-16 shows how the addition of a media hub can incorporate the home theater (or any audio/visual equipment) into the home network.

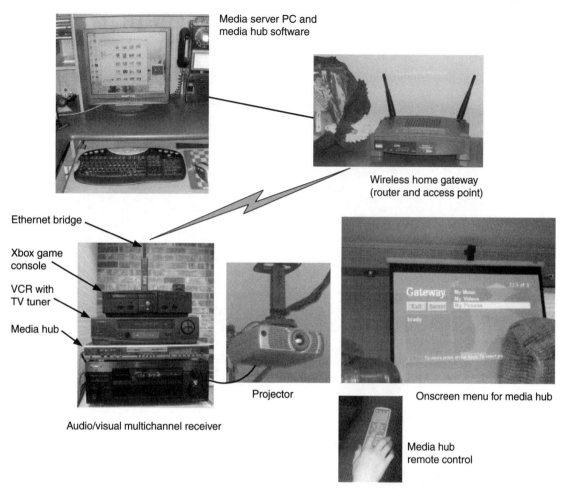

Figure I-16 Media files on networked PCs, including recorded TV programming, can be selected via a remote control and played directly to audio/visual equipment through a media hub interface.

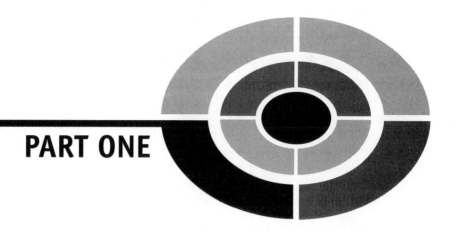

PART ONE

Home Networking: The Basics

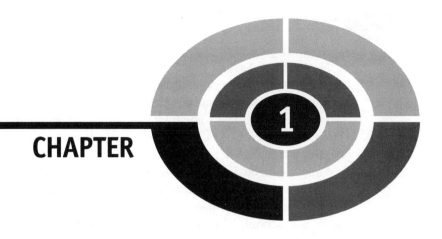

CHAPTER

1

What Is a Home Network?

Do you have two or more personal computers at home—for at least a portion of the day? If so, your family is primed for home networking. Do you have a home network, but it's not meeting your needs? If so, you are ready for an upgrade to any of a wide range of innovative home networking technologies that offer more speed, flexibility, and applications. One of these applications defines a new era in digital home entertainment. This book demystifies the home network by introducing you to the options; showing you what it can do; and explaining how to design, install, and maintain one in your home. It also prepares you for the exciting, and somewhat mysterious, future of home networking.

A *network* is any group of PCs or network devices linked via wired and/or wireless media. Until a few years ago, computer networks of any kind were for businesses that could afford expensive data communications equipment and a substantial salary for at least one highly trained network administrator. These expenses and the required technical expertise made networking in the home prohibitive. Now, however, you can have and enjoy a network in your own home— at an affordable price and without a network guru living in your spare bedroom.

Networking. Aackk! The term *networking* is a bit threatening to some users, but creating a home network is surprisingly easy to do once you understand networking terminology, concepts, and options. Moreover, the results of the effort are immensely satisfying. There's just something exhilarating about having domestic connectivity. The moderate cost of home networking is easily justified when you consider the savings you realize in resource sharing.

Families are buying second, third, and fourth PCs to keep up with their insatiable demand for personal computing and Internet access. Often the number of PCs in the home increases when parents and children bring their notebook PCs home from work and school. This spread of PCs throughout the house has prompted an explosion in home networking. Within the decade, we can expect the home network to be as much a part of the structure of the home as the phone system. If fact, it's likely that our phone systems will be integrated into our networks.

The PC Competency Assumption

To make expeditious progress with the demystification process, I will assume that you have acquired a basic level of personal computer competency. That competency would include the following:

- *An ability to work with Windows.* I am assuming that you are familiar with basic Windows operations and concepts, the implication being that you will be able to navigate around windows, manage files, request online help, work with dialog boxes, and so on.

- *An understanding of personal computing terms and concepts.* You really don't need to be a PC expert, but you will need to understand the basic terminology associated with personal computing. For example, I will use common personal computing terms without explanation (for example, USB port, flash memory, PCI card, and RAM).

- *An ability to install and use personal computing hardware and software.* Any experience you might have gained during setup and maintenance of your PCs will prove valuable when you do the same with your network components and their software.

Of course, everything associated with home networking will be described and illustrated in detail.

If you feel a need to boost your confidence in any or all of these competency areas, I have a great recommendation for a resource you can use to level your knowledge: *Personal Computing Demystified* (McGraw-Hill/Osborne, 2004) by

Larry Long. Besides the explanations of relevant terms and concepts, this book should open up new vistas in your personal computing horizons, even if you're a veteran PC user.

Think of home networking as the second step in your personal computing adventure. This book helps you take that next step and is basic in its approach. It is no more or less complex than is needed to get you into a home network. To minimize any perception of difficulty, I will feed you the "net talk" in plain English and in easily digestible portions. If you run across an unfamiliar term as you read the book, just review the definition in the comprehensive glossary in the back of the book.

Home Networks: Yesterday, Today, and Tomorrow

Home networking, one of the hottest domestic trends in America, has a short history. Prior to 1980, the cost of any kind of computer network could run into tens of thousands of dollars and would be unaffordable for the home. Even if you could afford it, you would probably need to hire a network administrator to maintain it. In the 1980s and 1990s the cost of the hardware plummeted, but like thrifty politicians, home networks remained a rarity. You might find one in the home of a computer guru with too much time on his hands or, perhaps, in the home of someone with a high-tech background that works at home.

Home networks didn't surface in any significant numbers until the late 1990s. The home networking movement was ignited by the widespread availability of high-speed broadband access and the emergence of affordable networking equipment. Today, broadband is approaching universal availability and home net gear is flying off the shelves. It's only a matter of time before the home network becomes commonplace and serves as the central nervous system for domestic computing, communications, entertainment, security, and much more.

Home Networking: A Historical Perspective

I have lived through most, if not all, of the history of home networking. My experiences are representative of its plodding growth between 1980 and the late 1990s, so I offer my story to give you some historical perspective. I'm a self-employed consultant, lecturer, and writer in the information technology arena and have worked out of my home since 1980. My wife, Nancy, and I worked together in the second floor of our turn-of-the-century home in Pennsylvania along with a part-time college student who helped us with programming jobs. The personal computers of that period were but toys compared to the high-performance systems of today, but each of us had and used one, and the only communication between them was the "walknet"—literally carrying floppy disks between the three upstairs offices (converted bedrooms).

Having worked with big-iron mainframe computers in the past, I felt frustrated enough with the minimal capabilities of the PCs of the era to look around for an alternative. AT&T had just introduced an innovative desktop server computer with minicomputer power. Most importantly, its UNIX operating system had built-in support for networking! Although they were a bit pricey, I purchased two of these PC look-alikes, an intelligent terminal, and 150 feet of coaxial networking cable. The increased power and the ability to share files and a printer were enough to justify the cost, about $20,000, of this early "home network." Actually, the term *home network* would not be used for another 15 years. We were the first family in our neighborhood and probably in our city with a network of computers in our home. We called it the Longnet.

The AT&T UNIX–based system had the power but not the growing plethora of software available for IBM PC–compatible systems, so in the late 1980s we went back to the new improved PCs and the cumbersome, but reliable, walknet. The Longnet remained in place for a few more years but was seldom used. In 1991, we moved to Arkansas and I built an office 200 feet up the hill from our house and wired it for networking. I installed a simple, but limited, computer-to-computer link between the two PCs in my office at minimal cost (about $300). As it turned out, my wife decided to work in the house, instead of the office, and the somewhat cumbersome link was seldom used.

Although our home and office share a telephone and a security system, the considerable expense of the network gear and software required to span 200 feet was prohibitively expensive for home use, even along with a home office. Our family PCs remained separate entities until the late 1990s and the beginning of the modern home networking era. However, we went on the Internet in the early 1990s and were able to pass information between the home and office via Internet services.

Three things came together to make home networking affordable and easy to install:

1. The Microsoft Windows operating systems began to provide reliable support for home networking.

2. New connectivity technology enabled the use of existing home telephone lines and AC power lines to link PCs.

3. The availability of high-speed broadband Internet service was spreading rapidly, and people were subscribing to it in significant numbers.

It was the last point, broadband Internet, that gave home networking wings. DSL and cable modem broadband services came late to our city and especially to those of us on the outskirts of town. I decided not to wait for terra firma broadband, so I subscribed to broadband via satellite. Satellite is available to anyone in America with a southern exposure. Well, as soon as my wife and kids witnessed the wonders of fast Internet, they wanted it, too. I responded by installing the home network shown in Figure 1-1, using only Windows and home phoneline adapters (devices that enabled computer-to-computer communications over regular telephone lines). The new version of the Longnet worked fine, even though the link between the home and office exceeded the operational maximum of phoneline networks by 150 feet.

Satellite Internet service is an excellent alternative when DSL and cable modem are not available. However, the actual day DSL was made available in our neighborhood, I subscribed to DSL, tore down the satellite dish, and cut the cost of our Internet service in half.

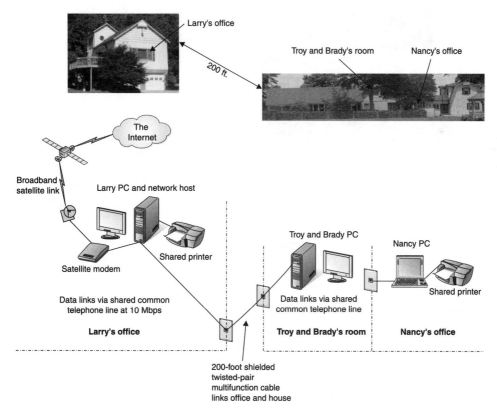

Figure 1-1   A Windows-based home network that uses phoneline connectivity

Today's Home Network

Many of today's home networks are wireless. They are relatively easy to install, are inexpensive, and provide plenty of flexibility in the placement of PCs. I chose to wait on wireless because the early wireless alternatives were slow, unreliable, and overpriced for the service offered. Today, however, wireless is five times as fast, extremely reliable, and a great buy. Needless to say, the current reincarnation of the Longnet features wireless connectivity, along with conventional Ethernet wiring, the type of wiring used to connect PCs in most networks in businesses and homes.

The current version of the Longnet, which seems to be in a constant state of change, is shown in Figure 1-2. Nancy has a desktop PC in her office, which is just off the kitchen area. Each of our teenage sons, Troy and Brady, has a desktop PC. I have two desktops adjacent to one another in my office up the hill, one of which is a beta

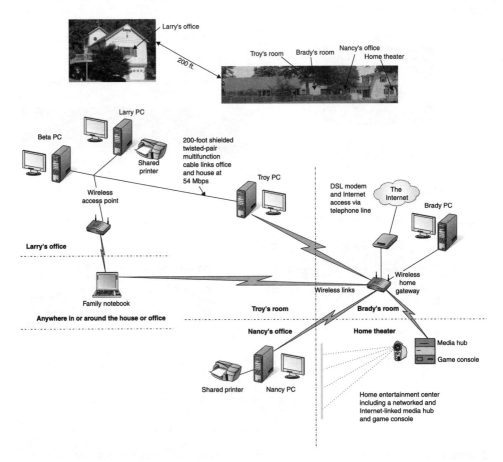

Figure 1-2   The Longnet: the home network at the Longs'

machine that is used exclusively for running prerelease software. We have a notebook PC for those many times when one of us needs a portable PC. All of these PCs are linked together, along with a media hub and an Xbox game console in the home theater, via a high-speed home network. The *media hub* provides the link between the network and the home entertainment center such that network- and Internet-based images and video can be viewed and music can be played in the home theater.

All PCs share an all-in-one printer (print, fax, copy, and scan) in Nancy's office and a printer in my office. Nancy's PC has two hard disks, one of which is the *backup server* for all PCs on the Longnet. A *server PC* provides some type of service for the others on the network. Brady's PC is the *media server* that stores the images, music, and video files that are shared throughout the network. The Longnet of Figure 1-2 illustrates the elements commonly found in home networks and will be used as an example throughout the book.

At the center of the network in Figure 1-2 is a *wireless home gateway* located in Brady's room. This multifunction device coordinates communication throughout the entire network and enables sharing of the DSL broadband Internet access. An additional *wireless access point* in the office extends the range for wireless communication. The Longnet is made up of a combination of wireless and wired links. We'll talk at length about wireless/wired links, home gateways (also called *residential gateways*), and other network equipment (not shown in Figure 1-2) in later chapters.

The Longnet includes several other peripheral devices that aren't illustrated in Figure 1-2. Only Nancy and I have scanners. Troy and Brady do their scanning in our offices and then transfer the files via Longnet to their systems. We have a couple of fist-sized desktop digital cameras that we share. They are easily plugged into any USB port on the network and used as a webcam or for videoconferencing. We also share a couple of megapixel digital cameras and a couple of digicams (digital video cameras). Once captured (at any PC) and edited, the images are stored on the media server, which is Brady's PC.

The greatest challenge to installing the Longnet was the distance between the home and the office, about 270 feet between my PC and the centrally located wireless home gateway. Attempting to span this distance using wireless technology was too expensive. The 350-feet wired distance exceeded the operational maximum of Ethernet cable; nevertheless, I strung the cable and it works very well with relatively little loss in transmission speed. This tells us that the capabilities of Ethernet cable are conservatively stated.

No two networks are alike. Each is designed to fit the networking needs of a specific family. The Longnet was designed to meet our needs today. It may look different tomorrow. Expect your home network to grow and expand with your hardware, your ever-changing network needs, and your desire to use an expanding variety of innovative home networking applications.

The Home Network of the Future

To this point in the short history of home networking, the focus has been on the connectivity of multiple PCs in the home. Home networks, however, have the potential to encompass more than PCs and the sharing of computer peripherals and services. In the not-too-distant future, the home network will emerge as a foundation structure for the "e-home," an electronic home in which computers, electronic and audio/visual equipment, and electro-mechanical components throughout the home are linked to the network and given "intelligence" (see Figure 1-3). Already, people are expanding their home networks to include their home theaters, game controllers, security, and lighting.

We are witnessing a slow, steady digital convergence of consumer electronics, including durable goods, such as kitchen appliances. The home network already is changing the face of home entertainment. When we are able to control kitchen appliances from anywhere in our homes and even in our offices, it is sure to change the way we cook and eat. Today, the foundation of most home security systems is an automated telephone call to the security company. The next step in home security is for the control unit, the sensors, and possibly video cameras to be integrated into the home network. The foundation is laid for the home network of the future to extend to control of everything in the home, from the heating/air conditioning unit to the swimming pool's chlorinator. And yes, your onboard automobile PC can be part of the network, as well.

Courtesy of Intel Corporation

Figure 1-3 An e-home with structured wiring and wireless links that enable connectivity between all PCs, audio/video appliances, the Internet, and the security system

NOTE *By 2010, virtually all new home construction will include structured wiring and wireless transceivers in support of home networking along with wiring for AC power. Telephone wiring as we know it, however, will no longer be necessary, since terrestrial telephone service will be delivered over the Internet through home networks.*

Networks and Networking

Whether in a business environment or in the home, a network is about sharing and communications between endpoints on the network, called *nodes.* The PCs in a home network, printers, and even home theaters are nodes that are linked physically by wires or by wireless links. Most of the nodes on a home network communicate or "talk" with each other; however, this is not always the case, because some may be output-only devices. For example, the linked media hub in your home theater has little to do with the upstairs printer.

Generally, networks are classified by their size and scope. A home network is a *local area network,* or *LAN,* which connects nodes in close proximity. The Internet is a *wide area network,* or *WAN,* which connects nodes in widely dispersed geographical areas. One of the primary reasons people install home networks is to share broadband Internet access among all PCs in the home. This means creating a link between the home LAN and the Internet WAN. One of the functions of the home gateway is to control the flow of information between your home network and the Internet.

Personal computers can be linked in a number of ways to create a LAN, but the approach used most often for home networking is called *peer to peer,* or *P2P.* In a peer-to-peer network, the PCs are peers, or equals. The transfer of information between nodes is controlled by a *protocol* that is built into the logic of a *network adapter.* A *protocol* is a set of transmission rules that govern how computers "talk" with each other. The most widely used network protocol is *Ethernet.* Each PC on the network must be configured with an internal or external network adapter, which can also be called a *network interface card (NIC).* Ethernet transmits messages at 10 Mbps (megabits per second or million bits per second), 100 Mbps, or 1 Gbps (gigabits per second or billion bits per second). The 100 Mbps speed is called *Fast Ethernet,* and the 1 Gbps speed is called *Gigabit Ethernet.*

Although the Ethernet is the most common network protocol for local area networking, both in the home and at the office, there are other ways to link PCs in a home network. PCs can even be linked directly with a USB cable or via existing telephone or power lines. Rapid advances in *Wi-Fi (Wireless Fidelity)* technology has caused wireless networks to emerge as the most popular form of connectivity in home networks.

What You Should Know about Home Networking

Before you dive head first into the meat of this book, there are seven things you should know about home networking:

- *Home networking is not as complex as you might think.* Home networking support is built into modern Microsoft Windows operating systems, which are on the vast majority of PCs. Manufacturers of networking hardware have done an admirable job of simplifying complex networking gear for the home user.

- *The biggest hurdle to having a home network is having a good grasp of all the options.* Contrary to popular thinking, the setup and installation of a home network is the easy part. The greatest challenge is to understand the alternatives and what each can contribute to your network. That knowledge, which you will get from this book, is all you need to create an efficient, cost-effective design that fits your networking circumstances and needs. Installation should be a piece of cake.

- *Home networking is not as expensive as you might think.* Wireless home networking kits that contain everything you need for a two-PC wireless network can be purchased for under $80. A couple of computers can be linked directly in a simple network for the price of the cable, possibly under $10. All of the network gear for the Longnet of Figure 1-2 was purchased for under $800. Your net cost may actually be a savings that results from resource sharing.

- *Built-in security measures can provide protection for you and your family.* I won't lie to you—home networks, like business networks, are vulnerable to a laundry list of cybercrimes, such as identity theft, virus attacks, and cyberstalking, and to a variety of annoyances ranging from spam to pop-up ads. This is the world we live in. However, with the judicious use of available hardware and software tools and with the constant vigilance on the part of all family members, you should be able to shield yourself and your family from most, if not all, of this nonsense.

- *You can do it yourself.* Millions of people just like you have installed home networks, and you can, too. Some may have paid too much and not purchased exactly what they needed or wanted, but they have an operational network. You, however, should have the background knowledge to avoid their pitfalls.

- *Having a home network can be frustrating.* Yes, some of the home networking horror stories are true, albeit probably embellished for effect. Sometimes it seems as if home networks have personalities and, like people, just do strange and unexplainable things. Fortunately, there is usually a fix for most problems. For example, you can solve most problems by resetting the network devices (often just turning them off and then on again). These maddening moments are the price we pay to enjoy the benefits of a home network.

- *Help is everywhere.* Everyone eventually needs help—even veteran power users. In home networking, it's okay to ask for directions. Most of us learn the common features of our net gear, and then we learn about other features as we need them. Fortunately, help is readily available and easily accessible. Windows has plenty of help for installing, maintaining, and troubleshooting a home network. Also, all of the network equipment manufacturers have extensive technical support web sites with helpful step-by-step tutorials, FAQs, and searchable knowledge bases.

Frequently Asked Questions

Most of my friends know me as a tennis player, a Rotarian, a church member, a community volunteer, and so on, and most have a vague notion that I know something about computers and networking. And like anyone in this day and age who has a perceived technical knowledge, I get peppered with questions. The questions I hear most often are these.

- *Where do I begin?* Now that this book is out, my answer to this FAQ is "Chapter 1 of this book." However, I invite you and them to feel free to jump directly into any chapter. The chapters are relatively independent, so you can hopscotch about the book depending on your level of networking knowledge and your information needs. Throughout the book, information is presented in small chunks to make it easy for you to skim content in search of specific material. If you read ahead and get hung up on a specific term, the glossary and the index are always there to help you out.

- *Should I upgrade my current home network?* Probably so, if you installed your network in 2003 or before. Chances are that all or part of your network is a lot slower than is possible with state-of-the-art connectivity technologies, that you may wish to enhance your network to have the flexibility of high-speed wireless connectivity, or that you may wish to integrate elements of your home entertainment or other systems into the network.

- *What network gear do I buy?* Networks are designed to fit the hardware and computing needs of a particular family, so the equipment you purchase depends on your circumstances. Much of this book is devoted to giving you the background information you need to make good purchasing choices.

- *What can I do with a home network?* The answer to this question is a little more involved, so I've devoted the next chapter to answering it. Chapter 2 gives you a guided tour of the home network's capabilities along with the advantages and potential of having one.

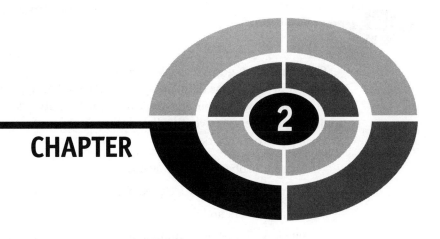

Applications of Home Networking

With a home network, sister can print a document from a PC in the upstairs bedroom to a printer in the downstairs den—without leaving her chair. Brother can watch television shows he recorded the night before on any networked PC or in the home theater. Dad can check stock quotes on the Internet. Mom can take her notebook PC and work under a shade tree in the backyard and still be able to interface with her company's customer database. The scope and variety of applications for home networks is growing as rapidly as the number of home networks. For example, soon you will be able to convert songs on your CDs to MP3 format and then use the network's wireless interface to upload the songs from your PC to your car's entertainment system. Your car stereo will no longer be limited to the songs on the CDs in the changer.

There are many good reasons to create a network in multi-PC homes, and they all revolve around home networking applications. The applications listed here pretty much describe what you can do with a home network. To help you put these applications in perspective, I've listed them in order of importance (the best reason for home networking first).

- Share broadband Internet access
- Share files among PCs on the network
- Share printers and other resources
- Integrate home entertainment and personal computing
- Play multiplayer games
- Enhance PC and network security
- Go wireless with PCs and other devices
- Create an e-home

The list reflects my home networking experiences. Others might see it differently. As new innovations in home networking technology hit the shelves, our ratings are sure to change anyway. For example, I would expect that home entertainment will continue to climb this ladder of importance.

Sharing Broadband Internet Access

The number one reason people make the decision to install a home network is to give them the ability to share a high-speed Internet connection. Typically, these are people like you who have known the despair of having to wait their turn for the privilege of having their shot at slow, click-and-wait dial-up Internet access. Or they are families in which only the chosen one has the screaming fast Internet and the other family members just scream about their sluggish dial-up access.

The difference between broadband and narrowband (dial-up) Internet access may be unexplainable for those who have not experienced the two for themselves. It's the difference between watching a Harry Potter movie on a nine-inch portable TV and watching it at a movie theater with Dolby Digital surround sound. It's the difference between chicken broth and pot roast. Well, you get the idea. Broadband offers an entirely different experience, and now, through the wonders of home networking, everyone in the house can enjoy broadband for the price of a single DSL or cable modem line.

Every PC on a home network can share a single always-on broadband link to the Internet. Users in a home network setting seldom access the Internet at exactly the same time, so more often than not, users can enjoy the full capacity of the broadband line (see Figure 2-1). Chapter 9 addresses the alternatives and considerations and explains how to set up Internet sharing on your home network.

Figure 2-1 Sharing the Net: brother does instant messaging (top), mom shops (middle), and dad uploads files to the publisher (bottom).

> **NOTE** *Internet access sharing has become very popular, actually, too popular for some Internet service providers (ISPs). Under normal circumstance, a single broadband line can handle the Net needs of your family—and your neighbors, too. And that's a problem for the ISP. Because some subscribers have chosen to illegally share their single-location connection, many ISPs offer services that limit the number of PCs that can share an Internet line. Choose an ISP (or a service option) that can provide Net access to all PCs on your home LAN.*

Sharing Files among PCs on the Network

The ability to share files is one of the great advantages of having a home network. Once you have your LAN set up, sharing files between PCs and other network devices that use files is no more difficult than working with files on your PC. That's because we use the same familiar Windows Explorer interface to work with files on a network that we use for file management on our PCs.

You can perform copy, delete, move, rename, open, and other operations on your personal files and on those shared with other PCs on the network. Each user on the network can choose which files he or she wishes to share. The other files are protected from unauthorized access. You can drag and drop files from shared folders among network PCs just as easily as you would between your hard disk and CD burner. Network file sharing is covered in detail in Chapter 9.

At our house, files are continually passing between PCs and the media hub in the home theater. Arguably, our most important application for file sharing is file backup. The members of my family use each other's PCs to back up our important files. Because my office is in a separate building, we have the added advantage of off-site storage within our home network.

Brady's PC is the multimedia server for music, image, and video files. Having a multimedia server gives each of us ready access to our family's growing MP3 music collection, the ever-changing family photo album, and a wide variety of videos that accumulate in a family with a couple of digicams (see Figure 2-2). This access extends to the multimedia hub in the home theater, too.

When one of us needs to go mobile with the family notebook PC, we just copy applicable folders to the notebook, do our work, and then reverse the process to update the master folders on our desktop PCs. When I download a new device driver program, I notify everyone so that they can pull it from my computer at network speeds, which are much faster than broadband speeds. These are just a few of the endless number of applications for file sharing on a home network.

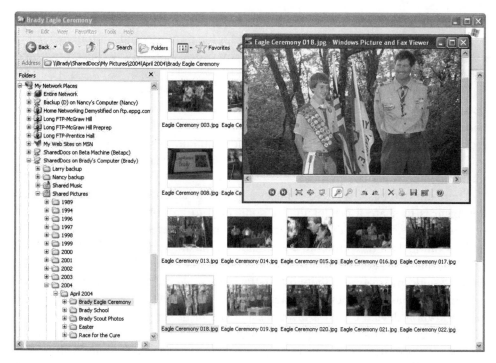

Figure 2-2   The family photo album is shared and can be viewed from any networked PC.

CAUTION You need to be ever vigilant about what files you share and with whom you share them. I would suggest that you protect all of your important personal files (work, school, and so on) and in those infrequent instances in which you wish to share them, do so indirectly. That is, copy the original to the special Shared Documents folder set up by Windows for network sharing so that you share a copy and not the original.

Sharing Printers and Other Resources

The ability to share a single printer can easily justify the relatively modest expense of a home network. It is not unusual for non-networked homes to have printers and their costly print cartridges scattered throughout the house. A single networked printer or any all-in-one multifunction device (print, fax, scan, and copy) can handle

the printing needs for most families. My family uses the all-in-one printer connected to Nancy's PC, which is more than adequate for the printing needs of four heavy PC users (see Figure 2-3). I have a printer in my office, but only because my home office is in an outbuilding 200 feet from the house.

Home printers range in cost from around $100 to $500. On those infrequent occasions that we need printed materials, it is a minor inconvenience to walk to Nancy's office to pick up the printed pages. It would be, however, a major inconvenience and expense to purchase and maintain printers for each PC. Save your printer dollars. One good printer will suffice, even for a family actively involved in personal computing.

There are two basic ways to connect a printer to a network. The most common approach is to share a printer that is connected to any of the network PCs. The obvious disadvantage of this approach is that the connected PC must be turned on and operational for the printer to be available to the other PCs on the network. Both of our printers are connected to PCs, but Nancy and I use our PCs throughout the day and seldom if ever turn them off. In the homes where PCs are turned on and off on a regular basis, the best approach may be to connect printers directly to the network via a device called a *print server*. The print server is built into an ever-higher percentage of modern printers, primarily because of the explosion in the number of home networks. The pros and cons of each approach along with printer sharing specifics are covered in Chapter 9.

Printer sharing is a natural application for networking in that printers are output-only devices and no device/media preparation is needed unless special paper is required. Wireless video cameras are easily shared on the network, too. Any PC on the network can switch to a camera view of the backyard and/or the baby's room.

Other resources can be shared, but not so easily. It is possible to share fax services, CD/DVD burners, and scanners directly, but honestly, it is not worth the effort in a home setting. The best way to use any of these devices is to use file sharing and copy appropriate files to the PC hosting the fax or CD/DVD burner capability and then fax or burn CDs or DVDs on the host PC. Do your scanning from the host PC and then move your files via file sharing to your PC. If you have a lot of scanning to do and would prefer to use your PC, just load the driver software for the scanner to your system and temporarily move the plug-and-play USB scanner to your PC. If you do, don't forget to lock and secure the scan bar before moving the scanner.

NOTE *More and more printers will be networkable until 2010, when virtually all mainline printers will be sold network ready.*

Figure 2-3   This multifunction all-in-one printer is the primary printer on the Longnet.

Integrating Home Entertainment and Personal Computing

For better or worse, our society is experiencing a remarkable transformation to a digital lifestyle. Anything in the physical and communications world that can be represented as binary ones and zeros in a computer is a candidate for *digital convergence.* Digital convergence is making our world more integrated and accessible, but in so doing it has made our world look very different. Electronic books (e-books), tiny MP3 players with thousands of songs, electronic mail (even via cell phones), instant messaging, digicams, wireless palm PCs, PC networks on-the-fly, linked automobile PCs, and videoconferencing are part of a new technology lexicon. Moreover, they are becoming part of our lives, too. In our new digital lifestyle, the home network is emerging as the glue that ties all of these devices and their applications together.

Shortly, we will be able to watch any movie, hear any song, or read any book—anytime from anywhere in the house. You can watch, listen, or read at your desk on your PC, but most of us would prefer a more comfortable setting, such as the living room, a bedroom, the deck, or a home theater (see Figure 2-4). The home network is evolving to fit our new digital lifestyle and give us a variety of home entertainment options, from Internet-based gaming to downloadable movies on demand.

Figure 2-4   This home theater is linked to the Longnet via a media hub.

To meet the demand for the integration of entertainment into our home networks, we can expect to see a continuous string of innovative network devices that complement the capabilities of the PC. For example, I would expect that the typical networked home will have linked media hubs strategically placed throughout the house that can receive multimedia content from linked PCs or the Internet for playback on the home theater, the bedroom TV, and other media players. Media hubs are available that can record your favorite TV shows for playback at your convenience on any monitor in the house. Game consoles, such as Microsoft's Xbox, are going live—that is, live on the Internet for multiplayer gaming.

A number of portable devices are on the horizon. For example, we will have wireless stereo headsets that give us the flexibility to move about the house while listening to music from distant radio stations or the network's music server. Wireless electronic readers will let us read the latest bestseller or today's online news from our favorite chair or the comfort of our bed. Of course, handheld PCs, cell phones, and just about any other digital appliance will have the ability to interface with the home network for any of a number of applications, from synchronizing calendars to uploading/downloading images.

Combining a variety of linked devices with power of the PC, access to the Internet, and the connectivity of the home network has and will continue to redefine home entertainment at a mind-boggling pace over the next decade. This new multimedia experience will be something to behold, so get ready. Chapter 12 illustrates the integration of entertainment and PCs on a home network.

NOTE *It's inevitable that digital convergence will bring us a plethora of home entertainment services, including video on demand. I would expect that online movie subscription services will preempt video stores by 2010, maybe sooner, depending on the rate of penetration of home networks and home theaters. Current services allow you to download as many movies as you want for about $12 per month, while others charge a per-download fee. Movies can be downloaded in 30 minutes or less via broadband, about the time it takes for a trip to the video store.*

Playing Multiplayer Games

Walk into any retail store that sells PC software and observe the mix of available software. It is not unusual for 75 percent of the shelf space to be devoted to gaming software. The gaming craze passed me by, but the interactive exhilaration of a wide variety of imaginative and challenging games grabbed my teenage children and millions of adults, too. The high-resolution graphics, realistic animation, and accompanying Dolby Digital sound give players the you-are-there feeling. At any given time, millions of games are being played on the Internet—and you are invited to join. Or you can have a private LAN gaming party in your house (see Figure 2-5).

Response time is critical in multiplayer gaming. A few milliseconds of lag time, which is common with Internet-based gaming, can mean the difference between you blasting the bad guys or being the blastee. The Internet gamer with the fastest response time has a built-in advantage. That advantage is rendered nil when gaming is played within the confines of a high-speed home network.

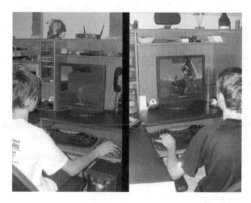

Figure 2-5   Multiplayer gaming on the Longnet

My teenage boys often invite their friends over for gaming parties. Sometimes the boys' friends will bring their own PCs and plug them into our network via a wireless or Ethernet link to expand the number of possible players. Usually, they will consolidate the PCs in one or two rooms so that they can interact with each other as well as the games. Multiplayer gaming for both PCs and game consoles is discussed in Chapter 14.

Enhancing PC and Network Security

Throughout much of the 1990s, each member of my family was connected to the Internet directly via a dial-up connection, placing each system at great risk to intrusion by a malicious hacker. The communications hardware associated with a home network provides an extra layer of protection from hackers, viruses, cyberthieves, and all the other bad things floating around the Internet seeking vulnerable prey (see Figure 2-6).

When it comes to cyberspace, I have never had that warm feeling one gets when wrapped in a cocoon of safety. I do, however, feel much better knowing that my home network provides some front-end protection that is not available with a direct link to the Internet. Firewalls, antivirus software, and other Internet security measures that can be employed in the home networking environment are presented in Chapter 10.

Figure 2-6 The firewall that sits between the Internet and the Longnet permits only authorized traffic to reach Larry's office PCs.

Going Wireless with PCs and Other Devices

Clearly, the trend in home networking is to go wireless with all or at least part of the network. Therefore, it is likely that you will enjoy the freedom and flexibility of working with PCs that are not tethered to one another or a DSL/cable modem (see Figure 2-7). Moreover, most new PC sales are notebooks. If you have one or more notebook PCs, you may as well give these mobile nodes the flexibility to stay connected to the network and the Internet from anywhere in or around the house.

The primary PC for all of us on the Longnet is a desktop; however, our lone family notebook gets plenty of use during those occasions that call for mobile computing. For example, Brady will sometimes take the laptop to bed and talk with his friends via instant messaging. The notebook gives Troy an extra gaming station when he has LAN gaming parties. Nancy moves the notebook to the kitchen so that her 90-year-old mother can view recent family photos rather than asking her to descend the stairs leading to the desktops. All of us enjoy taking the laptop to the home theater so that we can surf the Internet on the seven-foot screen. On nice days, there is a good chance you might find one of us working or doing homework under a shade tree. When we have guests, we move the notebook PC to the guest room to give them a tool for personal computing and that all-important access to the Internet and their e-mail.

Once you equip notebook PCs for wireless communication (a wireless network adapter), you give that PC the capability to establish a link to any wireless network as long as you are within the network's *hotspot*. The *hotspot* is defined by the coverage

Figure 2-7   With wireless connectivity, you are online anywhere in and around the house.

area of the network's wireless access point(s). The same wireless network adapter that gives you access to your home network gets you on your company's network within seconds after you arrive at the office. Also, you can go online at any of thousands of free wireless hotspots at schools, colleges, coffee shops, and so on, and at a growing number of fee-based wireless hotspots at airports, hotels, retail stores, and many other locations. Commercial airplanes are becoming flying hotspots. In some parts of the world, the hotspot is called a *coolspot.*

Creating a Smart Home

The e-home, sometimes called a *smart home*, has been around for a long time in our technical lexicon, but it is in very few homes. In an e-home, a variety of systems and appliances are linked and placed under program control. Smart homes have been a sound economic investment since the early 1990s, but few people have been willing to spend the five-figure amount needed to give their home intelligence. The home network is giving the smart home new life in that it already has two of the most expensive elements of any smart home: processing/control capabilities (the networked PCs) and a wired and wireless infrastructure for connectivity throughout the home.

The e-home includes computer-based controls that can be programmed to optimize, functionally and economically, a variety of domestic systems. For example, an integrated home security system might involve lighting, an alarm and police notification system, and security cameras. One of the major applications for e-homes is climate control, where temperatures are adjusted automatically to minimize energy consumption. Blinds throughout the house can be timed to open and close in sync with the season and the family's activities. Hot water temperatures can be raised and lowered to meet cyclical demands.

A number of home network–compatible consumer devices are being developed and introduced. For example, coffee makers, oven/refrigerator combos, dishwashers, and other kitchen appliances will be given programmable control. You will be able to control some of these appliances from remote locations via the Internet. Pet care devices are coming on the market that can be programmed to feed fish, dogs, cats, and other pets at predetermined times. If you prefer, you can release the food manually from a remote location via an Internet link.

Home networking has hastened us toward the day when the e-home will be commonplace in your neighborhood. I fully expect that we will be able to communicate with our e-homes via ever-improving speech recognition as we walk from room to room, probably within this decade.

The Downside of Home Networking

Everything has a downside, even something as helpful and life-changing as a home network. That downside, however, is relatively minor. Sure, you will need to invest a little time and money, from a few hours and around $100 to several days and up to $1000. The benefits of these expenditures in effort and dollars, though, are returned many times over.

A home network is more dynamic than a twisted-pair phone system or your AC power structure, both of which can provide unattended service for decades. Your home network, however, will evolve with your changing needs; thus, you have one more thing in life to maintain. Although home networks can be hassle free for months at a time, it is inevitable that you will need to do some minor troubleshooting. Perhaps a wire is jarred loose or you need to reposition wireless network adapters for better reception. Occasionally, you might lose Internet access. Chapter 11 provides troubleshooting hints on how to proceed when problems occur.

Home networking demands cooperation among family members. Security is an ongoing concern that requires constant vigilance and adherence to security maxims by everyone who uses the LAN. A home network is about sharing, and sharing can mean that you may have to plan ahead to use resources wisely. For example, all of the kids can't print their homework assignments on the network's solo printer five minutes before the school bus arrives. If you wish to download a movie from a subscription service, the courteous thing to do would be to download it during off-peak hours so as not to bog down Internet access for others in the family.

When you put home networking's upside and downside alongside one another, the downside elements seem relatively insignificant. As you will soon see (if you haven't already), a home network is like a dishwasher or a car—once you've had one for a while, you just can't imagine yourself without it.

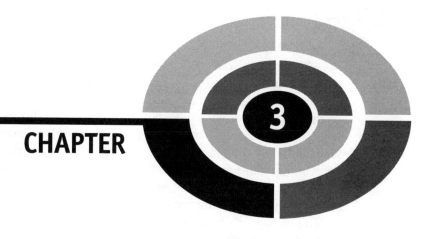

CHAPTER 3

Network Concepts and Strategies

We live in an increasingly connected world. If you work in an office, there's a good chance you and your PC are linked to your company's local area network. Because you are reading this book, you are either planning or already enjoying an Internet-ready home network. Whether at work or home, you're connected.

During the first three decades of widespread networking, networks existed in an experts-only domain for the business world. These past few years, however, we have experienced an amazing transformation in network technology. Network technologies are now readily available consumer items. Communications gear that cost in the four figures a decade ago can be purchased today at Wal-Mart, Best Buy, and many other retail stores for less than $50. Now, millions of PC users like you purchase, install, and maintain network hardware and communications channels.

Although hardware and software vendors do their best to shield us from the complex inner workings of networks (and they can be extremely complex), the use of some network terms, such as IP address and DHCP, is unavoidable. Even though network gear with easy-to-install diagrams on the boxes peppers the shelves of every big-box retailer, installing a home network is considerably more involved than installing a toaster oven. Therefore, a little knowledge about networks and networking will prove beneficial during the installation process and make you a more effective network user both at work and at home. Just knowing the basics saves you plenty of time and money.

This chapter, which is a bit more technical than the others, is about unraveling the mystery of networks. It introduces you to those networking concepts and strategies that will prove helpful as you go about installing, maintaining, and growing a home network.

Types of Networks

Networks facilitate the collection and distribution of information between two points. Were you aware that you have been communicating on a network for most of your life? Yes, the telephone system is a network, and a telephone is an endpoint, or node, connected to a network of computers that routes your voice signals to any one of a billion other telephone nodes around the world. The node can be a terminal, a computer, or any destination/source device (for example, a printer, an Xbox game controller, or even a telephone). Computer networks can have two nodes or thousands of nodes, depending on the specific requirements of an organization. The typical home network will have two to five nodes. Home networks with three PCs or two PCs and a print server, for example, are very popular.

The proximity of a network's nodes defines the type of network, the most popular types being the LAN and the WAN.

- *Local area network.* The local area network (LAN) connects nodes in close proximity, such as the rooms in a home or a suite of offices in a building. Home networks are LANs. The LAN also is called a *local net.*

- *Wide area network.* A *WAN,* or wide area network, connects nodes and local area networks in widely dispersed geographic areas, such as cities, states, and even countries. The WAN normally will employ the transmission services of a common carrier to transmit signals between nodes in the network. Many national and international corporations support WANs. The world's grandest WAN is the Internet. Even a stand-alone PC connecting via a dial-up link is a node on the Internet WAN.

When we refer to a LAN or WAN, we refer to all hardware, software, and communications channels associated with it.

Local Area Networks: LANs

LANs link the workstations/PCs in just about any office building and the PCs in millions of homes. Because of the proximity of nodes in local nets, a company or a family can install their own communications channels, such as Cat 5 cabling or wireless transceivers. The LAN can operate in isolation of other networks or common carriers, but they seldom do. In the business world, LANs often are linked by WANs, and virtually all home networks (LANs in the home) bridge to the Internet via DSL or cable modem. The DSL signal is delivered over a common carrier's telephone lines, and the cable modem gets its signal from a cable company, also a common carrier. A small percentage of home networks get their Internet access via satellite.

LAN Topologies

A network's *topology* describes the physical relationship between the nodes on the network. The most popular local area network topologies are star and bus. The *bus topology* permits the connection of PCs, print servers, and so on along a common coaxial cable called a *network bus*. The term bus is used because people on a bus can get off at any stop along the route. I mention the bus topology because, at one time, the bus-based LAN was popular, and because it remains installed in many businesses. Because the bus topology can be slow and difficult to maintain, virtually all modern home networks are based on a star topology.

In a *star topology,* devices on the network are connected to a central hub, creating the appearance of a star. In a home network, the hub normally will be a multifunction home gateway (see Figure 3-1). Multiple hubs and their stars can be linked and, often, are combined into a single network. Figure 3-2 illustrates a home network that combines two hubs (each a star topology), one of which is a wired home gateway that links three PCs, the DSL/cable modem, and another hub. The second hub is a *wireless access point* (*WAP*) that provides wireless links to two PCs and wired links to a network printer and the home gateway. The wireless access point, or simply *AP, (WAP)* is a transceiver for radio signals. Devices can be added to either of the hubs in Figure 3-2, and another hub can be linked to either of the hubs to expand the network.

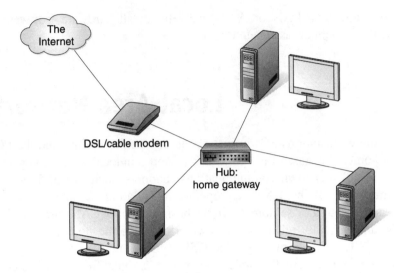

Figure 3-1 A home network with one hub

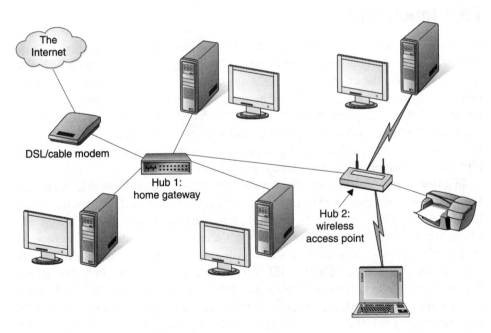

Figure 3-2 A home network with two hubs

The Ethernet LAN Protocol

Each PC/network device must have a network adapter. The transfer of information between nodes is controlled by a protocol embedded in the logic of the network adapter's memory. A *protocol* is the set of rules by which networks determine usage priorities for a shared medium—the wired and wireless links. The protocol acts like a series of traffic lights, but instead of keeping cars from crashing into each other, it keeps messages from colliding along the transmission medium. The most popular access method for business and home LANs is Ethernet.

Ethernet, a wired protocol, uses *CSMA/CD* (*Carrier Sense Multiple Access/ Collision Detection*) and Cat 5 cabling. CSMA/CD is a set of rules that describe what happens when devices on a network attempt to use the same transmission media at the same time (data collisions). Ethernet sets the stage for communication such that all devices uses a common format for messages and a standard method (queries and responses) for communicating with one another.

In your basic Ethernet network, the nodes on the LAN compete for the right to send a message. A node with a message sends it and its signal over the network, possibly to all nodes. Only the addressee node recognizes and accepts the message; the other nodes ignore it.

One of the most important functions of the Ethernet adapters is to detect when two messages collide en route to their destination. Collisions are a normal and expected part of Ethernet communications. When this happens, the adapters return "line busy" signals to the senders. Then, each node waits a few microseconds and tries again, and again, until the line is free. The typical network user doesn't know about all of this contention and is unaffected by the imperceptible wait. Essentially, Ethernet LANs operate like a conversation between polite people. When two people begin talking at the same time, one must wait until the other is finished.

Communications technology has improved in the last few years, so today's Ethernet networks don't have all of that contention and colliding. Most networks have "intelligent" gateways and switches that can route messages more expeditiously to their destinations, often directly. Computer equipment is covered in more detail in Chapter 5.

Ethernet transmits messages at 10 Mbps, 100 Mbps (Fast Ethernet), or 1 Gbps (Gigabit Ethernet). The choice for most home networks is Fast Ethernet. The hardware for Gigabit Ethernet is still a bit pricey for the home market, and the extra speed is overkill for domestic applications, anyway.

Wireless communications, an alternative to wired Ethernet, adhere to the rules of *CSMA/CA*, which emphasizes collision avoidance rather than collision detection. This collision avoidance technique requires that the wireless network adapters get permission to send information before actually transmitting it. Wireless uses radio waves to transmit information between the nodes instead of wire. Virtually all wireless

LANs are *Wi-Fi (Wireless Fidelity)* certified. Wi-Fi is an interoperability certification based on one of the Institute of Electrical and Electronics Engineers (IEEE) 802.11 standards. The term Wi-Fi is often used as a generic reference to wireless networks.

The two protocols, Ethernet and Wi-Fi, can and do coexist in home networks. In fact, home networks with a combination of the two technologies are common (see Figure 3-2). In the Longnet introduced in Figure 1-2 in Chapter 1, the media hub and the Xbox in the entertainment center, both Ethernet devices, are connected via a wireless link to the home gateway. Ethernet and Wi-Fi devices can be connected to networks based on phoneline and powerline technologies, too. These alternative wired technologies are introduced in Chapter 4, Connectivity: Wired and Wireless.

IEEE 802.11 wireless is not really "wireless Ethernet," because 802.11 networks do not use CSMA/CD but use CSMA/CA instead. I would avoid using that term. (Of course, even Ethernet is not really Ethernet anymore; it's IEEE 802.3.)

Peer-to-Peer and Client/Server LANs

There are several ways to connect PCs and other devices to form a local area network, but most families opt for the least expensive, easiest-to-install approach to home networking—*peer-to-peer.* In Windows terminology, a peer-to-peer LAN often is called a *workgroup.* In a peer-to-peer LAN, all PCs on the network are peers, or equals, and a central server computer is not required to manage network resources. Each peer PC on a peer-to-peer network can share its files, printer, and other resources with its peers.

A much smaller percentage of home networks, mainly the homes of network wizards, install the more sophisticated *client/server networks,* which offer capabilities more aligned with the information processing needs of a business. In client/server networks, one or more central computers, called *server computers,* manage the resources on a network and perform a variety of functions for the other computers on the network, called *client computers.*

Most of us are very familiar with the client/server concept. The World Wide Web on the Internet is an example of a client/server network. Most businesses have a web server, and we use our client web browsers (such as Internet Explorer) to interact with web servers to access Net-based information. Also, we use an e-mail client (such as Outlook) to send e-mail to an incoming e-mail server (POP3 server) and receive e-mail from an outgoing mail server (SMTP server).

Client PCs are linked to the server computer to form the network. A client/server network can have one or many servers depending on need and application. The various types of servers include file, print, web, database, applications, and backup. Sometimes, a server is dedicated to one of these functions, and occasionally, a single server may perform multiple functions (for example, a print and file server).

In contrast to peer PCs in a peer-to-peer network, client computers in a client/server network generally do not share resources with other clients. Table 3-1 summarizes the characteristics of peer-to-peer and client/server networks.

	Peer-to-Peer Networking	Client/Server Networking
Where to use	Mostly in homes and small businesses	Mostly in businesses, government agencies, and education institutions
Size of network	Small (usually 10 or fewer nodes)	Medium (10–30 nodes) to large (30–150 nodes)
Ease of installation	Relatively easy	Usually requires a trained network administrator
Ease of maintenance	Relatively little	Usually requires a trained network administrator
Administration	Individual users can control sharing options	Sharing is tightly controlled by a network administrator
File sharing	All PCs share files	Shared files are centralized on one or more servers
Server options	Clients can be servers to peer PCs and share files, printers, the Internet, and other resources	Depending on need, types of servers (which normally are dedicated to one or more server functions) can include file, print, backup, web, database, applications, and so on
Authentication	The use of passwords is optional	Username and password must be entered by each user
Intranetwork security	There is an implied trust that fellow users on the network will act responsibly when sharing and using files	Users can access only their local files and shared files on the server(s)
Applications	Primarily local applications (each PC runs its own software)	Can support networkable applications where client PCs run applications from a server and share server-based databases
Network performance	Network overhead at the PC level can reduce performance	By relegating certain network tasks to servers, overall performance is optimized
Backup	Each user is responsible for his/her backup	Backup of important shared files is done at the server level

Table 3-1   Comparison Between Peer-to-Peer and Client/Server LANs

Because peer-to-peer networking is the overwhelming choice for home networks, our emphasis throughout this book is the *peer network*. Anyone installing a client/server network in the home doesn't need this book and probably enjoys the extra administrative work, expense, and headaches that come with the more sophisticated client/server network. Installing a client/server network in a home would be a good example of communications excess.

The line between peer-to-peer and client/server networks is beginning to blur. In a peer network, any PC can be a client to another peer PC or any PC can be a server and share its resources with its peers. Still, peer networks are less sophisticated than the business-oriented client/server networks, but they offer more than enough features and capabilities for home networking applications. Because they are relatively easy to install and maintain, peer-to-peer LANs are popular when small numbers of PCs are involved (for example, from 2 to 10). Most home networks are Windows-based peer-to-peer networks.

NOTE *The capabilities of peer-to-peer networking will continue to grow with the needs of home users and eventually look very much like client/server networks, but without the administrative hassle. For example, I would expect that a future version of Windows will support (and possibly encourage) the use of networkable software. This means that the PCs on the network interact with an applications server to load programs such as Word, Excel, and PowerPoint. Networkable software is licensed for sharing.*

LAN Servers

A *server* is simply any computer or device on a network that provides some service for other PCs on the LAN. Peer networks have servers, too. The most popular servers on a home network are the Internet access server, the file server, and the print server. The server can be a dedicated PC or a device, or the server function can be embedded in a multifunction PC or device. Figure 3-3 illustrates a home network that includes a wireless home gateway, which performs the function of an Internet access server. The gateway includes a *router*, which is a device that controls the flow of information between your home network LAN and the Internet (a WAN). It can be a stand-alone device, too. Other servers in Figure 3-3 include a network print server and a desktop PC that doubles as a multimedia and backup file server.

- **Internet server**   The Internet access server is a PC or a device that controls the flow of information between the PCs on your home network and the Internet. Sometimes a network PC does the work of a router, but in most modern home networks, the router is built into a home gateway or is a stand-alone single function communication device.

- **File server**   The file server normally is a PC with one or more high-capacity hard disks that are dedicated to storing the information that can be shared by network users. Sometimes, the file server is given a label that defines its function. For example, the Longnet has two such servers. A hard disk on Brady's PC serves as the multimedia server (stores images, music, and videos). A dedicated hard disk on Nancy's PC is the Longnet's backup server (provides backup storage for the other PCs).

- **Print server**   The print server handles user print jobs and controls at least one printer. The print server can be a network PC that shares its connected printer, or it can be a printer that is connected directly to the network with a stand-alone or built-in printer server device (see Figure 3-3). If needed, the server spools print jobs; that is, it saves print jobs to disk or memory until the requested printer is available, and then routes the print file to the printer.

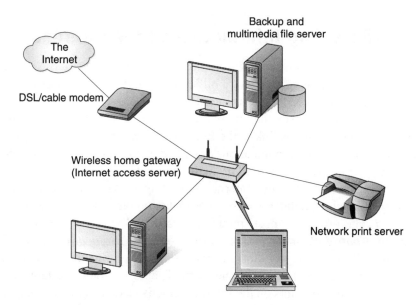

Figure 3-3   A home network with an Internet access server (the home gateway), a backup/multimedia file server, and a print server

Sharing Internet Access on a Home Network

You probably have two or more stand-alone PCs in your home, each of which is connected directly to the Internet via a dial-up or broadband link. If this is the case, there is no direct connection or communication between the PCs and each interacts independently with the Internet. A home network provides connectivity among the PCs and enables sharing of Internet access.

Communications-wise, there are two things happening in a home network. First, there is communication among the PCs, such as file and printer sharing. This transfer of information is made possible by the networking software built into the Windows operating system. PC-to-PC communications within a home network is relatively straightforward and is explained in later chapters. The second element of communications within a home network deals with sharing the Internet among the PCs on the network. Internet-related communication is not difficult either, but it has a few more points of potential confusion. So, if you wish to maintain a cheery nature during your home networking adventure, I would recommend that you become familiar with the principles and terminology associated with how information travels between nodes in your home network and the Internet.

Sending/Receiving Information on the Internet

The Internet is a network of networks. Your home network is one of those networks, and each PC in your network is one of a billion or so *nodes* with access to the Net. Your personal LAN is served by your Internet service provider, which has at least one *point of presence (POP)* on the Internet for use by its subscribers. ISPs maintain a high-speed communications link to the Internet's *backbone*, which is a system of high-level networks and communications devices that facilitate the interconnection of those computer networks with a POP on the Internet.

Data are transmitted over the Internet according to several *communications protocols*, each of which defines a set of rules that computers follow when they talk to each other. The protocols most frequently associated with the Internet are the *Transmission Control Protocol (TCP)* and the *Internet Protocol (IP)*. You'll see references to *TCP/IP* as you work through the process of setting up and maintaining an Internet connection on your home network. The TCP protocol establishes the guidelines by which two points on the Internet establish a connection and exchange information. The IP protocol describes an addressing scheme that enables information sent over the Net to reach its Internet destination. TCP/IP and Ethernet are both communications protocols, and both can be used to facilitate transmissions between computers. The typical home network will use both of these protocols.

The TCP and IP protocols combine with other protocols to enable the packaging of Internet transmissions into independent *packets*. Each packet on the Net contains an *IP address* of the destination, a portion of the user data, and the address of the sender. The packets travel independently through the Internet, and those from the same message may actually take different paths. Once all packets associated with a particular transmission have arrived at the destination, they are reassembled as an e-mail, a photo of grandfather, a colorful web page, or the like. If, for some reason, a packet is lost or is corrupted in transit, the destination computer notifies the source computer and requests that the packet(s) be resent to complete the transmission. This communications process, which happens very quickly, is called *packet switching*.

NOTE *The slow migration from traditional telephone systems to Voice over IP (VoIP) Internet-based telephone systems has begun. Over the next few years, I would expect that you will hear more about this transition and the difference between* circuit switching *and* packet switching. *When we call someone on a tradition telephone, we talk over a dedicated circuit (a channel) that spans the distance between the phones and lasts for the length of our conversation. This is circuit switching, and it wastes much of the capacity of the communications channel. In contrast, VoIP and the Internet use the more channel-efficient, digital packet switching technique.*

The IP Address

The year was 1969 and a U.S. Department of Defense sponsored project, named ARPANET, was underway to unite a community of geographically dispersed scientists by technology. The first official demonstration linked UCLA with Stanford University, both in California. Ten years later, the ARPANET had 200 sites, each with an IP address to facilitate communication. By 1990, ARPANET had evolved into what we now know as the Internet.

Who could possibly have imagined that the Internet would explode to encompass hundreds of millions of computers throughout the world? Apparently the wise people who designed the Internet were thinking ahead, because they created an addressing scheme that would permit over four billion unique addresses! Every node on the Internet could be assigned one of these addresses. The entire population of the world is only six billion and change, so we're okay for decades, right? Wrong.

Although the engineering end of the Internet was solid, the administrative end dropped the ball when assigning IP addresses. While some companies have IP addresses spilling out the door, some countries are left screaming for more. The

reality is that the Internet is running out of IP addresses. A new IP addressing scheme has been developed with enough address space to provide 1564 addresses for each square meter of the Earth's surface (over 35 trillion). That should suffice. This new version of IP addressing will replace the current scheme, but a complete conversion may take a decade or more. In the meantime, designers have given us an interim solution that adds another step to the transmission process, but it seems to work pretty well.

Dynamic IP Addressing

Each point of presence on the Internet, such as an Internet service provider, has one of those four-plus billion *IP addresses*, each of which consists of four numbers (0 to 255) separated by periods (for example, 65.70.230.81). Typically, when you log on to an ISP, your stand-alone PC is assigned a temporary IP address, called a *dynamic IP address*. Your computer has this address for as long as you are connected, and then it goes into a pool of addresses that can be reassigned. By assigning IP addresses as they are needed, the number of IP addresses required to serve ISP customers is minimized, since not all customers are online at any given time.

Because of the paucity of IP addresses, the ISP assigns a home network a single dynamic IP address when the network's modem/router requests Internet access and establishes a connection. So, with only one IP address per network, how is Internet information routed to the correct PC on your home LAN? This is done using a couple of technologies created to solve the problems created by a shortage of IP addresses. Before discussing these technologies, however, we need to look at the two different types of IP addresses they use.

The Public IP Address and the Private IP Address

In a perfect cyberworld, there would be enough IP addresses for every node on the Internet to have a unique IP address. As you know, the Net is less than perfect and there just aren't enough IP addresses to go around. To solve this dilemma, Internet designers had to create two types of addresses, the *public IP address* and the *private IP address*.

Public IP addresses are the addresses recognized throughout the Internet world as source/destination nodes, and they are in short supply. When IP addresses were passed out in the early days of the Net, universities and businesses, primarily in the United States, gobbled up large blocks of these addresses. And guess what? They're not giving them up.

IP addresses can be static or dynamic. A *static IP address* is one that is permanently assigned to an Internet node. The original plan for the Internet was for each node to have its own address, but explosive and continued growth of the Internet has made meeting this design objective impossible. Many points on the Internet have permanent addresses, such as businesses, government agencies, universities, and ISPs. But most of us who rely on ISPs for Internet access are assigned a *dynamic IP address*. ISPs have a pool of reusable IP addresses that they assign dynamically when a PC or network logs on to the Internet. The home network normally is assigned a single public IP address, even if the network has five PCs.

But how does the Internet know to send your e-mail to your PC and route the contents of a web page to your spouse's PC? Actually, it doesn't. Internet traffic destined for your home network is routed to that single dynamically assigned IP address. From there, your network gear uses private IP addresses, sometimes called *internal IP addresses*, to route information to the appropriate PC. Internal addresses are visible only within the confines of the network and cannot be reached from the Internet.

Your network's router monitors traffic between networked PCs and the Internet. The router uses the private IP addresses assigned to each networked PC to ensure that Internet traffic is routed to the appropriate destinations. International Network Standard RFC 1918 set aside several blocks of IP address for use as private IP addresses (see Table 3-2). You or your router can assign the addresses to the PCs on your network from one of these three blocks. The default setting for most home networks is the block of private addresses that begins with 192.168.0.0.

Dynamic Host Configuration Protocol (DHCP)

The *Dynamic Host Configuration Protocol,* or *DHCP* for short, is a protocol that works with TCP/IP to assign dynamic IP addresses. A *DHCP server* provides this service to its clients. Figure 3-4 illustrates two of the client/server relationships. First, there is the relationship between an ISP and the home networks and dial-up clients it serves. The figure also illustrates the client/server relationship between the home network's router and the PCs on the network.

Block Size (Number of Available IP Addresses)	Beginning Private IP Address	Ending Private IP Address
16.7 million	10.0.0.0	10.255.255.255
1 million	172.16.0.0	172.31.255.255
65 thousand	192.168.0.0	192.168.255.255

Table 3-2   Blocks of IP Addresses Available for Exclusive Use as Private IP Addresses Within a Network

The DHCP server in the ISP's router automatically assigns dynamic IP addresses to its clients from the ISP's pool of reusable public IP addresses (see Figure 3-4). The assignment of a dynamic IP address is part of the process that takes place when a stand-alone PC or a home network establishes a connection with an ISP. Typically, the PC or network will have the assigned IP address until the connection is broken. Another address is pulled from the reusable pool the next time a connection is made to the ISP.

Your home network's router, which probably will be built into your home gateway, uses an Internet standard called *Network Address Translation,* or *NAT.* A NAT router, which sits between the home LAN and the Internet WAN, will also have a DHCP server. This home network–level DHCP server assigns private IP addresses to the PCs on a home network (see Figure 3-4), probably those that begin with 192.168 (see Table 3-2). The primary function of NAT is to facilitate the routing of Internet communications between the outside network (the Internet) and the inside network (the home network). NAT keeps track of all information exiting the network into the Internet and all information entering the network from the Internet. When a user requests a web page or e-mail, NAT ensures that the requested web page or e-mail is returned to the correct PC.

An important side benefit of NAT is that it provides some measure of protection from the bad elements of cyberspace (and there are many). NAT shields internal IP addresses from the Internet; therefore, all of the internal (private) IP addresses are unknown by and inaccessible to the hackers and crackers who constantly prowl the Net for vulnerable networks and PCs.

TIP *To find the public IP address of your network (the address from which Internet service is requested), enter* **find IP address** *into any Internet search engine to get a list of sites that will return your network's IP address when displayed. To view the private IP address assigned to your PC by your home network's DHCP server, click Start | All Programs | Accessories | Command Prompt and then enter the command* **ipconfig** *to view the IP address (key in* **exit** *to terminate the command window).*

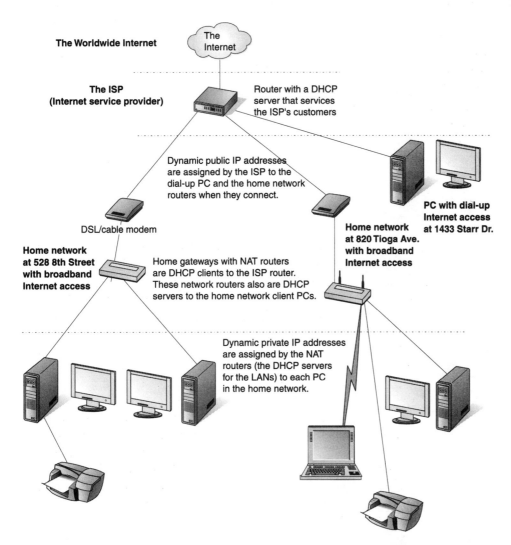

Figure 3-4   Assigning dynamic public IP addresses via an ISP's DHCP server and assigning dynamic private IP addresses via the home network's DHCP server

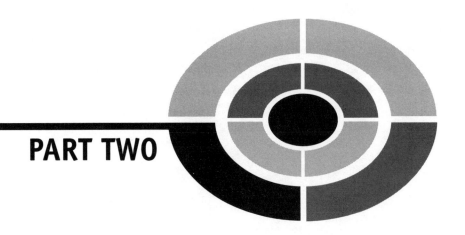

PART TWO

Home Networking Technologies and Equipment

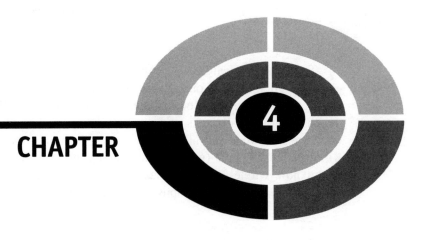

Connectivity: Wired and Wireless

My first exposure to computers was in college in the early 1960s. All engineering students were required to take a course on FORTRAN, a scientific programming language. We wrote our instructions with pencils on coding sheets and then went to the "computer center" to keypunch our programs into punched cards. A typical program would be a stack of 50 to 200 cards, each containing a program instruction. After we placed our programs on the "in" shelf, an operator loaded them into the computer's card reader. The programs and their printed output (usually containing lots of error messages) were returned to the "out" shelf. The process was repeated until the program did what it was supposed to do—without errors. Did I mention that the turnaround time was unknown and could be minutes, hours, and even days? We would return to the computer center throughout the day (and night) to check if our program had been run.

Today, the typical college student will have his or her own PC. And that PC, usually a notebook, is on the college's network no matter where the student or PC is located—in the dorm room or under a giant oak tree. College campuses are strewn with Ethernet wall jacks and wireless hotspots that enable an easy link to the college's network and all of it resources, including the Internet and the campus information systems (grades, assignments, library access, and so on). Our wired (and now wireless) society has come a long way since punch cards. We are connected, whether on campus, at work, or now, at home.

Connectivity Technologies: The Transmission Media

Because home networking has a smorgasbord of options, home networks are like snowflakes—no two are alike. Your home, your personal computing hardware, and your personal preferences are unique, so it stands to reason that your home network will be one of a kind. One of the primary contributors to the uniqueness of your home network is how you choose to connect the nodes in your network.

An important design consideration revolves around whether you want a wired network, a wireless network, or a network with a combination of these connectivity options. Wired and wireless technologies for home networking are the focus of this chapter. These options are summarized in Table 4-1 and explained in the sections that follow.

Wired Networking Technologies

If you choose to link the PCs in your home network with wires, the most popular technology is *Ethernet,* but *HomePNA* and *HomePlug* are viable options. The primary difference among these wired alternatives is that you will need to install cabling for Ethernet links, but existing telephone wires and electrical wiring provide the wiring structure for HomePNA and HomePlug connectivity, respectively. Also, Ethernet has a transmission speed advantage, at least for now. The advantages and disadvantages of these proven technologies are summarized in Table 4-1 and discussed in the following sections.

	Wired Networks			Wireless Networks
	---	---	---	---
	Ethernet	**HomePNA**	**HomePlug**	**Wireless-B, Wireless-G, enhanced Wireless-G, and Wireless-N**
Maximum speed	10/100/1000 Mbps	10 Mbps (HPNA 2.0) 128 Mbps to 240 Mbps (HPNA 3.0)*	14 Mbps (HomePlug 1.0) 100 Mbps (HomePlug AV)*	11 Mbps for Wireless-B 54 Mbps for Wireless-G 108 Mbps for enhanced Wireless-G 200 plus Mbps for Wireless-N
Operational speed	4 Mbps 55 Mbps 500–600 Mbps	5 Mbps 60–100 Mbps*	6 Mbps 30–60 Mbps*	4–6 Mbps 15–40 Mbps 25–60 Mbps 100-125 Mbps
Effective Range	328 feet	1000 feet	1000 feet	For Wireless-B/G: 100–300 feet (indoors) Up to 1300 feet (outdoors, unobstructed) For Wireless-N: 1000-plus feet (indoors) up to .5 miles (outdoors)
Cost of hardware	Least expensive	Moderately priced	Moderately priced	Most expensive
Transmission media	Cat 5 or Cat 5e cabling with RJ-45 connectors	Standard telephone lines with RJ-11 connectors	AC electrical power lines	Wireless-B (802.11b) and Wireless-G (802.11g) Wireless-N (802.11n)
Cost of transmission media	Most expensive Cost: From $50 to $100 for Cat 5 or Cat 5e for a typical three-PC network	Minimal (if existing telephone lines used)	Minimal (if existing power lines used)	Least expensive (no wires)
Cost of transmission media installation	Most expensive (new wiring)	Minimal (if existing telephone lines used)	Minimal (if existing power lines used)	Least expensive (no wires)
Pros	High-speed, low-cost, reliable, and proven hardware technology; *de facto* standard in office LANs	Offers excellent balance among cost, ease of installation, and speed	Offers excellent balance among cost, ease of installation, and speed; multiple AC outlets in every room	Flexibility in location of nodes; notebook PCs have network portability; easy to install (no cables to buy and run); Wireless-B and -G *de facto* standards in office wireless LANs
Cons	Running cables between rooms/ floors can be cumbersome and expensive	Requires a telephone jack near each PC	Security (vulnerable to unauthorized access from immediate neighbors)	Signal speed affected by location and obstructions; possible interference from devices on same frequency band (Bluetooth devices, portable phones, etc.); security (vulnerable to unauthorized access)

*Announced standards to be implemented in the future as support software and hardware become available.

Table 4-1   Home Networking Wired and Wireless Technologies

Ethernet

Most modern PCs and home networking communications gear are set up to handle Ethernet connectivity. The additional cost to a manufacturer to add Ethernet compatibility is less than $5, so virtually all new desktop PCs and all new notebook PCs are sold Ethernet ready.

The Ethernet Wiring Challenge

The greatest challenge associated with installing Ethernet links between network nodes is the installation of the wiring. People-friendly houses allow freedom of movement between rooms; however, they are not Ethernet friendly. Few of us would be satisfied with Ethernet wiring running through doorways, along hallways, and down the stairs. Getting Ethernet wiring from room to room in an unobtrusive manner is, at times, cumbersome. The amount of effort and expense involved in the installation of Cat 5 (Category 5), Cat 5e, or Cat 6 cabling depends on where you place your PCs and the structure of your home.

If the installation of cabling takes place during new construction along with telephone and electrical wiring, a qualified electrician can install the cabling that terminates at standard Ethernet wall jacks for about $50 a room. However, if the wires are to be installed in an existing house, the cost can be two to five times that amount per room, depending on how unobtrusive you wish to make the wiring and jacks. If all you wish to do is run a cable between adjacent rooms, you may simply need to install and connect RJ-45 wall jacks on either side of the wall. However, if you plan widely dispersed PCs throughout the house, that's an entirely different and more complicated project.

Over the last 25 years my family and I have strung several thousand feet of cabling in two existing homes for our security system, phone/intercom system, home theater, and home network. We spent many hours contemplating how to get cables from one room to the next and sometimes just across the room. We used attics, narrow crawl spaces, soffits, windows, and external eves. We have run wires among and through wall studs, within ceiling rafters, in basements, and through cabinets. The wiring process can be time-consuming and, frequently, difficult, even if you have some expertise in carpentry and electrical wiring. Nevertheless, we chose to do all the wiring ourselves to save money, but most importantly, to get it done on a timely basis. Contractors tend to slip "small retrofit jobs" into their schedules just after the twelfth of never.

TIP *Stringing Ethernet cable in existing homes can be challenging, but it is not rocket science. Anyone with the motivation to save some money can install the necessary wiring. It just takes time and a little forethought. Who knows your home, its layout, and its idiosyncrasies better than you? So, before you decide to hire it done, think it through and come up with some solutions. If you have the skills, tools, and confidence to do it yourself as a weekend project, you can save some serious money, possibly hundreds of dollars.*

Ethernet may be the best wired solution for a home network, that is, if you don't mind the added expense and effort required to string Ethernet wire between the nodes. Ethernet cabling is relatively inexpensive and offers speeds at 10 Mbps and 100 Mbps; normally the latter, which is faster than the current HomePNA and HomePlug technologies. If you wish to plan for the future and higher speeds, you can upgrade to gigabit Ethernet cards that support Gigabit Ethernet at 1000 Mbps. With the trend toward Gigabit Ethernet, many new PCs already have integrated 10/100/1000 Ethernet cards.

Ethernet Wiring: Cat 5, Cat 5e, and Cat 6

Most Ethernet home networks use Cat 5, Cat 5e, or Cat 6 cabling. These cables have four insulated copper twisted-pair wires (eight wires) within a common jacket terminated by Registered Jack–45 (RJ-45) male connectors (see Figure 4-1). Each pair of wires is color coded so that pairs can be easily matched when splicing wires or installing to wall jacks or connectors. Two wires are twisted around each other to reduce crosstalk or electromagnetic induction, thus the twisted-pair name.

The four-pair RJ-45 connectors are similar to and slightly larger than the familiar RJ-11 connectors used with telephones. The RJ-11 jack is designed to handle three twisted pairs (six wires) but is usually implemented with one or two pairs. Most lines used to connect telephones to an RJ-11 wall jack have only one pair (see Figure 4-1). One pair is all that is needed to carry voice conversations or data over a telephone line.

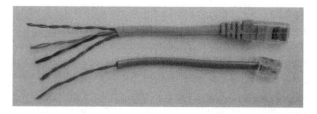

Figure 4-1   An eight-wire Cat 5e Ethernet cable with a four-pair wire RJ-45 male connector (top) and a two-wire telephone cable with a three-pair RJ-11 connector

The generic name for these types of wires is *unshielded twisted pair,* or *UTP.* UTP wire is fine for cabling inside the house. However, *shielded twisted pair,* or *STP,* may be needed to shield and protect the twisted pairs whenever the possibility exists for crosstalk between adjacent cables or to protect the copper wires from external elements. An STP cable containing 25 twisted pairs (50 wires) runs between my house and office. The 200-foot cable, which is buried about one foot deep in an electrical conduit, carries signals for our computer-based telephone/intercom system (12 pair), the security system (4 pair), and an Ethernet line for the home network link (4 pair). Regular UTP cables are spliced to either end of the STP cable to complete the connections to the systems at the house and the office.

The difference among the categories is performance, with performance and cost increasing from Cat 5 to Cat 5e to Cat 6. All support Fast Ethernet, the target speed for most home networks. Most current wiring structures for Ethernet-based home networks are built with Cat 5 cable, which works well for 10 Mbps or 100 Mbps networks. However, an increasing number of home networks are using high-performance Cat 5e (Cat 5 enhanced) and Cat 6 cables that enable gigabit networks (1000 Mbps or 1 Gbps). The cost of the Cat 5 cabling for a representative three-PC home would be in the range of $50 to $150. Add a little extra for Cat 5e or Cat 6. The cost of the cable is relatively small when compared to the cost of the network gear, so I would advise against trying to save money on cabling.

Cat 5, Cat 5e, and Cat 6 cabling can be purchased in bulk or in a variety of *patch cables* (premade cables with RJ-45 male connectors on both ends). You can save a little money if you purchase Cat 5 in bulk, but you will need a special crimping tool and some electrical savvy to attach the RJ-45 connectors to the cable. The actual installation of wiring is covered in Chapter 7.

NOTE *All Ethernet wiring and components, such as the RJ-45 connectors and wall jacks, must be rated at the same category (Cat 5, Cat 5e, and Cat 6).*

HomePNA: Phoneline

HomePNA (HPNA) technology enables home phoneline networking, where PCs are linked and communicate over the home's existing telephone wiring at speeds up to 10 Mbps. If the next generation of HomePNA, called HPNA 3.0, lives up to its promise of reliable speeds of 128–240 Mbps, the decision between Ethernet and home phoneline networking will be made more complex. The typical home is peppered with RJ-11 jacks and already has the wiring structure for an HPNA-based home network.

Telephone lines, you say? Well, aren't these used for our telephone conversations? Indeed, they are. The same lines may also carry the DSL broadband signal, too.

Because each service uses a different frequency band, voice and multiple data signals can be transmitted simultaneously over the same twisted-pair telephone line.

The first Longnet in our current home was based on HPNA technology, and it worked very well, but at a relatively slow 10 Mbps. We used both internal PCI cards and external HPNA network adapters to complete the network. The adapters were connected to the phoneline system in the same way and with the same twisted-pair male-to-male cable that you use to connect your telephones. HPNA external adapters are connected to PCs via a USB cable.

The length of the telephone line between the house and my office was over 300 feet. Even so, the signal was strong enough to transmit 4 Mbps to the house, more than enough to share the 1.5 Mbps broadband access from the satellite dish pointed skyward outside my office. Eventually, we replaced the expensive satellite service with DSL. The three—DSL, HPNA, and voice—used the same phonelines and coexisted in harmony for several years. Now that we have converted to the Fast Ethernet, it's just DSL and voice on the phonelines.

HomePlug: AC Power Lines

HomePlug technology uses the AC power lines throughout the house as the transmission media in the network. On average, an electrical outlet is placed every eight feet along the walls of homes, providing a convenient conduit for data transmission around the walls of every room in the house. Power outlets are everywhere in the typical house—in every room, the garage, and often, at points outside the house—so the wiring structure for a HomePlug network is conveniently intact.

HomePlug 1.0, the current technology, has a rated line capacity of 14 Mbps. The future of HomePlug technology, however, is much faster, up to 100 Mbps. Called HomePlug AV, the improved power line standard will support the streaming of audiovisual (AV) multimedia content, including high-definition television (HDTV), high-quality audio, and voice over IP telephony. The term *telephony* often is used to refer to the integration of computers and telephones.

HomePlug is a relatively easy way to set up a home network. Simply plug in as many wall-mount HomePlug network adapters (see Figure 4-2) into electrical outlets as you have PCs. They are connected to one another through the home's existing system of AC power lines. Depending on which adapters you choose, connect the wall mount adapters to the PCs via USB cables and/or Ethernet patch cables. To use Ethernet cable, you will need an Ethernet adapter for your PCs. Most modern computers are equipped with an Ethernet adapter. HomePlug wireless access points can be plugged into electrical outlets in the same manner to extend the network to link devices with wireless adapters.

We have three nationwide wired networks: the telephone system, the cable TV system, and the electrical power grid. The Internet is actively flowing on the first

Figure 4-2   HomePlug wall mount network adapter (courtesy of NETGEAR Inc.)

two via DSL and cable modem. It now appears that the nation's power grid is being primed to deliver Internet access *to* homes as well as *within* homes. Several telephone and electricity companies are currently testing a plan for providing broadband Internet access over power lines. Current tests have shown that the power grid can be used to deliver a 13 Mbps capacity to wireless access points embedded in street lampposts. Nearby homes can receive up to 3 Mbps of wireless Internet access. Far more homes have electricity than do fixed-wire telephones or cable TV. Will the power grid be our primary mechanism for Internet connectivity? Time will tell.

TIP As a general rule, use Fast Ethernet and/or Wireless-G (or Wireless-G enhanced) technologies for LAN connectivity whenever possible. The data rates for these transmission media are fast enough to support multimedia applications involving image, audio, video, and recorded TV files or to perform backups. When these faster solutions are impractical, HomePNA at 10 Mbps and HomePlug at 14 Mbps will work well, albeit at a slower data rate. Circumstance for using existing wiring might be that the installation of Ethernet wiring is prohibitively expensive or physically very difficult or that achieving a consistently strong wireless signal is unlikely. Also, if your primary application for home networking is Internet access sharing, then the slower wired options have more than enough capacity to deliver broadband Internet access, which normally is in the 1–3 Mbps range.

Wireless Networking Technologies

Not too long ago, wireless was too slow and way too expensive for home networks. Not anymore. Wireless is emerging as a viable, if not preferred, networking technology for all or part of home networks.

Going Wireless: A Historical Perspective

Wireless is nothing new, even to those of us who have been around for a while. Radio signals have traversed the airwaves for as long as I can remember. I do, however, remember the first television in our neighborhood and how truly amazed we were that the television can pull moving pictures from thin air and display them on a huge seven-inch screen. Equally amazing is the fact that broadcast radio and television were developed as wireless technologies from the beginning but that now they are being delivered via cable, too.

We are living in an increasingly wireless world. Fifteen years ago, wireless pagers were worn by a select few who needed that type of connectivity. Today, cellular phones are worn by the masses and have all but eliminated geography from the voice communications equation. Cordless phones with ranges that enable people to walk their neighborhoods now outsell wired phones two to one. Radio, TV, pagers, cell phones, satellite HDTV, garage door openers, keyless entry, and so on are commonplace. We accept their range and flexibility as part of what we do.

Only within the last few years have wireless home networks been installed in any numbers, so wireless in the home is still in the emergent stage of development. In time, however, I would expect wireless networking to become part of the fabric of our lives—at home, at work, or just about anywhere else, even along the highway.

NOTE *A decade ago, the Long household had six fixed traditional terrestrial telephone lines coming into the house: three data lines for dial-up modems (one for the 56 Kbps dial-up modems in the house and two for a 128 Kbps dial-up ISDN modem that required two lines), one for fax, and two for voice. Today we have two voice lines and only need one, primarily to deliver DSL broadband access. If we had cable modem access, we wouldn't need any. All four of us carry our cell phones with us wherever we go, and our cells give us unlimited calling and lots of services. Moreover, much of the personal communication that at one time was done via landline telephone is now done via e-mail, instant messaging, and other Internet-based applications. My family and millions of others are asking: Why do we need landlines? The migration is on from wired telephone to a world that depends on wireless telephones and Internet-based communications. In retrospect, we may look back at this era of technological development and mark it as the beginning of the end of wired voice connectivity. Our grandchildren will be truly puzzled when we tell them that there was a time when we actually had to sit at a desk to talk on the telephone and that computers were linked to the Internet via wires.*

Why Wireless?

A home network can be entirely wired, entirely wireless, or both. Wired links are consistently reliable, and Fast Ethernet connections can offer faster transmission speeds than wireless links. My recommendation would be to consider linking stationary desktop PCs on the network with Fast Ethernet cabling in those circumstances when cabling can be run with ease and at limited cost. All other situations invite the possibility of wireless links. The following are the reasons most often cited for why people choose to design all or part of their home network with wireless connections.

- **Portability**   One of the key benefits of wireless networking is portability, which is having the ability to physically relocate PCs, printers, and other network components within the home. Moving a desktop PC to the other side of the room or to another room is a non-issue with a wireless network. The same is true with rearranging the linked audio/video equipment in the home theater.

- **Flexibility**   Having the flexibility to enjoy connectivity and Internet access on notebook PCs, PDAs, and other mobile devices from anywhere within and around the house is a huge advantage. Our house guests appreciate being able to use their notebooks and PDAs to tap into our home network's broadband Internet service.

- **Ease of growth**   All you have to do to add a wireless-ready PC to the network is turn it on. The network and PC quickly find each other. There is no need to string wires.

- **Speed**   You can avoid the hassle of running Fast Ethernet wiring and simply use either your existing telephone or AC power wiring structure. However, current implementations of HomePNA and HomePlug technology operate at 10 Mbps and 14 Mbps. These speeds are significantly slower than the 54 Mbps data rates in state-of-the-art wireless networks.

- **To take advantage of mobile computers and devices**   Notebook PCs now outsell desktop PCs, and we can expect an even greater percentage of PC sales to be notebooks in the future. People want mobility in the office, when they travel, and at home. If you have a house full of notebooks and PDAs, you may as well have wireless networking so that you can realize their full potential. This includes being able to create an *ad hoc network* among wireless-ready PCs. This type of *spontaneous network* is great for a variety of applications, from gaming to working on a team project.

The Wireless Options

For most of my professional life, networks were wired, mostly with Ethernet interfaces. In the late 1990s, the wireless LAN became an "alternative" networking strategy. Today, the "alternative" tag no longer applies and wireless is fully capable of serving as a primary LAN solution.

The most popular connectivity standards used for short-range wireless networking are the IEEE 802.11 communications standards.

- **IEEE 802.11b (Wireless-B)**   The *IEEE 802.11b* standard, often called *Wireless-B,* permits wireless transmission at 11 Mbps up to about 300 feet from an access point (up to 1300 feet outdoors). *Wireless-B* and the other options evolved from the original 802.11 standard. At this time, Wireless-B is the most widely deployed standard. It sends data via radio waves over the 2.4 GHz ISM frequency band (ISM stands for industrial, scientific, and medical), the same band used by modern cordless telephones.

- **IEEE 802.11a (Wireless-A)**   The *Wireless-A* standard permits a transmission rate of 54 Mbps, but because the effective range can be less than 25 feet in a house, this standard is not a player in home networking. This newer standard transmits over the 5 GHz U-NII frequency band (Unified National Information Infrastructure).

- **IEEE 802.11g (Wireless-G)**   The *Wireless-G* standard, which also uses the 2.4 GHz band, offers Wireless-A speeds (54 Gbps) with Wireless-B distances. Wireless-G has emerged as the clear choice for wireless home networking. Virtually all Wireless-G communications devices are backward compatible with Wireless-B net gear.

- **IEEE 802.11n (Wireless-N)**   At this writing, Wireless-N, the next generation standard is still in development in an IEEE task group and has not been approved as an industry standard. The task group's objectives are to create a standard for high-performance wireless networks that provides for throughput performance that quadruples that of Wireless-G. Wireless-N speeds are expected to be in excess of 200 Mbps with a range in excess of 1000 feet indoors and much further outdoors. It's likely networking products based on an approved 802.11n standard will be available by the next edition of this book.

Most major manufacturers of Wireless networking equipment jumped the gun on the Wireless-N standard and have introduced Wireless-G enhancements that enables data rates of up to 108 Mbps, twice that of Wireless-G. This enhancement also extends

the coverage (the effective range of the signal), as well. Enhanced Wireless-G network equipment is backward compatible with all IEEE 802.11 standards, so the equipment would automatically choose the highest possible data rate for connected devices.

These 802.11 standards are the result of efforts by a worldwide consortium of engineers. Their work is ongoing, and they are continually reevaluating the standards and adding new features and capabilities. These standards become the basis for improved products for wireless communication. In contrast, enhanced Wireless-G products are the result of entrepreneurial innovation by for-profit companies to meet a growing need for faster data rates on wireless networks.

TIP *Wireless-B has the largest installed base for home networks, but it will soon give way to Wireless-G or proprietary enhanced Wireless-G options (for example, Linksys's SpeedBooster and Belkin's Pre-N), which offer data rates that are five to ten times faster than Wireless-B. You may be able to purchase a Wireless-B home networking kit at a dramatically reduced price. Please don't. For a little more money, you can purchase Wireless-G net gear. With significantly faster data rates more in line with multimedia requirements and, generally, better wireless technologies embedded in the devices, Wireless-G is a great buy. Of course, wireless technology marches on as Wireless-G products soon will be pushed aside for Wireless-N products.*

The speeds and effective ranges of wireless options are summarized in Table 4-1. The actual range of wireless transmission may vary markedly, depending on the quality of the wireless hardware and whether or not the point-to-point transmission is impeded by obstructions. The wood and wallboard construction in the typical home has relatively little impact on wireless transmission speeds. Water and metal, however, can slow or block wireless transmissions.

NOTE *Some companies sell enhanced Wireless-G products that deliver better "real-world" performance with up to a 40 percent improvement over regular Wireless-G network gear. This technology is packaged under several names. Broadcom calls it Wireless-G Afterburner. Linksys terms its solution Wireless-G SpeedBooster. Belkin's entry is the Wireless-G 125 High Speed Mode or Pre-N. These products are primarily for bandwidth-intensive applications, such as the sharing of multimedia files. If you don't anticipate frequent use of audio/video files, you may be best served to stay with products based on the original Wireless-G standard. Plain old Wireless-G has more than enough speed to play DVD-quality video and is working extremely well in millions of homes. Afterburner technology is relatively new and unproven. Although backward compatible, the performance benefits are lost unless all network devices include the enhanced technology.*

CAUTION *Whenever you purchase products based on a ratified communications standard, such as Wireless-B, you can be reasonably assured that the next generation of the standard, in this case Wireless-G, will have backward compatibility. This means that your Wireless-B hardware will work with Wireless-G hardware. When you purchase products with proprietary enhancements that do not conform to ratified standards, there is a very real possibility that you may end up with orphaned technology that may not work with future ratified standards.*

Wireless Modes: Infrastructure and Ad Hoc

When you talk wireless, you need to talk in terms of its two modes: infrastructure and ad hoc (see Figure 4-3). *Infrastructure mode* is what you normally would deem to be a wireless LAN. In this mode, the network would have at least one access point (AP) that enables wireless communication between multiple wireless PCs and devices on a network. The typical wireless infrastructure, including one in the

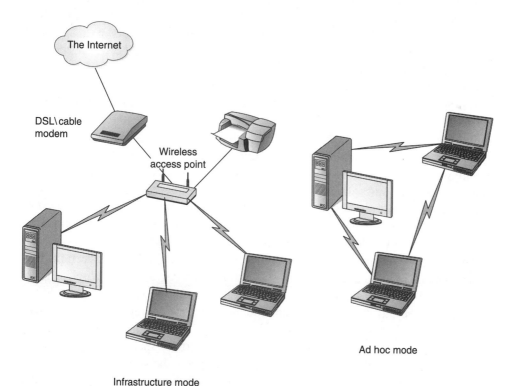

Figure 4-3   Wireless modes of operation: infrastructure and ad hoc

home, would include the ability to communicate with wired components as well, such as a printer or a multimedia file server.

Having an AP is highly recommended for home networks with wireless communication, but the AP is not essential for wireless networking. PCs and devices equipped with wireless network adapters can communicate directly with one another without using an AP. Use *ad hoc mode* to form spontaneous or on-the-fly networks. Any group of people with wireless-ready PCs can easily form an impromptu LAN using ad hoc mode. The ad hoc mode works extremely well for any type of gathering of people with PCs: company meetings, study groups, classes, and so on. To create a spontaneous network, participants simply turn on their PCs while within close proximity of one another. The PCs recognize the presence of the wireless links.

Fallback: Data Rate Versus Reliability

Wi-Fi networking uses radio-based technology, which means that the radio waves carrying the signals can be absorbed or blocked by walls, furniture, appliances, fish tanks, and even other computers. This interference with the signals may result in dead spots in which the radio signal is lost. Fortunately, dead spots often are small and may encompass only a portion of the room. Repositioning the wireless access point or the PC can usually solve this problem.

Optimally, all devices on a wireless network would communicate at the maximum operational speed of the devices (54 Mbps for Wireless-G). This is a realistic goal for some home networks; however, network performance (the speed of the connection) will vary with the signal strength. Therefore, the data rate may vary, depending on the distance between communicating devices, the types of objects blocking the line-of-sight radio wave paths between these devices, and the level of interference from other devices that use the same frequencies. Although cordless telephones and microwave ovens operate on the same frequency band, they use slightly different frequencies within the radio frequency (RF) range and, generally, are not a threat to wireless network reliability.

The objective of wireless LAN technology is to make the link between devices as reliable and consistent as possible. As performance degrades, the wireless LAN activates the *fallback* feature. This feature falls back or switches to a slower connection speed to maintain a reliable connection. For example, when a weaker signal can no longer maintain a reliable data rate of 54 Mbps, the LAN components (AP and wireless network adapter) fall back to a slower speed, perhaps half the maximum speed. If reliability is a concern at that speed, the system falls back to an even slower speed, eventually falling back to a speed that is consistent with a reliable connection. A reliable connection at a slower speed is always preferred over one that offers a higher speed but may be unreliable.

There are devices and strategies that can be employed to boost wireless performance throughout the network. These are discussed in Chapters 5 and 6.

TIP *There is a good chance that one or more of the PCs on your wireless network will operate at less than Wireless-G capacity. Therefore, I would recommend that you position your wireless access point to give the most-used PC the highest possible level of wireless performance.*

The Need for Speed

There will always be a need for more speed in computer networks, especially with all the new multimedia network applications on the horizon, such as Internet telephony and movies on demand. And, there will always be engineers and entrepreneurs doing what they can to meet that need.

As with any area of technological innovation, it's difficult to predict the winds of change in how the various technologies will sort out in the coming years. For now, the standard for wired home networks is Fast Ethernet (100 Gbps), but I would imagine that Gigabit Ethernet (1000 Gbps) will evolve as the standard as supporting network gear drops in price and as it becomes the standard implementation in new PCs.

If I were building a new home, I would install a Gigabit Ethernet infrastructure. The vast majority of homes, though, are existing structures that are difficult to retrofit with network wiring. Fortunately, virtually all existing homes have a twisted-pair telephone system and electrical outlets in every room, both of which can carry high-speed network signals. If the network industry embraces the new HomePNA 3.0 standard, which has an operational maximum of 240 Mbps, or the new HomePlug AV standard at 100 Mbps, then one or both of these may evolve as the de facto wired standard for home networks. That, however, is a big "if." For this to happen, the industry would have to commit not only to the research and development of supporting equipment, but to an expensive, protracted, and risky marketing campaign, as well.

The baton for the wireless standard has been passed to Wireless-G, but a series of entrepreneurial enhancements, such as Pre-N and SpeedBooster, give us cause to question how long Wireless-G will hold the baton. Retail shelves are filled with enhanced Wireless-G products, thus pressuring the IEEE 802.11n Task Group to complete its work on Wireless-N, a standard that is expected to quadruple throughput performance. The only thing I can say with some confidence is that the next edition of this book will present new and ever-faster network technologies.

CHAPTER

5

Net Gear: Gateways, Modems, and More

Those of us who do personal computing are somewhat familiar with PCs, printers, scanners, and other common hardware, but it's not these devices that enable the wired and wireless links in a home network. It's a family of communications equipment that, for the most part, will be new to you if you are building a home network for the first time. This chapter provides a survey of network gear commonly found in home networks, showing you the functions and applications for a variety of these devices. When you initially build your network, it is unlikely you will use all of them. But in time, your network will grow and you will appreciate having this knowledge when it comes time to purchase the additional devices.

Approaches to Networking: ICS and Home Gateway

Home networks are created by linking the internal or external network adapters for the PCs in the network via some type of data transmission medium, either wired or wireless. There are two viable ways to do this and enjoy shared Internet access. One approach is to designate one of the PCs as the *host PC*. In this network design, the host becomes the central point in the home network and handles the communications duties between the networked PCs and the Internet sharing. This approach, which is illustrated in Figure 5-1, uses the *Internet Connection Sharing (ICS)* feature built into Microsoft Windows. The other, more modern and, in my opinion, preferable approach is to use a multifunction home gateway (see Figure 5-2).

In the late 1990s, I chose and installed a host-based home network that used ICS. ICS was the obvious solution for the cost-conscious consumer at that time because communications gear was very expensive. Today, we can purchase the convenience and flexibility of a wireless home gateway for under $100 (versus $1000 or more in the late 1990s). This relatively small investment has one of the best, if not the best, paybacks in personal computing. I highly recommend that you consider the second approach and go with a multifunction home gateway.

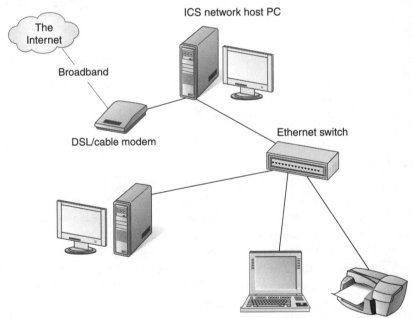

Figure 5-1   Home networking via Internet Connection Sharing (ICS)

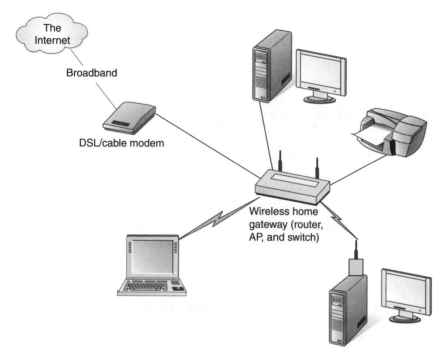

Figure 5-2   Home networking via a multifunction home gateway

There is no comparison between the two approaches when it comes to convenience and overall network functionality. For example, the ICS host PC in Figure 5-1 must be on and running to enable Internet Connection Sharing (ICS). When it's down or off, the other PCs are without Internet access. The ICS software runs on the host PC, so Internet access speeds can suffer if the ICS host PC is running a processor-intensive application, such as a video game or a disk scanning utility. No matter which way you view the situation, the home gateway approach of Figure 5-2 wins easily over the "PC as gateway" solution shown in Figure 5-1. For example, the home gateway's firewall offers a greater degree of protection from Internet intruders because the gateway has no files or folders and, therefore, can't be hacked to manipulate network PCs.

The advantage of not having to buy a home gateway for a host PC network is more than offset by the overwhelming advantages of building a network around a relatively inexpensive home gateway. Moreover, it's likely your DSL or cable broadband ISP is promoting the use of gateways for delivering Internet access to home networks. Indeed, the argument for gateways is so compelling that this

approach is assumed throughout the remainder of the chapter. If you are currently maintaining an ICS host-PC network, I would encourage you to switch to one based on a home gateway.

The Hardware: Network Gear

In the business world, the number and variety of communications devices needed to link PCs in a local area network can easily fill a half-inch thick catalog. Professional network administrators choose the required devices to meet their company's network needs. The LAN in the home, however, is on a smaller scale and is not nearly so complex. Home networking is vastly simplified because communications manufacturers have wrapped much of the necessary LAN functionality into a single unit—the *home gateway* or *residential gateway*.

Ethernet and Wireless Network Adapters

To set up a home network, you need a *network adapter* installed on each PC. The PCI card and CardBus/PC card versions of the network adapter also are called *network interface cards (NICs)*. Most new desktop PCs and all new notebook PCs are equipped with internal Ethernet adapters. If not, PCI card adapters are easily installed in desktop PCs and CardBus/PC Card adapters are easily inserted into one of the notebook's external expansion slots. The external adapters are connected via USB cable. Also, small USB devices with Ethernet ports are available that can be inserted directly into USB ports.

Each PC in the home network of Figure 5-2 has a network adapter. The wired desktop PC has an internal PCI Ethernet adapter. The other desktop PC is linked via an external USB Wireless-G network adapter. The Wireless-G network adapter in the family notebook PC is a PC card, which is inserted into a PC card slot.

Table 5-1 summarizes the most popular wired and wireless network adapter options for desktop PCs, including relevant points and concerns. Table 5-2 does the same for notebook PCs. Figures 5-3 and 5-4 show several popular options for desktop and notebook network adapters. The USB Wireless-G and compact USB Ethernet network adapters in Figure 5-5 can be used with any USB-ready PC.

	Desktop PC Network Adapters	
	Wired Link	**Wireless Link**
Integrated (built into motherboard)	*Preferred*: No installation required. Most new desktops have built-in Ethernet.	
PCI card	Installation involves opening the system unit.	Clean appearance with no wires. Installation involves opening the system unit. The system unit can block the line-of-sight signal.
USB	Easy to install (plug USB cable or device into USB port).	*Preferred*: Can be positioned to achieve the best possible signal.

Table 5-1   Ethernet Network Adapters for Desktop PCs

NOTE   *Until 1996, the technology for cards inserted into a notebook PC's external expansion slots was PCMCIA (Personal Computer Memory Card International Association). Rather than use this cumbersome acronym, people just called it the PC card. We still call it the PC card, but today's PC cards are CardBus technology. The new PCs will accept either PCMCIA or CardBus cards. The copper contact strip on the CardBus cards distinguishes them from the original PCMCIA cards (see Figure 5-4).*

	Notebook PC Network Adapters	
	Wired Link	**Wireless Link**
Integrated (built into motherboard or implemented as a miniPCI card)	*Preferred*: No installation required. All new notebooks have built-in Ethernet.	*Preferred*: No installation required.
CardBus/PC Card	To use, simply insert into slot and connect Ethernet cable. PC cards frequently are lost.	To use, simply insert PC card into slot. Easy to upgrade to a new technology. PC cards frequently are lost and/or antennas are broken.
USB	Easy to install (plug USB cable or device into USB port). Small, one-piece devices stick out and are easily broken.	Can be positioned to achieve the best possible signal, but can be excess baggage in a mobile environment.

Table 5-2   Ethernet Network Adapters for Notebook PCs

Courtesy of US Robotics

Figure 5-3   Internal network adapters for desktop PCs: PCI Ethernet card (left) and Wireless-G PCI card (right)

Courtesy of Intel Corporation; Courtesy of US Robotics

Figure 5-4   Network adapters for notebook PCs: miniPCI Ethernet card (left) and Wireless-G PC card (right)

Courtesy of US Robotics; Courtesy of Linksys

Figure 5-5   USB network adapters: USB Wireless-G adapter and compact USB Ethernet adapter

TIP *Most integrated Ethernet network adapters will support 10/100 Mbps. Some support 10/100/1000 Mbps. Nevertheless, it's a good idea to check the adapter's specifications to ensure that it will run the speeds you plan for your network.*

HomePlug and HomePNA Network Adapters

Other popular types of wired home network adapters are the *HomePlug powerline adapter* and the *HomePNA phoneline adapter.* These technologies are introduced in Chapter 4. Whereas Ethernet and Wireless-B/G network adapters often come installed on PCs, the adapters for these technologies typically are installed separately. These technologies can, and often do, exist on the same network with wired Ethernet and/or Wireless-B/G.

The HomePlug adapter usually is an external or wall mount unit that links to the PC via an Ethernet or USB cable. In either case, you plug the unit into a normal AC power outlet just as you would any other appliance. Both electricity and data flow to the adapter through the same plug you use to power your TV and refrigerator.

The HomePNA adapter usually is a PCI card in a desktop or an external unit connected to the PC via a USB or Ethernet cable (see Figure 5-6). In either case, a regular telephone wire with RJ-11 connectors links the adapter and telephone wall jack. The phoneline adapters link PCs via the regular phone lines that run throughout the house. Just as a TV cable employs different frequencies to carry the signals for a hundred TV channels plus broadband Internet access, a twisted-pair telephone line can carry multiple signals, too. Our first Longnet was built on HomePNA technology, so our voice conversations and HomePNA shared the telephone system for several years. During the last year we used HomePNA, we switched from satellite to DSL broadband, thus adding a third signal to the system of telephone lines in our house.

Figure 5-6   PCI and external USB HomePNA network adapters

NOTE At this point in the development of home networking technologies, HomePNA and HomePlug have lost some of their luster. They offer a convenient solution to a wired network, but at speeds that top out at 10 Mbps and 14 Mbps, they are considerably slower than Wireless-G at 54 Mbps. Why not spend a little more and choose the speed and flexibility of a Wireless-G LAN? In fact, consumers are doing just that and probably will continue to do so until the emergence of the next generations of these technologies in the marketplace: HomePNA 3.0 (128 Mbps to 240 Mbps) and HomePlug AV (100 Mbps).

The Wireless Access Point and Signal Booster

If you design a home network with at least one wireless link, you will need a *wireless access point,* or *WAP.* The "wireless" tag is redundant, so frequently, this device is simply the *access point,* or the *AP.* The AP is a communications hub that enables the transceivers embedded in the wireless network adapters to link to the home network via short-range radio waves, like those used by cordless telephones. The AP can be a stand-alone unit or can be integrated into a home gateway (see Figure 5-7). Under normal circumstances, a single AP is all that is needed to link the PCs in a home network.

If a single AP does not provide sufficient wireless coverage, you have two choices. You can add an additional stand-alone access point, or you can use a *wireless signal booster* (see Figure 5-7). If your choice is the stand-alone wireless AP, it must be linked to the gateway via a data cable (see Figure 5-8). If installing cabling for the additional AP is cumbersome, you can extend the wireless range with a wireless signal booster, which doesn't require extra cabling. The signal booster, also called

Photo courtesy of Cisco Systems, Inc.

Figure 5-7 Wireless-G cable modem home gateway with access point (left) and a wireless range expander (right)

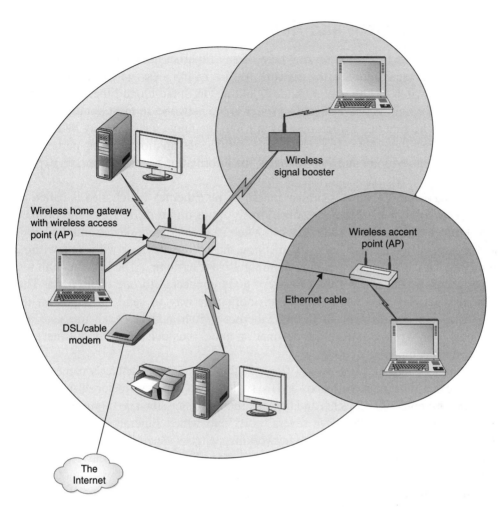

Figure 5-8   Extending wireless coverage: access point and signal booster

a *wireless range expander,* is placed within the AP's range, usually on the perimeter of the range, to extend the coverage to another area of the house, to an outbuilding, or to an area outside the house.

You can create an ad hoc wireless network without an AP, but this is not a viable solution for a home network. Creating an ad hoc mode wireless network is great for networks on-the-fly, but to have a full-featured home network, you'll need an infrastructure mode network, which requires an AP.

Ethernet Switch and Hub

The *Ethernet switch* is the unsung hero of any Ethernet network because it serves as a central clearinghouse for network traffic. Every message passes through at least one switch on the way to its destination. The stand-alone Ethernet switch in Figure 5-1 connects two PCs and a printer to the network. In most home networks, however, the Ethernet switch that is built into the home gateway may be the only switch (see Figure 5-2). The switch interprets the destination address, perhaps the PC in the game room, and then forwards the information to the appropriate port, an RJ-45 jack.

Because they perform a similar function, the Ethernet switch also is called an *Ethernet hub*. In fact, they are functionally quite different devices. The primary difference between the two is that the switch is an *intelligent* device and the hub is *dumb*. (The technology industry distinguishes those devices with and without processing capabilities by calling them intelligent or dumb.) The Ethernet hub just passes on whatever it receives to every node connected to one of its ports. This wastes network bandwidth and is an inefficient way to send messages on the network. In contrast, an intelligent Ethernet switch analyzes each message and routes it only to the port of the destination node, thus delivering the full network speed to each port.

What distinguishes one switch from another is the manufacturer's name on the outside of a rather nondescript box and the switch's two important major attributes—the number of ports (RJ-45 jacks) and the maximum transmission speed (see Figure 5-9). An Ethernet switch will have several ports into which Ethernet devices or other switches can be connected. Home networking switches usually have 4, 5, or 8 ports; however, they are available with 16, 24, and more. Switches can be daisy-chained to enable the addition of more Ethernet devices to the network, possibly in another area of the house. For example, you might put a switch on the main floor, one upstairs to service the bedrooms, and another in the basement for the entertainment center audio/

Courtesy of US Robotics

Figure 5-9   Five-port Fast Ethernet switch (front and back)

video devices. There are limitations; however, it's unlikely that these limitations would be a factor in home networking. Only four additional switches can be daisy-chained on an Ethernet link (10 Mbps), only two on a Fast Ethernet link (100 Mbps), and only one on a Gigabit Ethernet link (1000 Mbps).

Most switches used in home networks are 10/100 Fast Ethernet switches; that is, they can handle both data rates of 10 and 100 Mbps. The 10/100/1000 Gigabit Ethernet switches are more costly, and the gigabit capacity does not come into play unless the communicating devices have Gigabit Ethernet ratings, too. Switches have an autosensing feature that enables them to detect the speeds of connected devices and then adjust their port speeds to fit the capabilities of connected devices (10, 100, or 1000 Mbps).

Until recently, Ethernet switches were too expensive for home networks and the only economically feasible option for many of us was the simple-minded Ethernet hub, even with its built-in inefficiencies. These days, the switch is not that much more expensive than the hub. The extra amount you pay for an intelligent switching hub is easily justified when you consider what it can do to expedite the flow of information through your network and provide an improved level of security.

NOTE *If you purchase a modern Ethernet switch, this note will be irrelevant. That is because modern network gear has made the distinction between the two types of Ethernet ports a moot point to the end user. The ports on switches are called* switch ports. Device ports *are the Ethernet RJ-45 connectors on PCs, print servers, and other Ethernet devices. The standard Ethernet cable is designed to link an Ethernet device to a switch. It is possible that you will encounter an older switch or hub with a specifically designated* uplink port *(usually the one with the highest number). Use this uplink port to connect to a regular port on another switch. To link one Ethernet device, such as a PC, to another Ethernet device, you need a special cable called a* crossover cable. *A crossover cable is like a normal Ethernet cable except that the transmit data pair at one end is connected to the receive data pair at the other end. You may need a crossover cable to link one switch to another switch. Modern switches, however, automatically detect whether a port is connected to a switch or an Ethernet device, and then make an electronic adjustment, thus eliminating the need for a crossover cable.*

The typical home Ethernet switch, which also is called a *network switch*, has four or five ports and is housed in a box about a fourth the size of this book. It could be made smaller, but it needs a little size to give it some stability. A switch has some amazing electronic capabilities, but visually it's a bust. I supposed the most exciting part of the switch is the LED lights. When an LED light is lit, the corresponding port has a successful Ethernet connection. The light flashes to indicate activity on the port; that is, LAN traffic is moving through the indicated port.

In a home network environment, a Fast Ethernet switch often is built into one of the multifunction devices, such as the home gateway, wireless access point, or even the DSL/cable modem. Typically, these multifunction devices will have at least a four-port Ethernet switch into which four Ethernet cables can be connected.

NOTE *In the wireless world, the wireless access point does the work that the Ethernet switch does in the wired world. However, an important distinction between the two is that a wireless access point also provides a bridge to a wired LAN to enable the integration of wired and wireless devices on the same network. Wireless access points normally will have an Ethernet port or a built-in Ethernet switch with up to five ports.*

The Home/Residential Gateway

The central component in a home network is a *home gateway,* also called a *residential gateway.* The home gateway doesn't have a specific function; instead, it embodies a variety of functions needed to control a home network, it interfaces with the Internet, and it provides security for the network. Earlier Figure 5-7 is representative of an all-in-one home gateway in that it includes a cable modem, a router, a Wireless-G access point, a four-port Ethernet switch, a firewall, and a parental control feature for Internet access. In the business environment, these capabilities often are in separate pieces of net gear. A home gateway, however, may include some or all of these capabilities.

- **Router** In home networking, the router function is always embedded in a multifunction device, usually some type of home gateway, although it might be called by some other name. For example, it might be called a router/AP, a router with firewall and 4-port switch, an all-in-one AP, or something else that may or may not indicate the presence of the router function. The router provides a link between the home network (a LAN) and the Internet (a WAN) such that the entire home network can share a single high-speed Internet connection. Sometimes the connectors on routers are labeled LAN and WAN. An explanation of how routers use DHCP (Dynamic Host Configuration Protocol) and NAT (Network Address Translation) to enable the interface between the Internet service provider (ISP) and the nodes on the home network can be found in Chapter 3. If you don't use a home gateway but opt to base your home network on the Windows ICS (Internet Connection Sharing) feature, the router function is handled by host PC.

TIP The router is a special-purpose computer that runs one program directly from its flash memory. The term firmware *is used to describe this combination of software (the program) and hardware (flash memory). The firmware includes a firewall and other security features that may need to be updated to reflect changes in technology. I recommend that you periodically visit the router manufacturer's web site and download the latest version of its program. Follow the web site instructions to install the update.*

- **Cable and/or DSL modem**   Although some home gateways may have both a cable modem and a DSL modem for broadband Internet access, most will have one or the other. When you subscribe to broadband Internet service, your ISP probably will give you an opportunity to purchase a DSL/cable modem or a multifunction home gateway with a built-in modem. During promotions, which seem to be an ongoing activity with most ISPs, they may sell them at a reduced price or they might give you one of the devices in trade for your signature on an extended contract.

- **Access point**   The AP works with wireless network adapters to permit wireless communications over the network. Gateways enabling wireless access normally have two or three antennas (see earlier Figure 5-7). Most wireless gateways include a data encryption feature that protects transmissions within the network. Without encryption, wireless signals on the network are vulnerable to external interception. For example, someone could park in front of your house and tap into the Internet through your broadband access.

CAUTION Wireless security is discussed in Chapter 10. However, in case you've decided to do the quick start and set up your network now, you should be aware that the default for wireless protection is "off." I highly recommend that you toggle wireless protection to "on." This should thwart attempts by people within the range of your AP to tap into your network. It happens all the time.

- **Ethernet switch**   A home gateway will have a built-in Ethernet switch with at least four RJ-45 ports into which four Ethernet cables can be connected. Often, one of the ports connects to another switch or to an AP with a built-in switch.

- **Firewall**   The convenience of always-on Internet comes with a price—the ever-present threat of Internet intruders. A built-in *firewall* keeps Net intruders and attackers out of your home network. The firewall is the electronic version of a sentry that protects your network from unauthorized Internet traffic. Firewalls, which are described in depth in Chapter 10, let you decide during setup what traffic will be allowed to pass through the firewall and into your network. Most have a parent control feature that gives parents peace of mind by blocking Internet transmissions that contain selected keywords and by enforcing Internet access time limits.

- **USB port**   Home gateways often have a USB port. This port can be used to connect another PC to the network via a USB cable, thus eliminating the need for a network adapter.

Some home gateways are more encompassing than others. The more extensive all-in-one gateways may include these optional features, as well:

- **Print server**   The *print server* feature allows you to connect a USB printer directly to the network, thus eliminating the need for a PC to perform printer server duties. In a network without a print server, the PC that shares a printer must be on all of the time. The print server function is built into some high-end printers and all-in-one devices.

- **Modem**   Some home gateways have a traditional dial-up modem embedded into the unit. This feature is designed to provide backup Internet access if the broadband signal fails. Also, it gives you the flexibility to send faxes (over telephone lines) from your PC.

- **Voice over IP**   Some gateways have a couple of standard phone jacks and a feature that permits telephone service over the Internet, called *VoIP* (*Voice over IP*). VoIP is addressed in Chapter 13.

The Wireless Network Bridge

The Wireless-B/G communication protocol is different than the Ethernet protocol, so a *wireless network bridge* is required to link the wired Ethernet segment of the network to the wireless portions of a network. The wireless network bridge is also called a *wireless Ethernet bridge*. Some wireless network bridges are multifunction devices that include a multiport Ethernet switch (see Figure 5-10). The bridge performs whatever protocol conversions are necessary to enable a seamless flow of information over the Ethernet and Wireless-G portions of the network.

If the nerve center of your home network is a wired home gateway that is linked via Ethernet cable to a wireless access point, you probably won't need any network bridges. Every AP used in home networking is a multifunction device that includes a built-in network bridge that can be used to connect Ethernet devices.

Photo courtesy of Cisco Systems, Inc.

Figure 5-10   A wireless network bridge with a built-in five-port switch

The Longnet Revisited

It is a good time to revisit the Longnet because it includes implementations and uses of the home networking communications equipment discussed in this chapter. The Longnet, originally shown in Chapter 1, Figure 1-2, is illustrated again in Figure 5-11. However, this time the PCs and nodes are shown in relation to all of the communications gear. Keep in mind that the Longnet has considerably more PCs and pieces of network gear than the typical home network. Also, keep in mind that networks grow and it's possible that yours might expand to include most or all of the PCs, Ethernet devices, and communications equipment pictured in Figure 5-11.

If you will remember, the Longnet links five desktop PCs, a notebook PC, a media hub, and an Xbox game console. My wife, Nancy, each of my teenage boys, Troy and Brady, and I have desktop PCs, all of which were built by Troy. I have a second desktop PC adjacent to my primary PC that I use exclusively for running beta software (prerelease software). The laptop is used daily on a first-come, first-serve basis for a variety of mobile computing applications. The media hub and Xbox game console normally are in the home theater; however, both of these Ethernet devices can be and are easily moved to different locations.

Home Networking Demystified

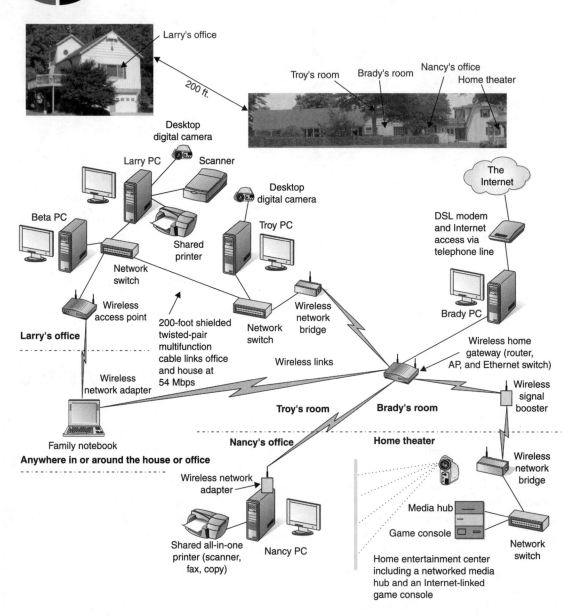

Figure 5-11   The home network at the Longs with network gear

At the center of the Longnet is a *wireless home gateway* in Brady's room, which is centrally located within the house. The gateway coordinates communication throughout the entire network. Its built-in *router* enables sharing of the DSL broadband Internet access. Wireless network adapters for the notebook PC (PC card) and the desktop PC in Nancy's office (external USB) facilitate wireless communication between the wireless home gateway through its built-in transceiver *wireless access point.*

The Longnet in Figure 5-11 provides two examples of when you might need to use a wireless network bridge. The center of the Longnet is a wireless home gateway, however, two parts of the network contain Ethernet devices wired directly to Ethernet switches. As you can see in Figure 5-11, each of the network bridges enables a wireless link to an Ethernet switch, which serves as a hub by which to connect Ethernet devices to the network. One provides a bridge to systems linked by wired Ethernet in Troy's room and my office. Another bridge links the media hub and the Xbox game console, both Ethernet devices.

The Longnet has four *Ethernet switches,* three stand-alone switches and one that is built into the home gateway. The switches permit network connectivity of several Ethernet devices at a single location. The five-port switch in my office links my primary PC, my beta PC, and a wireless access point to a five-port switch in Troy's room, which connects the office PCs, the office AP, and Troy's PC to a wireless network bridge. Another five-port switch in the home theater links the media hub, Xbox game console, and, occasionally, other PCs (not shown in figure) during a gaming party.

In the Longnet of Figure 5-11, the AP function is built into the wireless home gateway, the nerve center of the network. When we added a couple of devices in the home theater to the network, the signal was weak and the fallback data rate was a fraction of the network's rated capacity. The distance between the home theater devices and the AP is over 60 feet, and several large, unmovable metal obstacles are in the signal's path. We had two choices. We could install another AP and the associated Ethernet cabling, or we could add a *wireless signal booster.* We chose the latter, primarily because of the difficulty involved in stringing the required Ethernet cable. Now, that part of the house has a strong signal and the full Wireless-G data rate of 54 Mbps.

The Cost of Net Gear

By now, you are probably wondering how much all this communications equipment will cost. The total cost of the net gear for a home network depends on the scope of the project and the technologies you choose to employ. The network equipment can

	Wired Networks			Wireless Networks
	Ethernet	HomePNA	HomePlug	Wireless-B and -G
Residential/ home gateway	Includes a router for broadband Internet access and any or all of these features: cable/DSL modem, firewall, 2- to 6-port Ethernet switch, print server, and/or wireless access point (AP): $40–$250			
Network adapters: cost per PC (NICs for USB, PCI, and PC card)	A standard feature on most modern PCs: $15–$35	HPNA 2.0: $20–$50 HPNA 3.0: $40–$60	$50–$100	$40–$70
Ethernet switch	Ethernet switch: $40–$100			Access point (AP): $100–$150
Ethernet bridge		$100–$160		$80–$160
Wireless access point				$40–$100
Wireless signal booster				$40–$90
Cost of hardware	Least expensive	Moderately priced	Moderately priced	Most expensive

Table 5-3   The Cost of Network Hardware

range from as little as a wireless gateway with a wireless PC card to something like the network in Figure 5-11. The net gear for a sophisticated home network might cost as much an entry-level desktop PC. However, the hardware for an entry-level network probably won't cost as much as a good printer.

Pricing for network equipment follows the same rules as everything else. Name brands cost more than off brands. You'll pay a premium for state-of-the-art devices that move data more quickly. Last year's models are priced to clear the shelves. Table 5-3 is provided to give you a feel for the relative costs for common network devices.

Home Networking Kits/Bundles

Typically, you would design your home network and then purchase the necessary communications components. However, there is an alternative called the *home networking kit* or *home networking bundle*. When you purchase a kit, you accept the kit's network design. The kit should include "everything you need" to create a specific type of home network. These are representative bundles:

- *A wireless gateway/router with a wireless PC card network adapter.* This mix of net gear represents the most common home networking kit. The kit will enable wired links for up to four PCs and a wireless link to a notebook PC. To add other wireless PCs, additional wireless network adapters will be needed.

- *A wireless gateway/router/DSL or cable modem with a wireless PC card network adapter.* This is the same as the kit in the preceding item, but the home gateway includes either a DSL or cable modem.

- *A wireless gateway/router/DSL or cable modem with PC card and PCI wireless network adapters.* This is the same as the preceding kit, but a PCI wireless adapter is included as well, enabling wireless links to both a notebook PC and a desktop PC.

- *Two PCI network adapters and a crossover cable.* This bundle includes the necessary equipment to connect two PCs via a crossover cable. This limited approach to networking (two desktop PCs) does not include the gateway.

These are common home networking kits/bundles, but you may find others with different combinations of net gear. If you purchase a kit with a wireless gateway, you will always be able to expand your network with additional wired and wireless links.

CAUTION *You might be able to find a seemingly great buy on a home networking kit. Before buying, however, it's important to assess the contents of the kit relative to available technology. I would recommend that you avoid kits that do not offer Wireless-G (54 Mbps) and/or Fast Ethernet (100 Mbps) connectivity or better.*

TIP *The shrink-wrapped boxes that line the shelves of retail stores may not provide all the information you need to make an informed decision. To find out more about a device, navigate to the vendor's web site and then to its support page. Typically, this page will have a detailed description of the device, operational specifications, and hyperlinks to more information, including the complete user manual.*

PART THREE

Building a Home Network

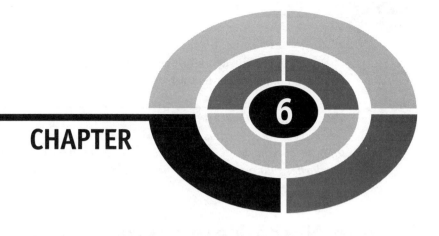

CHAPTER

6

Designing a Home Network

The first five chapters introduce you to the tools and options for home networking. If you feel confident with the material in these chapters, you are ready to design a home network that will meet your family's needs now and for the foreseeable future. The two most important results of the home network design process are the following:

- **The network diagram** The purpose of the network diagram is to graphically illustrate the physical locations and connectivity of all PCs, networked devices, and communications equipment in the network.

- **The shopping list** This list identifies everything you need to purchase. These items are combined with existing hardware/software to turn your network diagram into a working home network. The shopping list could include all PCs, PC upgrades, peripheral devices, and network gear. It may also include cabling and cabling accessories; however, cabling needs may not always be clear during the design stage.

Before you begin work on the network diagram, you may need to resolve some issues and make some decisions.

TIP *I invite you to resist the urge to buy until you have had an opportunity to give this project some serious thought. A little planning now can save you big bucks later. By starting with a well-conceived design, you'll be able to avoid the massive headaches that plague those who shortchange this planning stage.*

Making Home Networking Decisions

You need to set the stage for decision making regarding the design of your home network: you need to prepare a budget for this project, assess the general personal computing needs of your family (now and in the future), resolve the wired/wireless issue, identify important networking applications, and make a realistic assessment of your technical capabilities.

Assessing Your Budget for Home Networking

Each increment in convenience, speed, and flexibility has a cost. In the scheme of things, however, the actual cost of the network equipment is relatively small, usually from $100 to $500. Add an additional $500 to the high end if you plan on integrating your audio/visual equipment into the network. This amount is not much when you consider your investment in personal computing (the PCs, peripheral devices, and software).

Let's put the cost of a home network into perspective. The cost of the communications equipment for a typical three-PC network is a small percentage of the overall cost of all hardware and software in the network. Depending on the sophistication of the network, the net gear cost would be only 5 to 10 percent of the total cost. If you need to trim or hold down expenses, I would suggest that you do so with the purchase of your next PC or peripheral device. The incremental cost for purchasing quality communications equipment is but a small element of the overall cost of domestic personal computing, which can easily exceed $5000 a year when you consider the cost of hardware and software upgrades and related services (Internet access, security services, and so on). Moreover, if you purchase off brands or net gear that is a year or more off the technology, you run the risk of compatibility problems. You might even be disappointed with network speeds when you find out that your neighbor's network runs faster than yours.

TIP *Think big. It doesn't cost that much more to buy name brands, proven technologies, and devices with capabilities that you may not need at this time. For example, for an extra $10 or so you can purchase an Ethernet switch with eight ports rather than four ports. For another $40, you might be able to purchase another hundred gigabytes of disk space that you could use for a backup server and/or a multimedia server. Even though you might not envision a need for eight ports in the den or a massive hard disk, keep in mind that you need a network that is as flexible as your imagination. Ports and disks are like closets in the house. Eventually, you will fill them.*

Place the activity of budgeting for personal computing in networking within the context of your family's priorities. What percentage of each day does each family member spend with personal computing, networking, and the Internet? It is not unusual for members of the family to spend more time on the network than they do eating, driving, or watching television. If personal computing is a big deal in your family, then its cost should be in line with other family priorities, including automobiles and vacations.

TIP *If one or more of your family members is a teleworker, there is a good chance that at least a portion of the expenses associated with home networking might qualify as a tax deduction. Your accountant can provide details on this potential "rebate" on network expenses.*

The Family Meeting on Home Networking

Now is an excellent time to hold a focused family meeting to gather input for the network design. Every member of the family will eventually use the network, and each deserves a say in its design. You won't be able to resolve every design issue, but this type of meeting will invariably surface issues that you overlooked. Also, you can take solace in that you have done the politically correct thing by including those affected by the decision-making process.

Families and their immediate and future expectations for networking will vary considerably. Your family's issues and concerns will be different than those of your neighbors. These, however, are representative questions that you might wish to address:

- Where should we locate our three PCs and Dad's office notebook?

- Should we locate the children's desktop PC in brother's room or sister's room?

- Should we replace the three-year-old PC in the office? If so, should we buy another desktop or a notebook PC?

- If we go wireless, what areas of the house should be covered?

- What would be the best location for the wireless home gateway?

- Should we integrate the home entertainment center into the network? If so, which components should be included? If not now, should we make plans to do so in the future?

- Whose PC(s) should be designated as the backup server and/or media server?

- Do we purchase a new high-speed, high-resolution all-in-one printer to serve the entire network or continue to use the three older printers?

- Will we be able to string an Ethernet cable between the downstairs office and the upstairs front bedroom?

- Should we run the printer off a print server directly on the network or as a shared peripheral on one of the networked PCs?

- Should we upgrade mom's old Windows 2000–based PC to Windows XP or by a new one?

- Will the kids want to subscribe to Xbox Live (an online gaming service)?

Wired and/or Wireless?

The fundamental question facing anyone confronting the design of a home network is this: should connectivity within the network be wired, wireless, or both? A follow-up question to a wired/wireless response would be: which PCs will be wired and which will be wireless? Chapter 4 offers an in-depth discussion of the advantages, disadvantages, and costs associated with these options.

I recommend that anyone implementing a home network include wireless capabilities. It's fast, easy to use and install, and relatively inexpensive. Plus, it adds an entirely new dimension to domestic personal computing—mobility with connectivity to the Internet and the other PCs. Wireless has a lot of positives, but a couple of negatives can impact network design: signal interference is an ever-present possibility, and wireless is vulnerable to intruders who might tap into the signal.

Wireless-B/G operates on an unlicensed band of radio frequencies (2.4 GHz); that is, the Federal Communications Commission does not require a license for radio transmissions over these frequencies. As you might imagine, an unlicensed band attracts other commercial radio devices, such as cordless telephones, which can interfere with the signals in a wireless home network, and vice versa. Fortunately, the better cordless telephones are able to sense an active frequency and will seek a clear channel before transmitting. Microwave ovens remain a problem for home networks, but only if they are actively operating and in the line of sight of a network signal.

Wired connectivity is as fast as or faster than wireless connectivity, and it's not susceptible to radio frequency interference. My recommendation would be to use wired links for stationary desktop PCs whenever cabling is relatively easy to install. As good as wireless is, wired connectivity will provide a more consistently reliable link and will involve less maintenance over the long term.

In the recent past, the speed of wireless connectivity in the home topped out with Wireless-B speeds (11 Mbps), so the best strategy was to provide Fast Ethernet (100 Mbps) wiring to stationary PCs whenever possible. With Wireless-G at 54 Mbps and enhanced Wireless-G at 108 Mbps, wireless becomes a very real possibility for any PC, especially if you're facing a weekend crawling through the attic rafters and drilling holes in walls. Wireless-N, the next generation standard, will offer in excess of 200 Mbps. Generally, wireless network gear is more expensive, but you have to weigh this relatively small incremental cost against the costs associated with installing the Ethernet cabling.

The difference between the speeds of popular wired and wireless transmission media is quickly becoming a non-issue. So, ultimately, the decision for each workstation boils down to whether you want (or need) the flexibility and mobility of wireless connectivity or the reliability of a wired link.

Desired Networking Applications

When our boys were in elementary school, they asked if we would buy them fold-up push scooters. I asked them why they wanted scooters when they already had bicycles and a go cart. "Well, dad, we just really need them." They didn't have a clue as to what they would be doing with them. Eventually, the boys got their scooters, and they became transportation to school and to friends' houses, they became racing machines over obstacle courses, they became the tools for seemingly impossible tricks, and they were much more. Now the boys drive cars, but they still grab their scooters to pick up the mail and to expedite the trip between the house and the office. Occasionally, I do, too.

There is an important parallel between these clever scooters and home networks. Most of us don't actually know what we plan to do with a home network; we just know that we want one. Once we get one, we never stop finding new applications for it. You need to think ahead regarding applications, whether the scooter or the network. Fortunately, we envisioned the inevitable crashes and purchased knee pads, elbow pads, and helmets—for the scooters, not the home network.

Home networking applications expand in numbers and sophistication with your networking experience and imagination. However, now is a good time to identify as many potential applications as you can, especially those that can impact the design of your network.

The primary applications associated with home networking include the sharing of broadband Internet access, the sharing of user files across the network, and the sharing of printers and other resources. These are explained and illustrated in Chapter 2. If your current Internet access is dial-up, then you should research the broadband options available in your area. Keep in mind that some broadband ISPs place a limit on the number of PCs that can be serviced on a home LAN. Identify which PC or PCs will act as the media server and/or the backup server. You may wish to equip one or more of your PCs with an extra internal or external hard disk, depending on your expected volume of file sharing. You will want to assess your current printer(s) relative to its (their) ability to become a network printer(s) and whether or not you want it (them) to be connected directly to the network via a print server. Assess your current peripherals, such as scanners, desktop digital cameras, and rewritable optical disks, relative to how they can and might be used in a network environment.

If your plans are to integrate home entertainment into the network, then your current research will need to be extended to include the media hubs, digital video recorders, and Internet-based multiplayer gaming. These applications are discussed in Chapter 13.

Your Networking Expertise

So, whad'ya know? This opening line from Michael Feldman's popular show on National Public Radio (NPR) is apropos for anyone who has made the decision to install a home network. Installing a home network is relatively straightforward; however, some solutions are more challenging than others. My advice is to keep it simple for your initial effort and just keep the possibility of expansion in your mind during the planning. A properly designed home network is easily expanded to meet changing needs. If you choose the wired Ethernet option, carpentry and electricians' skills may come in handy.

TIP Let your home network evolve with your expertise and needs. You don't have to do everything at once. Home networks are built around wireless access points and switches, both of which can take on new nodes as needs evolve. For example, if you decide sometime in the future to add an external security camera at the entrance to your drive, all you will need is the wireless-ready camera and, perhaps, a signal booster.

Security

It is likely that your home network and the linked PCs will have always-on Internet access. Cyberspace is filled with exciting applications, informative people, and interesting information, but it also has a darker flip side. The dark side includes viruses, hackers, and criminals who will steal your identity if given an opportunity. Plan to have security software installed on each PC on your network from the moment it is linked to the network. Network security is discussed in detail in Chapter 10.

You may need to address physical security within your home. Consider these very realistic scenarios. Suppose that curiosity gets the best of your PC-savvy housekeeper and she decides to open Quicken and peruse your financial records. Or, suppose your sitter's boyfriend drops by for a visit after you've left for the evening, and he decides to use your PayPal account to purchase a few hip-hop CDs. Or, suppose your children's teenage friends ignore your instructions regarding what they can and cannot do on your network. Or, suppose your neighbors, who can detect your network's wireless signal, become more curious about the contents of your computers than they are about the contents of your garage?

A home network can span the far corners of the house, and you can't be everywhere at once. If your house has a lot of foot traffic, you might wish to install locks on selected doors and set up password-protected user accounts.

Mapping a Home Network

After you have made the important decisions discussed in the preceding section, especially those regarding nodes and technologies, you are ready to draw a schematic of your home network. The diagram should map all PCs, peripheral devices, communication equipment, and connectivity media. You can use the old-fashioned paper/pencil approach, or you can use a *drag-and-drop program,* such as Visio. If you choose the traditional approach and are artistically challenged (as I am), you can purchase an inexpensive networking stencil at a business supply store. In the end, the two approaches are equally effective, but you'll save time if you have access to Visio, ConceptDraw, SmartDraw, or some other diagramming package. Figure 6-1 illustrates the use of Visio to prepare a map of the Longnet (as presented in Figure 5-11 in Chapter 5).

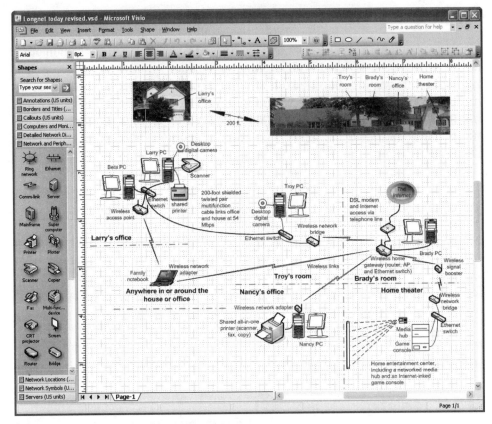

Figure 6-1 Visio (drag-and-drop software) used to create a home network diagram

Maxims for Network Design

Computer networking has been around for decades in the business world, so companies that manufacture communications equipment have had plenty of field feedback. Much of the feedback has been along these lines: give us plenty of flexibility to meet our unique and ever-changing communications needs. Communications companies listened, and many offer a full line of network gear that can handle any design we can dream up. This built-in flexibility eliminates the need for a long list of design rules; nevertheless, there are a few maxims you should to keep in mind during the design process.

- *Choose wireless over wired if you are uncomfortable with the labor-intensive work associated with cabling and/or the visual impact that wired connections might have on aesthetics.* Stringing wire between rooms and floors can be messy, time consuming, unsightly, and expensive.

- *Wire new houses for networking.* Ideally, you are building a new house and will be able to install the network wiring along with television, telephone, security, and electrical wiring. If your new home construction coincides with creating a home network, sprinkle Ethernet wall jacks liberally. Installation of Ethernet wiring during construction is relatively inexpensive. Connect most of the rooms in your new house to a central switching hub, perhaps in the basement or utility room, with Category 6 Gigabit Ethernet cabling.

- *Locate the wireless access point near the center of the network.* A central location for the AP maximizes the coverage within your home and minimizes the possibility that neighbors and passersby will eavesdrop on your network signal.

- *Locate wireless components such that the line-of-light signal between the transceivers is relatively uncluttered.* Avoid devices that interfere with radio signals. Large stationary objects, such as water heaters, refrigerators, wood-burning stoves, air-conditioning units and their ducting, and fish tanks, that contain metal or water will impede or block the signal. Avoid having microwave ovens and cordless telephones in the line of sight and, to a lesser extent, keep the signal path free of radios and televisions, too.

Home Network Design Sampler

Network gear is like Legos, the popular children's building blocks. You have a variety of pieces you can use to build a seemingly infinite number of unique structures. The trick is to build a structure that meets your short- and long-term networking needs. In this section and throughout the book, I offer numerous examples of home network structures that are wired only, wireless only, or a combination of wired and wireless. The structures shown in Figures 6-2, 6-3, 6-4, and 6-5 are representative structures that use Wireless-G and/or Ethernet solutions. Figure 6-6 shows a wired HomePNA solution.

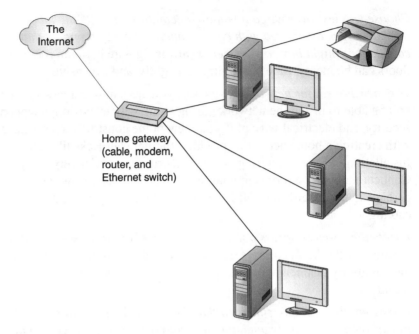

Figure 6-2   Ethernet LAN with all-in-one home gateway (shared host-based printer)

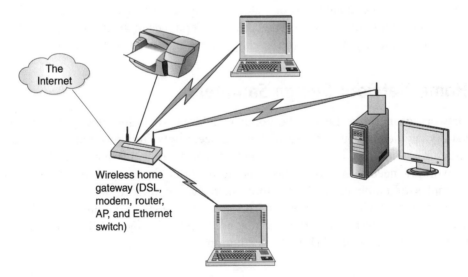

Figure 6-3   Wireless-G LAN with all-in-one wireless home gateway (wired network printer)

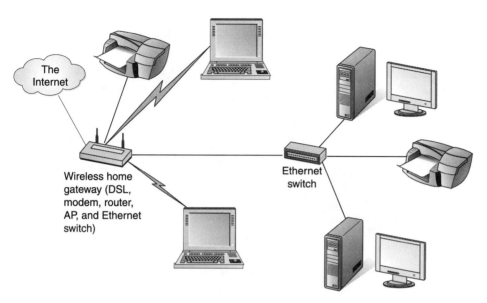

Figure 6-4   Wireless-G LAN with wireless home gateway connected to an Ethernet switch (two wired network printers)

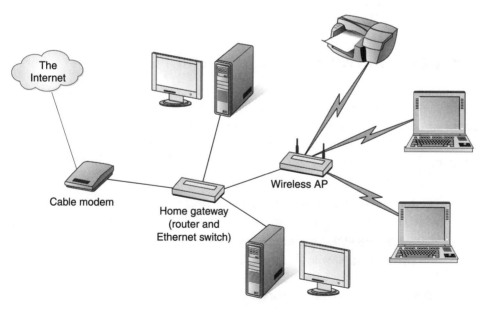

Figure 6-5   Ethernet LAN with home gateway and remote wireless AP (wireless network printer, separate cable modem)

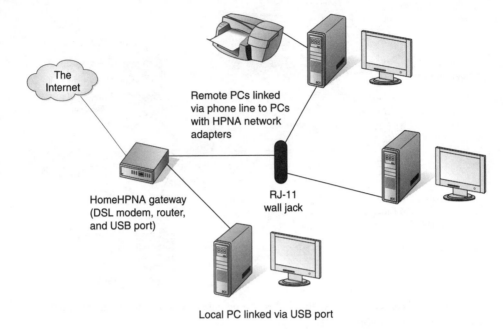

The
Internet

Remote PCs linked
via phone line to PCs
with HPNA network
adapters

HomeHPNA gateway
(DSL modem, router,
and USB port)

RJ-11
wall jack

Local PC linked via USB port

Figure 6-6   HomePNA LAN with all-in-one home gateway (USB link to local PC)

The Home Network Worksheet and Planner

The home network worksheet in Figure 6-7 is provided as a tool to help you formalize your thinking. Make a copy and use the tables to take inventory of your personal computers, modems, and networking equipment. You can also use the worksheet to document hardware and net gear needs and, ultimately, to create a shopping list and an estimate of overall cost. A completed example worksheet and planner is shown in the next section.

- **Modem Selection**   Use this table to indicate your current modem and which type of modem will be used for broadband Internet access on the home network and if it needs to be purchased.

- **PC Inventory: Now and in the Future**   Document your current PC inventory and note what PCs you plan for the initial network, the network after one year, and the network after three years.

- **Peripherals Inventory (Not Including Monitors or Audio): Now and in the Future**   Use this table to show an inventory of current peripheral devices and what will be planned for the initial implementation of the network. Think ahead and speculate what peripherals might be installed after a year and after three years (approximately the duration of a PC/network generation). Indicate the number of devices, if appropriate.

- **PCs and Network Adapters**   Use this table to summarize network adapter information and whether you anticipate a link to a particular PC to be wired or wireless. Now is a good time to name the PCs. Indicate E for existing and P for needs to be purchased, as appropriate.

- **Other Networked Devices to Be Purchased**   List and describe other networked devices, such as a print server or media hub, that you plan to acquire for the initial network. Also indicate the type of network adapter needed for each device.

- **Other Net Gear, Including Media, to Be Purchased**   List and describe all other network devices and media that you will be purchasing. Include the home gateway, switches, signal boosters, cables, and so on in this table. To help crystallize your thinking, describe each item's function within the network.

- **Other Peripheral Devices to Be Purchased**   Having a home network opens opportunities for new applications, such as security monitoring and printer sharing. Complete this table by listing peripheral devices that will need to be purchased to meet the requirements for new network applications.

- **Operating Systems**   This table summarizes the statuses on the current and proposed PCs, indicating any required upgrades.

- **Shopping List**   Use this table to compile a shopping list that contains everything you will need to buy to create home network of your design. Note desirable specifications, as appropriate.

Modem Selection

Type of modem	Current	To be used with network*
Cable modem		
DSL modem		
Satellite modem		
Dial-up		
Other		

* Indicate P for needs to be purchased

Figure 6-7   Home network design worksheet and planner

PC Inventory: Now and in the Future

PCs in the network	At present	Planned for initial network	After one year	After three years
Notebook PCs				
DesktopPCs				

Peripherals Inventory (Not Including Monitors or Audio): Now and in the Future

PCs in the network	At present	Planned for initial network	After one year	After three years
Inkjet printer				
All-in-one printer (print, scan, fax, copy)				
Desktop digital camera				
Scanner				

PCs and Network Adapters

Name of PC	Type of PC*		Type of link		Type of adapter*			
	Desktop	Notebook	Wired	Wireless	Integrated	PC card	PCI card	USB

* Indicate E for existing and P for needs to be purchased

Other Networked Devices to be Purchased

Device	Description	Type of network adapter

Other Net Gear, Including Media, to be Purchased

Device/Media	Description	Function in network

Other Peripheral Devices to be Purchased

Device	Description	Function in network

Operating Systems

Name of PC	Current operating system	Comment

Shopping List (Networking and Internet Access Equipment, Cabling)

Item	Model	Pertinent specs	Qty	Cost
Total Cost				

Shopping List (PCs, Peripheral Devices, Miscellaneous Network Devices, and Software)

Item	Model	Pertinent specs	Qty	Cost
Total Cost				

The Smith Family's Home Network

Let's walk through the design of a home network for the Smith family. Currently, the Smiths have two PCs. Generally, parents Jim and Mary share a notebook PC in the home office and their children Mike and Sally share a desktop PC in Mike's room. The whole family shares a dedicated dial-up data line for Internet access. Throughout the day, they take turns logging onto the Internet to check e-mail and surf the Web.

Members of the Smith family have grown tired of waiting for a slice of time to get on the Internet at click-and-wait speeds. Moreover, two PCs just aren't enough capacity for their personal computing needs. Expecting that they need to double the computing power, they plan to purchase a desktop for Mary and a notebook for Sally. Mary's desktop will be located in the home office and be the center of the network. The other desktop will remain in Mike's room, which is located over the home office. The desktops will be connected to the network via Ethernet. Wireless links are planned for the notebooks so that they can be online no matter where they are located in and around the house. Ultimately, the family plans to replace the desktop PCs with notebook PCs and make the entire network wireless.

The family strategy is to purchase an all-in-one printer that will be connected to the network via a print server, thus retiring the old inkjet printer and a low-resolution scanner. Mike's desktop PC will be upgraded from Windows 2000 to Windows XP so that all networked PCs will have the same operating system. Although DSL and cable modem broadband service are available throughout their neighborhood, the family chose DSL based on their neighbors' recommendations.

The Smith family wants to expand the network beyond the four PCs to include wireless integration with the home entertainment center. Jim plans to purchase a PDA with a Wireless-B adapter. The home entertainment center is located over 50 feet from the home office, so Jim has decided that a wireless signal booster will be needed to deliver the full capacity of Wireless-G to a media hub and game console. Jim and Mary worked together to create the network design shown in Figure 6-8. Figure 6-9 shows the completed home network design worksheet and planner (using the tables in Figure 6-7), which includes a shopping list for everything they need to purchase to build the network. The Appendix, "Home Networking Buyer's Guide," offers hints and strategies for purchasing network equipment.

TIP *Home networking is easier when all PCs use a version of Windows XP. An upgrade can be purchased for less than $100, a lot of money to most of us. However, Windows XP is a significant upgrade from the other Windows operating systems and has many advantages, especially in the area of networking and Internet security. When every PC has the same operating system, compatibility issues are seldom a concern. At this writing, Windows XP Media Center Edition 2005 is available only with new Media Center PCs.*

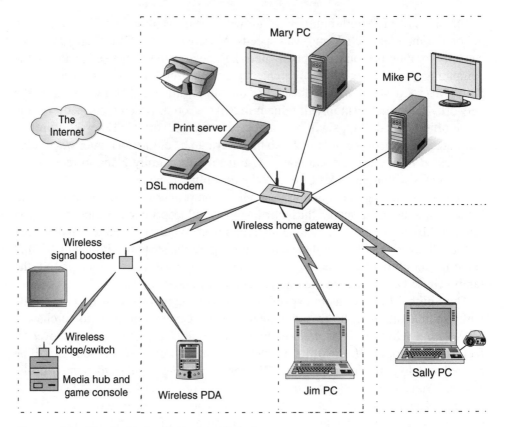

Figure 6-8 The Smith family's network design

Modem Selection

Type of modem	Current	To be used with network*
Cable modem		
DSL modem		P
Satellite modem		
Dial-up	X	
Other		

* Indicate P for needs to be purchased

Figure 6-9 Completed worksheet and planner for the Smith family's home network design

PC Inventory: Now and in the Future

PCs in the network	At present	Planned for initial network	After one year	After three years
Notebook PCs	1	2	2	4
DesktopPCs	1	2	2	

Peripherals Inventory (Not Including Monitors or Audio): Now and in the Future

PCs in the network	At present	Planned for initial network	After one year	After three years
Inkjet printer	1			
All-in-one printer (print, scan, fax, copy)		1		
Desktop digital camera		1		2
Scanner	1			

PCs and Network Adapters

Name of PC	Type of PC*		Type of link		Type of adapter*			
	Desktop	Notebook	Wired	Wireless	Integrated	PC card	PCI card	USB
Jim		E		X		P		
Mary	P		X		P			
Mike	E		X				E	
Sally		P		X	P			

* Indicate E for existing and P for needs to be purchased

Other Networked Devices to be Purchased

Device	Description	Type of network adapter
Print server	Connects printer directly to network	Ethernet print server
Game console	Zbox Live	Built-in Ethernet
Media hub	Enables playing of network-based multimedia content	Built-in Ethernet
Handheld PC	Pocket PC with integrated digital camera and phone	Built-in Wi-Fi (Wireless-B)

Other Net Gear, Including Media, to be Purchased

Device/Media	Description	Function in network
Wireless gateway	Wireless-G with router, firewall, and 4-port switch	Interface with Internet, provide Intrusion protection, and enable communication within the network
Wireless Ethernet bridge/switch combo	Wireless-G bridge with built-in 4-port switch	Connects to media hub and Zbox via wireless link to network
Wireless signal booster	Wireless-G	Expands range of wireless signal
Ethernet patch cables (2)	3 feet	Connects media hub and Zbox
Ethernet patch cable	15 feet	Connects print server to gateway

Other Peripheral Devices to be Purchased

Device	Description	Function in network
Desktop digital camera	Small USB desktop camera	To be shared by network users for videophone and other applications
All-in-one printer	Print, fax, copy, and scan	Network printer

Operating Systems

Name of PC	Current operating system	Comment
Jim	Windows XP Professional	
Mary	Windows XP Media Center Edition 2005*	Comes with new desktop Media Center PC*
Mike	Windows 2000	Upgrade to Windows XP Home
Sally	Windows XP Home	Comes with new notebook PC

*Windows XP Media Center Edition 2005 and Media Center PCs are discussed in detail in Chapter 13.

Shopping List (Networking and Internet Access Equipment, Cabling)

Item	Model	Pertinent specs	Qty	Cost
DSL modem	HomePort 2000W	ISP supplies with subscription to DSL service for reduce price	1	$50
Ethernet PC card	DigLink 100 Card	Fast Ethernet	1	60
Wireless home gateway	SysComp 1000	All-in-one Wireless-G gateway	1	150
Wireless Ethernet bridge/switch combo	DigLink Bridge/ Switch	Wireless-G with 4-port switch	1	120
Wireless signal booster	DigLink-G Boost	Wireless-G	1	80
Patch cable*	Category 5e cabling	Cat 5e snagless UTP Ethernet (3 feet)	2	10
Patch cable	Category 5e cabling	Cat 5e snagless UTP Ethernet (15feet)	1	10
Total Cost				**$480**

* More patch cables may be needed if cables are not distributed with network equipment.

Shopping List (PCs, Peripheral Devices, Miscellaneous Network Devices, and Software)

Item	Model	Pertinent specs	Qty	Cost
Notebook PC	Dellway X100	3.8 MHz, 200MB, DVD+RW, built-in Ethernet and Wireless-G adapters	1	$1800
Print server	DigLink Print	Stand-alone Ethernet print server	1	70
Game console	Zbox Live	Ethernet-ready gaming box	1	130
Media hub	Media Center Extender	Wireless, Ethernet-ready hub	1	250
PDA	Quarto Handheld IX	All-in-one Wi-Fi-ready handheld	1	500
Desktop digital camera	Logico Vision II	640 X 480 with zoom	1	100
All-in-one printer	Multifunction HiPrint IV	Print. Fax, copy, and scan	1	300
Windows XP Home	Upgrade to Windows 2000			80
Total Cost				$3230

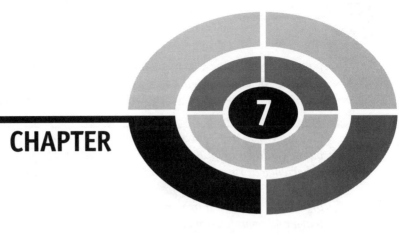

CHAPTER

Cabling a Home for an Ethernet LAN

If you have decided to go with a wireless home network, you can skip this chapter. However, more often than not, there is a place for wired links in a home network, even one that is mostly wireless. This chapter is for you, if you plan to cable your home to enable wired connections in your home network. We have talked about the advantages and disadvantages associated with wired and wireless connections in earlier chapters. If you're still undecided between wired, wireless, or both, and you do not consider yourself handy with tools and electronic wiring, let me be candid. I would encourage you to choose wireless over wired if you are uncomfortable with the labor-intensive work associated with cabling. I offer the same encouragement if you are concerned about the visual impact that wired connections might have on the aesthetics of your home. Running the cabling for an Ethernet LAN between remote

points in your house can be messy, time consuming, unsightly, and expensive. Cabling for an Ethernet LAN can be one of the biggest challenges you face in setting up your home network, whether you do it yourself or hire the work out.

CAUTION You don't have to be a skilled network technician to run Ethernet wire, but it would be helpful if you are adept with tools, in general, and have some experience at running wires around the house (any wire, such as speaker wire). If don't consider yourself to be "handy," let me remind you that every handyman or woman had a first project and you should never underestimate your ability to learn and complete this task.

If you are still with me, let's review the wired options. At this writing, it's difficult to justify using existing wiring, such as telephone lines (HomePNA) and power lines (HomePlug), when wireless solutions offer you five to ten times the data rates and the flexibility of mobile computing. Standards have been established for very high speed data transmission using existing telephone and power lines; however, these are paper solutions until reasonably priced supporting network gear shows up on the shelves at Best Buy, Wal-Mart, and other retailers/e-retailers. That leaves Ethernet, a fast and reliable networking solution. The problem with Ethernet is that you must install the cabling, and this project is the topic of this chapter. If you have prepared a network design that includes wired links and have identified all the cabling runs, then you are ready to wire.

CAUTION In most situations, wiring for a home network is a do-it-yourself project that won't involve civic paperwork; nevertheless, I suggest that you check out the building codes for your community to make sure that any modifications you make to your home will conform. If you rent, examine your contract. Some prohibit any alterations to walls or flooring other than picture hangers.

The Ethernet UTP Cable

Let's take a closer look at the UTP (unshielded twisted-pair) Ethernet cable, which comes in different grades or *categories* (Cat 5, Cat 5e, and Cat 6). Each has four pairs of wires (orange, green, blue, brown, with one of each pair solid and one with a white stripe), and each pair is twisted throughout the length of the cable to help minimize electrical interference. Cat 5 and Cat 5e cables use only four wires for Ethernet communication at 10 and 100 Mbps, those coming off pins 1, 2, 3, and 6. Even though only four wires are needed, all wires must be connected in both jacks.

Gigabit (1000 Mbps) data rates, however, require the use of all eight wires. Most wiring for Gigabit Ethernet is done with Cat 6; however, gigabit data rates can be achieved over Cat 5e and Cat 5 for shorter runs and in areas where the sources of line interference are minimal.

CAUTION *When using Cat 5 and Cat 5e for Ethernet cabling, you're running four unused wires. Although it's theoretically possible to use these extra wires for other applications (telephone, home security system, doorbell, and so on), I recommend that you leave them unused to avoid the possibility of line interference.*

Bulk UTP Ethernet cable comes in a variety of colors, quality levels (primarily overall durability), and lengths. Usually, it is less expensive to purchase an entire spool of cable (typically 250 feet, 500 feet, or 1000 feet), however, the cable can be purchased off the spool in any length at most home improvement stores, such as Lowe's or Home Depot. The completed Ethernet cable is terminated by an eight-pin *RJ-45 jack,* which is also called a *connector.* Virtually all new computers and all Ethernet devices, such as all-in-one gateways and switches, are outfitted with Ethernet ports. The RJ-45 connectors on the cables (the male ends) are inserted into the Ethernet ports (the female ends) to complete the link between devices on the network. Like the RJ-11 telephone connector, the RJ-45 connector has a flexible *tang* that locks it into the port. You must compress the tang to remove the connector.

You can purchase bulk cable and connectors to make your own cables. (This process is covered later in the chapter.) You can purchase a thousand-foot roll of Cat 5e bulk cable for as little as $0.06 a foot or as much as $0.15 a foot, depending upon where you buy them. RJ-45 connectors can be purchased for as little as $0.10 or as much as a dollar, again, depending on how carefully you shop and the quantity you purchase.

The alternative to making your own cables is to purchase preassembled cables. As a rule of thumb, if you consider only the materials you can make *patch cables* for about a fourth the cost of purchasing a ready-made cable. This comparison does not include your time and the amortized cost of the tools you will need to assemble the patch cables.

NOTE *UTP Ethernet cable comes with either solid or stranded wires in either vinyl or fire-retardant plenum sheaths. Usually, a spool of bulk vinyl-sheathed solid wire cabling suffices for home networking needs. Solid cable is designed primarily for runs between rooms because it is not designed to be flexed or twisted repeatedly; however, this type of cable abuse seldom happens in a home networking environment. You will need to use Ethernet cabling with stranded wires for patch cables (less than 20 feet in length) when you expect repeated flexing of the cable. Most preassembled patch cables have stranded wires.*

Preassembled Ethernet Cables

Preassembled *patch cables* (see Figure 7-1) can be purchased in a variety of lengths ranging from inches to 100 feet. Some stores, both store front and online, build and sell custom cables of any length you specify. All of your runs can be ready-made patch cables; however, the best use of these cables is for short runs within a room or places where it does not need to be threaded through a narrow hole.

You can run bulk cable through a relatively unobtrusive 1/4-inch hole, but you will need a potentially ugly 5/8-inch to 3/4-inch hole if you wish to pass the connector through a wall. Always buy *snagless patch cables,* which are designed to keep the cable from being snagged on the tang during threading. This is a common problem even when you are trying to pull a patch cable clear of entanglement with other system wires.

The standard patch Ethernet cable, which is designed to link an Ethernet device to a switch, is *straight through.* That is, the wires coming off connector pins 1, 2, 3, and 6 on one end are connected to pins of the same number on the other end. To link an Ethernet device, such as a PC or Xbox game controller, to another Ethernet device, you may need a *crossover cable.* A crossover cable is like a normal Ethernet cable except that the transmit data pair at one end is connected to the receive data pair at the other end. That is, the pin 1 wire on one end connects to pin 3 on the other end and the pin 2 wire goes to pin 6. Fortunately, modern network technology has pretty much made the use of a crossover cable a non-issue. All modern network devices are "intelligent" and are able to detect whether a port is connected to a switch or an Ethernet device. The device then makes an electronic adjustment to send signals over the appropriate wires.

TIP Some switches/hubs have a built-in uplink port. This port is internally crossed so that you can link switches with a regular straight-through cable. The uplink port is eliminated from most communications hardware because all have an autodetect feature that selects wires automatically.

Figure 7-1   Fourteen-foot Cat 5e snagless Ethernet patch cable

Making Your Own Ethernet Cables

There are three primary advantages to making your own cables. First, your cables will be the desired lengths. Second, stringing a cable in and through difficult places is much easier when the cable does not have a connector. Finally, you will save money by doing it yourself. Over the long term, there is another advantage. You will have gained the expertise and have the equipment and materials to make your own cables whenever you need them.

The downside of making your own patch cables is that it can be tricky if you're not used to working with electrical wiring and the associated tools. It's not difficult, but you have to be careful. If you make your own cable, you are sure to have a few frustrating moments. For example, I've crimped pin 1 into an orange wire (rather than orange/white) and I've cut a wire at 45 feet for a 55-foot run.

These are the only items you need to set up your own custom cabling shop:

- **All-in-one crimping tool**   You can purchase an easy-to-use crimping tool for as little as $20. Professional crimping tools that give you the flexibility to make a variety of cables can cost $50 or more. A good all-in-one crimping tool can perform three functions. First, use it to cut the cable to the desired length. Second, use it to strip away the insulation exposing the twisted pairs. Third, affix each RJ-45 connector by using the crimper function to press the eight copper contacts into the individual wires to complete the connection and the cables.

- **Bulk Catx cable**   Estimate the length of your runs and purchase enough *Catx* (a reference to Cat 5, Cat 5e, or Cat 6) to complete the job. I would recommend you give yourself an extra hundred feet because it is inevitable that you will need other patch cables to meet your growing needs.

- **RJ-45 connectors**   You will need two RJ-45 connectors for every run. These are inexpensive when purchased in bulk, so plan on buying at least a dozen extra.

- **Modular wall plates**   A more sophisticated solution to a hole in the wall is to terminate runs of Ethernet cable with modular wall plates. The wall plates have RJ-45 connectors into which patch cables can be inserted to complete the run. Wall plates are discussed further in the section "Ethernet Wiring for New Construction."

If you are just making patch cables for in-room connections, the cable can be made in its entirety any time. However, the connectors should not be affixed to long-run cables until they have been threaded through attics, walls, or wherever their paths take them. To make your own cables, follow these basic steps:

1. *Cut the cable.* Measure the run and cut the cable to the desired length.

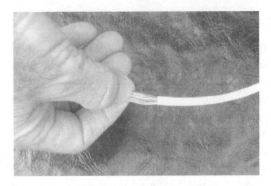

Figure 7-2 Flatten and arrange wires in the correct order.

2. *Strip off a couple of inches of insulation.* Use the stripper function on your crimping tool to remove about two inches of the insulation that protects the twisted pairs. Most crimping tools have a slot into which you can place the cable, twist it 360 degrees, and cut the insulation. The excess jacket is easily removed to expose the twisted pairs.

3. *Untwist the twisted pairs.* Take out the twists in the exposed wires and straighten them as best you can. I first wrap them about a quarter of the way around a pencil and then pull them the length of the exposed wire while holding my thumb across the wire.

4. *Spread the wires and put them in the proper order.* Pull, tug, rearrange, and do whatever you need to do to position the wires adjacent to one another, as shown in Figure 7-2 according to the order listed in Table 7-1.

Pin	Coding
Pin 1	orange/white
Pin 2	orange
Pin 3	green/white
Pin 4	blue
Pin 5	blue/white
Pin 6	green
Pin 7	brown/white
Pin 8	brown

Table 7-1 Wire Associations with the RJ-45 Pins on an Ethernet Cable

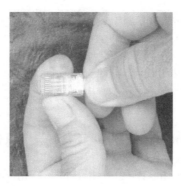

Figure 7-3   Insert wires into the RJ-45 connector.

5. *Trim the exposed wires.* Use your crimping tool's wire cutter to cut the wires about 5/8 inch from the insulation.

6. *Insert the wires into the RJ-45 connector.* Hold the connector with the copper contacts up, as shown in Figure 7-3. Check to ensure that wires are in the correct order (pin 1 and the orange/white wire are on the bottom in Figure 7-3). *Note that the even pins connect to wires with solid colors.* Carefully, shove all eight wires (flattened between your thumb and forefinger) to the end of the connector.

7. *Crimp the RJ-45 connector onto the Catx cable.* Insert the connector into the crimping area of the crimping tool and squeeze the handles firmly to affix the connector (see Figure 7-4).

Figure 7-4   Use the crimping tool to affix the connector to the wires in the Ethernet cable.

NOTE There are two wiring standards for four-pair UTP cable, Type-A and Type-B. Modular RJ-45 jacks normally are color-coded for both "A" and "B." Table 7-1 reflects the Type-B configuration, which is consistent with most off-the-shelf network gear and patch cables. Ignore the Type-A codes.

Ethernet Wiring for New Construction

The best possible scenario for the installation of Ethernet wiring is that you are building a home network and a new house at the same time. If this is the case, you should consider comprehensive structured wiring for the entire house. *Structured wiring* is simply the integration of all household communications wiring within a single wiring system. In structured wiring, the wires from the various household communications systems emanate from the convenient central location. The systems could include, but are not limited to, the home network (Ethernet), the telephone system (twisted pairs), TV/video (coaxial cable), security, audio (speaker wire), and anything else that involves wires and communications.

If I were building a new home, I would install a structured wiring system to handle all wired communications needs for the foreseeable future. And, I would contract the job out to the professionals. When all you see is wall studs, joists, and rafters, you can run several thousand of feet of relatively inexpensive wire in a fraction of the time it would take to do the same in a finished house and at a fraction of the cost. You would be surprised how quickly you can run through 1000 feet of Ethernet, telephone, or security wiring in a structured wiring system.

TIP I recommend that you find one or more good contractors with structured wiring experience to install the wiring in your new home. You may have to do some research to find a qualified installer. Some electrical contractors and computer companies do this kind of work. Also, you might find qualified installers at full-service audio/visual stores or home theater stores. Be advised that, if you choose to install your own structured wiring system, a lot of things can happen that have nothing to do with electronics and most of them are bad. You can bump your head on protruding roofing nails, step through the ceiling, get stuck in the crawl space, fall from the ladder, and so on.

As for the home network portion of the structured wiring system, I would recommend that you sprinkle Ethernet wall jacks liberally throughout the house, possibly in every room. Think ahead about the possibility of linking yet unknown Ethernet devices to the network (for example, a video camera, a lighting system, a swimming pool chlorinator, a refrigerator/range combo, and so on).

Household telephone twisted-pair wiring hasn't changed in my lifetime. Network wiring, however, has changed several times since I built my office up the hill from my home in 1991. At that time, my networking friends recommended that I use state-of-the-art coaxial network cable. It's still embedded in the walls and would work well with compatible network cards; however, I converted to Catx cabling several years ago to maintain compatibility with modern network equipment. I also wired my office for television, security, and audio. The security and TV wires are unchanged, but the two-channel stereo audio wiring is no longer in use. Today, I play everything through my PC's 7.1 audio system (six satellite speakers and a powered subwoofer).

As you can see, wiring technologies change, so I would recommend that you plan for the inevitable by embedding supplementary electrical conduits (1 inch inside diameter) along major horizontal (for example, the attic and basement) and vertical (between floors) runs in your new home. Use these conduits to install new wired technologies as they come available. A little planning now can save you considerable time, effort, and money in the future. The conduits, which would start at the central point in the structured wiring system, would terminate at empty junction boxes in walls. Be sure to install a *pull string* that will allow you to pull cables between the basement and the second floor or from one end of the house to the other.

When installing a structure wiring system, you would use modular wall plates that can be attached to standard electrical junction boxes. During construction, the wires are inserted into the boxes from within the interior walls. Eventually, they are attached to modular jacks by any of several methods, including screw-in contacts and the method shown in Figure 7-5. The modules, which are inserted into the wall plates, can include ports for telephones, Ethernet, cable TV, speakers, and so on. The wall plate in Figure 7-6 has ports for Ethernet and cable TV. The best place to find wall plates and modular jacks locally is home improvement stores, such as Lowe's and Home Depot. They can also be purchased from many e-tailers, such as Blackbox.com or Cables.com. Some A/V and computer stores stock these items as well.

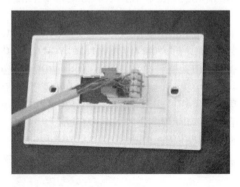

Figure 7-5   Ethernet cable connected to a modular RJ-45 jack

Figure 7-6   Modular wall plate with ports for Ethernet and cable TV

TIP *If your broadband service is DSL, you probably received several line filters with your DSL installation package. These filters are designed to eliminate "data noise" during voice conversations. You'll need to install filters for each telephone on your DSL line to eliminate the hissing sound. Extra filters can be purchased from your DSL provider or any electronics store.*

Ethernet Wiring for an Existing Home

Most of us are dealing with an existing home, which is not nearly as easily wired as a new home under construction. In an existing home, we tend to retrofit wiring according to immediate need. Seldom do we install structured wiring to accommodate all wired communications within the house. The more likely scenario is that we run speaker wires, security wires, and other wires as the need arises. Because you're reading this book, your immediate need probably is wiring for an Ethernet LAN. My comments here emphasize Ethernet wiring, but these approaches to wiring an existing home are generic and applicable to any type of wiring task.

When you retrofit an existing home with wiring, you must deal with the trade-off between aesthetics and utility, just getting it done. For example, you can simply thread an Ethernet cable through a hole in the wall or you can install wall plates with modular jacks on either side of the wall, the latter being the way professionals do it. However, some people might argue that a quarter-inch hole near the baseboard behind the sofa is less conspicuous than another wall plate.

CAUTION When installing wiring in an existing home, be ever aware of what lurks between the studs within your walls. When drilling or cutting, do so carefully, because that blade or drill has the potential to cut/penetrate a water pipe, a power line, an air-conditioning duct or wire, a natural gas line, a steam pipe, a security wire, and of course, nails. Since it is unlikely that you will be x-raying your walls, proceed with caution and stop the tool immediately if you feel anything other than wood. If this happen, try another spot.

The Parts, Materials, and Tools

Your first task is to gather the parts and materials you will need to wire your house for an Ethernet LAN. Work from your network design to identify specific needs (number and lengths of items). These might include the following:

- Bulk Ethernet wire
- Connectors
- Junction boxes with modular jacks
- Patch cables

I use a variety of common shop tools to install wiring, depending on the situation. These tools, however, would be considered the basic tools for wiring an existing house.

- **All-in-one crimping tool**   Use this tool (see Figure 7-4) to cut, strip, and crimp.
- **Cable staple gun**   Use this specially notched stable gun to affix wiring to baseboards, studs, rafters, and so on. From experience, I know that a regular staple gun won't work for this task, as it will eventually slip and penetrate your wire.
- **Power drill**   Chances are you will need to drill holes in walls, studs, and so on.
- **Extra long 1/4-inch drill bit**   Use this 12- to 18-inch drill bit to penetrate the entire width of a wall.
- **Spade bits**   You will need spade bits (5/8 inch, 3/4 inch, and 1 inch) to make holes big enough for multiple wires or for the connectors on preassembled patch cables.

- **Drill bit extension for use with spade bits**   Depending on the thickness of your walls, you may need this extension if you wish to penetrate the depth of the wall.

- **Handsaw**   Use the handsaw to cut the rectangular holes in the dry wall or plaster for the junction boxes.

- **Fish tape**   This thin, flexible band of steel (from 20 to 50 feet in length) about 1/8-inch wide can be used to push/pull cable through electrical conduits and tight places.

- **Coat hanger**   Use an unraveled and straightened coat hanger to pull the wire through a hole in the wall or, if you don't have a fish tape, to push it through a tight place. To attach the Catx cable, insert about two inches of a coat hanger into the insulation, and then wrap the insulation and hanger tightly together with electrician's tape such that you have a smooth taper between the insulation and the hanger.

- **Protective goggles**   It's a good idea to wear eye protection for any home improvement project.

- **Hard hat**   Wear a hard hat in the attic and crawl spaces where the sharp ends of numerous nails are exposed and joists/rafters abound.

- **Flashlight or head lamp**   I prefer a head lamp to illuminate attics, crawl spaces, closets, and dark corners so that my hands are free.

- **Tennis ball with pull string**   If you have drop or suspended ceilings, a tennis ball with a pull string taped to it and a good throwing arm can be very helpful.

Although not an absolute requirement, your cabling job can be made easier if you have a LAN tester, especially if you have to troubleshoot an Ethernet link. LAN testers cost from $25 to $100. One at the low end should suffice for home networking.

Installation of the Cable

Once you have the parts, materials, and tools, you're ready to install the cable. I'm certainly not a professional installer, but I've had plenty of on-the-job-training installing telephones (traditional 2 pair and 4 pair), security wires, network cable, TV cable, speaker wires, and cabling for a home theater in my own homes. The projects, which involved many runs between rooms and floors and some to outbuildings, were seldom easy.

The trick to wiring an existing home is to find a path that results in a functional run that is aesthetically acceptable. In the past, I have used all of these as paths to string wiring.

- **Attic**   The attic and basement are the first places I look when stringing wires between rooms. In the attic, I just lay the wire across the rafters and the insulation. It's not a pretty sight, but I don't see it very often (see Figure 7-7).

- **Basement**   Like the attic, a basement with exposed joists provides a great opportunity to run wires discreetly between rooms. If you must run wires between rafters, make the hole large enough for several cables.

- **Garage**   A garage with unfinished walls (exposed studs) can be used to transport vertical wires from the attic or basement into rooms adjacent to the garage.

- **Crawl spaces**   Homes with ground-level crawl spaces may not have a basement, but if you are willing and able to traverse this cramped area, it's an excellent conduit for runs between rooms.

- **Storage areas**   Our last house was a story and a half with six large dormers running around the top floor. These types of homes often have cubby hole accesses to the storage areas created between the roof line, wall, and floor. The storage areas make runs between the dormers easy to do.

- **Closets**   If you must enter the floor or the ceiling and you have a closet in the room, you might make your hole in the closet. Enter the room through a hole in the wall closet. Wall-length closets also provide a path between rooms.

- **Cabinets**   Built-in cabinets can be used to hide horizontal wires running between and within rooms and to hide vertical wires running between floors.

Figure 7-7   Ethernet, telephone/DSL, cable TV, AC power, and security

- **Lighting soffits**   The previous owner of our house installed almost 200 feet of soffits for supplemental and accent lighting. These gifts from heaven have given me long paths between and within rooms. Typically, I would enter the soffits from the attic and/or an adjacent closet.

- **External soffits**   Rooms with cathedral ceilings can put a damper on attic runs. When this happens, you can continue the run in an external soffit under the eve and reenter the attic on the other side of the cathedral room. Gain access to the soffits by removing an accent light or a vent.

- **Metal air conditioning ducts**   The air conditioning ducts are not the cleanest way to run wires within an existing house, but in a pinch, the ducts can be very helpful, especially in a slab home that has no ground-level crawl spaces. Use fish tape to snake around metal ducts such that you enter the air-conditioning vent in one room and exit a vent in another room.

TIP   *Avoid running any wiring (audio, video, or data) within two feet of fluorescent lighting and 12 inches of electric motors.*

Stringing wire is far from rocket science, but it does take some creativity and innovative methods to connect rooms with a wire such that the overall aesthetics of the home is not compromised.

TIP   *If you are running a cable through difficult places, give yourself plenty of room for error in measurement. Bulk cable is inexpensive, and cutting 20 percent extra is a good rule of thumb to follow. That's less than a dollar on a 50-foot run.*

The wall entry point may not be exactly where you want it, so you might need to use your imagination to get the wire across the room in the least offensive manner. One approach is to use a hand stapler and staple the wire to the baseboard, and possibly, around the door trim. Another is to use a snap-on conduit, which can be purchased in various lengths at any home improvement store. Mount one side of the conduit to the baseboard or wall, and then insert the wire and snap on the cover. Sometimes, the most effective approach is to simply lay the wire along the baseboard unobtrusively behind the furniture.

CAUTION   *When threading Catx Ethernet cable, avoid pulling with forces in excess of 25 pounds. Also, avoid sharp bends in the cable. As a rule, bend it no more sharply than the curvature of a golf ball.*

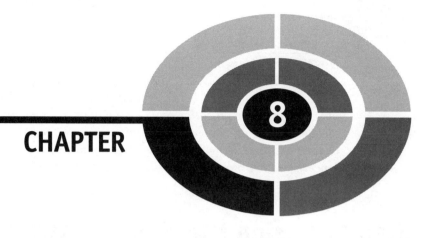

Setting Up and Installing a Home Network

At this point in your networking adventure, you are ready to set up and install a LAN in your home. In a nutshell, you design your network; purchase the necessary hardware, software, and cabling; establish wired and/or wireless links between network components; and configure the network for basic operation. Although Internet connection, printer, and file sharing methods are addressed in this chapter as part of the setup and configuration process, these topics are revisited in more detail in Chapter 9. Security issues are covered in depth in Chapter 10. The home network setup and installation process is presented as a seven-step process that includes concepts and tasks discussed in detail in earlier chapters. We begin with the home network design.

> **NOTE** *The wireless LAN can be constructed in* infrastructure *or* ad hoc mode. *Infrastructure mode involves the use of an access point (AP) and enables wireless communication between multiple wireless PCs. Infrastructure mode also enables communication with a wired network. Use ad hoc mode to create on-the-fly networks that do not require the use of an AP. The focus of this chapter is the steps involved in building an infrastructure mode home network; however, ad hoc mode is covered at the end of the chapter.*

Step 1: Design the Home Network

The home network design process is presented in detail in Chapter 6. A result of this process is a network diagram that graphically illustrates the physical locations and connectivity of all PCs, networked devices, and communications equipment in the network. Use the tables in Chapter 6 to complete an inventory of your hardware and software and what you need to build the network. Use the design and inventories to prepare a shopping list that includes everything you need to purchase and build the network, including all PCs, PC upgrades, peripheral devices, software, and network gear. The list may include general cabling and cabling accessory needs, too; however, these needs may not become clear until the actual installation of the cabling.

Step 2: Purchase the Hardware and Software

Purchase all of the hardware and software needed for your home network. The Appendix is a buyer's guide with lots of tips and recommendations about where to shop and how to get the best deals.

> **TIP** *If you purchased your PC prior to September 2004, you may need to download and install the Windows XP Service Pack 2 (SP2) update. SP2, which is available free from Microsoft to anyone using a certified copy of Windows XP, includes features that help you install and protect your home network. Also, certain wireless features, such as the Wireless Network Setup Wizard, are available only in SP2. If you have not upgraded all of your Windows XP PCs to SP2 (or the latest version of the Windows), I recommend you do so now. To install SP2 and/or the latest Windows XP updates, click Start | Help And Support | Windows Update.*

Step 3: Install the Cabling

This step is not applicable if you plan a wireless home network. Also, cabling is not needed if the wired portion of your home network design calls for the use of existing wiring and the use of HomePlug or HomePNA technology. However, if your design calls for running Catx Ethernet wiring between some or all of the nodes, now is the time to purchase and install the necessary cabling. Chapter 7 covers this task in detail.

TIP Before buying patch cables or bulk Catx cable, you should take inventory of the cables that came with your network equipment. These cables are interchangeable and can be used wherever they are needed. It's quite possible that some of the cables may be too short, such as those that come with the USB wireless adapters. If this is the case, you need to purchase one that is long enough to enable optimum placement of your wireless components.

Step 4: Install Network Adapters and Configure PCs

Most modern desktop PCs and all notebook PCs are sold with Ethernet network adapters. However, relatively few desktops and notebooks come with wireless adapters. If one or more of the PCs planned for your home network are not equipped with the necessary wired or wireless adapter, then you will need to install one for each networked PC.

You learned in Chapter 5 that you have a variety of network adapter options for both desktop and notebook PCs and for wired and wireless adapters. Some are permanently installed, some are connected via USB cables, and some can be inserted as needed. Ethernet adapter options are summarized in Tables 5-1 and 5-2 in Chapter 5. Other types of adapters, including HomePNA and HomePlug, are illustrated and discussed in Chapter 5 as well.

I don't have an exact count, but there may be more manufacturers of network adapters than there are bottlers of carbonated beverages. Certainly, there are as many flavors of adapters. The installation of adapters is normally straightforward; however, their unique idiosyncrasies preclude my providing you with detailed installation instructions. Fortunately, each product comes with its own instructions. Follow these carefully and you should have no problem with the installation of any network adapter.

TIP Given a choice, I would suggest that you use USB wireless adapters for desktop PCs rather than PCI wireless adapters. External USB adapters can be positioned to achieve the best signal, whereas PCI adapters are installed in the PC's system unit. If the system unit is positioned between the AP and the adapter's antenna, the signal can be blocked or dampened.

Installing the Network Adapters

Although Windows XP offers installation support for most network adapters, I would still recommend you follow the manufacturer's instructions. Typically, this involves installing a driver (and perhaps some support software) from the installation CD packaged with the adapter and then installing the adapter. You will need to remove the side panel from your system unit to install a PCI Ethernet or wireless adapter. External adapters are simply plugged into a USB port or a PC card slot on a notebook.

Upon recognizing the adapter for the first time, your PC will alert you that a new device has been installed. Network adapters appear in the Network Connections display (Start | Control Panel | Network Connections), as shown in Figure 8-1. This display shows net connection options for a particular PC.

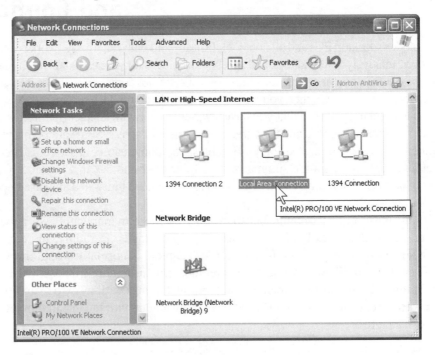

Figure 8-1   The Network Connections display

TIP Many new PCs have Ethernet adapters integrated into the motherboard functions. If your PC has an Ethernet port and the adapter is not showing on the Network Connections display, it's possible that the Ethernet card may be disabled at the BIOS level (see the next Note). If this is the case, you may need to enable it through the BIOS setup. To do this, keep tapping the DELETE key on startup to enter the BIOS setup. (Although most modern motherboards have standardized on the DELETE key, you might need to enter ESC, F1, F2, F10, or a key combination shown in your motherboard's user manual.) Often, you'll see "Press [whatever key your system uses] to enter Setup" during the boot process. Navigate to the network adapter preferences and toggle Disable to Enable.

The Windows driver support for wireless adapters, called *Wireless Zero Configuration (WZC)*, enables auto configuration for wireless network devices, such as wireless CardBus/PC Card adapters and USB wireless adapters. Without any action on the part of the user, the WZC service installs the drivers and begins seeking a wireless LAN as soon as you insert a wireless adapter into a PC card slot or a USB port.

NOTE Pronounced "bye-ose," BIOS is an acronym for Basic Input/Output System. The BIOS is built-in software that determines what a computer can do without accessing programs from a disk. On PCs, the BIOS contains all the code required to control the keyboard, display screen, disk drives, serial communications, and a number of miscellaneous functions.

Configuring the PCs to Work with the Gateway's Router

After successful installation of the Ethernet and/or wireless adapters, you need to configure each PC on the network to communicate with the router (one of the all-in-one gateway functions). To do this, change the PC's settings, if needed, such that it obtains an IP address automatically. This allows the PC to be a client to the gateway's DHCP server. Follow this sequence of steps to configure each Windows XP PC on the network:

 1. Open Network Connections (see Figure 8-1) through the Control Panel (Start | Control Panel | Network And Internet Connections | Network Connections).

2. Open the Local Area Connection Status dialog box shown here. To do this, double-click the Local Area Connection icon in Figure 8-1, usually the first one listed. The status dialog box includes information regarding connection status, duration, and speed.

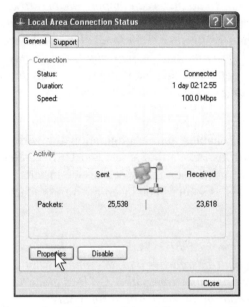

3. Click Properties to show the Local Area Connection Properties dialog box.

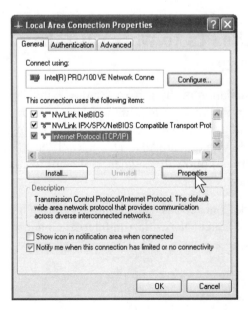

4. Scroll down, if needed, and highlight Internet Protocol (TCP/IP). Click Properties.

5. In the Internet Protocol (TCP/IP) Properties dialog box, select the radio button for Obtain An IP Address Automatically (if not already on). This is the default option and should be selected.

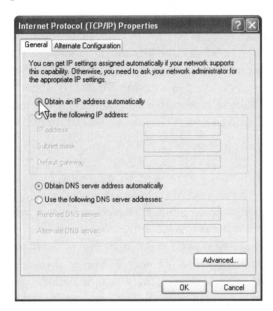

Step 5: Set Up Your Modem

Modems have come a long way in terms of installation ease over the last 15 years. I remember DIP switch settings, complicated preferences, lots of compatibility issues, and long conversations with technical support on my early 12 kbps modems, my finicky ISDN modem, and my weather-sensitive satellite modem. Now that Internet users number in the billions, ISPs have figured out that if they provide modems that are easy to install, they will save lots of money and require considerably fewer tech support people.

TIP *I recommend you use the modem provided by your ISP so that you are guaranteed support if you have problems. If you have problems with your Net connection and you are using an "unsupported" modem, your ISP's tech support people are instructed to send you to your modem's manufacturer. When this happens, you might be on a technical yo-yo where the ISP and the modem vendor blame one another for your problems.*

Once the ISP has activated your line for data, just follow the ISP's step-by-step instructions to install the always-on broadband modem. Typically, you would connect the broadband modem directly to a PC (without a gateway) to ensure that the Internet connection is active and working. To do this, shut down the PC and turn off power to the broadband modem (or the gateway, if the modem is embedded). Link the two, usually with an Ethernet cable, and then turn on the broadband modem and start your PC.

TIP *Usually, ISPs will provide several modem options, including a DSL or cable modem, an all-in-one home gateway (modem, router, firewall, switch, and so on), and an all-in-one wireless home gateway, which includes a wireless access point. If your home networking plans are humble and you don't anticipate expansion for two more years, you might want to consider one of the home gateway options, which have built-in modems and a lot more. However, if you expect your network to grow and would like to maintain a single-vendor philosophy with your net gear, I would recommend you choose the ISP's recommended stand-alone high-performance DSL or cable modem. In this way, Internet access remains functionally separate from the network that links the nodes.*

The ISP's instructions can appear on an interactive CD (see Figure 8-2) and/or in a manual. Most ISPs have the instructions online (see Figure 8-3) in case you have alternative access to the Net.

TIP *It's much easier to move a modem than computers and network gear. DSL signal strength is the same at all wall RJ-11 jacks. Although a cable modem can be installed on any available TV cable, it's best to choose a cable that comes directly from the cable feed line. The length of the cable and the number of splitters on the front end of the cable modem can have an impact, sometimes a dramatic impact, on signal strength and, therefore, speed.*

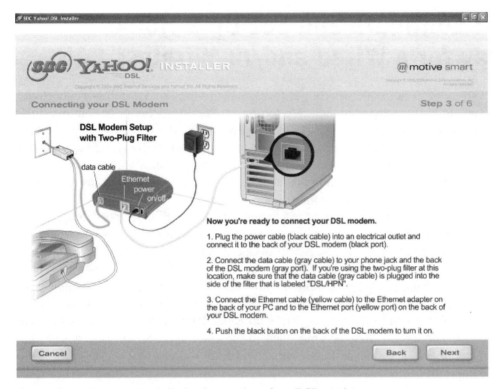

Figure 8-2 CD-based installation instructions for a DSL modem

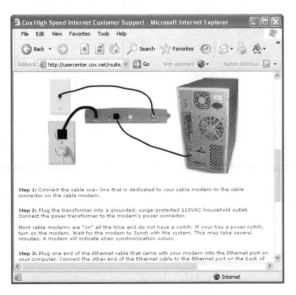

Figure 8-3 Online installation instructions for a cable modem

Step 6: Configure and Set Up a Home Gateway for a Wired and/or Wireless LAN

The trend in home networking is to have both wired and wireless connectivity. Therefore, I've integrated the setup for the gateway for either or both into a single step. Even if your initial network design calls for a totally wired LAN or for totally wireless connectivity, there is a high probability that you will expand your network to include both types of connectivity within the first year or so. For this reason, I recommend that you study all parts in this step, even if your current design calls for only wired or only wireless connectivity.

An all-in-one gateway will have a router, at least four Ethernet ports, and possibly a DSL/cable modem—everything you need to share an Internet connection, files, printers, and other resources. An all-in-one *wireless* gateway will have an access point (AP) as well. In either case, connect one PC directly to the gateway via an Ethernet cable so that you can configure the gateway from the PC. Connect the other PCs and Ethernet devices to the router via a Wireless B/G link or an Ethernet Catx cable. Connect the gateway to the broadband modem with an Ethernet or USB cable. The modem may be embedded in the gateway or an external device. The result of all this connectivity is a home network.

Choosing a Location for a Wireless Gateway

One of the most important considerations in setting up a home network with wireless capabilities is the location of the gateway and its access point (AP). In a wireless network, the connection speed and strength can vary considerably, so the location of the AP is critical. Table 8-1 offers some strategies to help optimize transmission speeds and minimize dead spots within your network.

CAUTION *If you choose to begin your home network with an all-in-one home gateway provided by your ISP and later choose to upgrade to a home gateway that is not supported by your ISP, then I recommend you replace your ISP-provided home gateway with your ISP's recommended stand-alone DSL or cable modem. You want to avoid having multiple gateways and, ultimately, conflicting routers in the same home network.*

Strategy	Explanation
Place AP in the center of the desired coverage area.	An AP is omnidirectional, so the best strategy is to place it in a central location, thus optimizing the signal strength among the nodes.
Position the AP at least four feet above the floor.	Most common household obstructions, such as chairs, tables, counters/cabinets, bathroom fixtures, and so on, are lower than four feet. You will get a better signal and more extended coverage if you mount your AP on a wall (most have wall-mounting accessories) or place it on top of a cabinet or any piece of furniture that gives it height.
Avoid positioning the AP such that the signal's line of sight would pass through large metal objects or water.	Wireless signals can be deflected or weakened by metal objects such as refrigerators, ranges, air conditioners and their metal ducting, metal cabinets, metal staircases, automobiles (in garages), and so on. The same is true of anything containing water, such as a fish tank or water heater.
Avoid potential conflicts with microwave signals.	Microwave ovens and 2.4 GHz cordless telephone base units are the main culprits. Whenever possible, position the AP well away from these devices.
Avoid positioning the AP near exterior walls that face neighbors or public areas.	Your AP signal can be picked up by passing motorists or neighbors in adjoining apartments, so the best strategy is to do what you can to minimize or eliminate this possibility (security issues and strategies are discussed in Chapter 10).
Avoid positioning the AP above or below one of the wireless nodes.	Devices used to facilitate wireless communication in the home use a collinear type of omnidirectional signal that decreases the vertical bandwidth to concentrate signal power on the horizontal plane. Therefore, the signal from the AP's vertical antenna is weakest in rooms directly above or below the AP.
A vertical antenna provides the most comprehensive coverage with the home.	Antennae on APs and wireless network adapters can be adjusted to optimize the signal. However, if you wish to maintain mobility throughout the house for wireless notebook PCs, you will want the AP's antenna to be vertical. You can, however, adjust the antennae on network adapters and signal booster units.

Table 8-1   Strategies for Positioning an AP

Set Up the AP/Router

The first step in configuring a LAN is to set up the router or, for a wireless LAN, the AP/router. These functions are usually part of an all-in-one gateway. The AP (sometimes called the WAP, or wireless access point) is the transceiver that enables data transmission via radio signals between the PCs and the router. Your gateway may not have an AP function if your LAN design is for wired links. Routers are network devices that enable a link between networks (in this case, your LAN and the Internet). If your AP is separate from your gateway, then you will need to link the two via an Ethernet cable.

Fortunately, the typical off-the-shelf gateway with AP and router functions is configured with common default settings and is ready to run as soon as you remove the wrapping paper. However, you may wish to change a few settings to personalize the gateway to your home networking environment. This section includes discussions of how to view and change common AP/router settings.

Although the topic was discussed in Chapter 3, let's review the basics of public and private IP addressing, an important concept in router functionality. Every device in your home network must have a private IP address that identifies its location on the network—something like 192.168.1.102. Private IP addresses are visible only within the network and are not known on the Internet. Routers depend on these private IP addresses to route information around the network. The IP address can be static or dynamic. Static IP addresses may be assigned manually or by default to a device or a PC. The router is assigned a private IP address for use within the network, usually a static IP address. Typically, PCs on a home network are assigned temporary dynamic IP addresses by the gateway's DHCP server function.

Most broadband connections with public ISPs give the router a single dynamic public IP address, which is used to establish the link with the Internet. Public IP addresses are the addresses known throughout the Internet. Through the magic of the router function, all PCs on the home network use this solitary temporary IP address to interact with the Internet.

Most gateways come with user-friendly setup CDs that contain interactive software to guide you through the AP/router configuration process (see Figure 8-4). Just load the software and follow the onscreen instructions that walk you through the setup procedure. As an alternative, you can use the router's browser-based utility that allows you to configure the AP/router with the settings provided by your ISP for your broadband Internet connection. To access the browser-based utility, open your browser and enter its factory-set IP address. This address, which is found in the manufacturer's documentation, will probably take the form 192.168.$x.x$ in a home network, although addresses can be in other ranges, too (see Chapter 3). Other network communications devices have similar IP addresses.

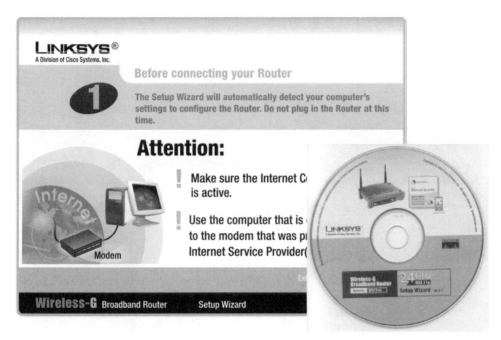

Figure 8-4   Interactive setup CD with interactive software for configuring a Linksys Wireless-G broadband router

Changing the Password

Security is an ongoing concern, and you want to do everything possible to keep intruders from poking around your router. During your initial session, I recommend you change the vendor-supplied default password (it's "admin" for Linksys gateway/routers) to one of your choosing. For a Linksys router, this is done via the browser-based utility. The IP address of the AP/router in the example of Figure 8-5 is 192.168.1.1.

To change the password using the Linksys browser-based utility, select the Administration tab, then Management (see Figure 8-5). I suggest you always include a mix of alpha and numeric characters in your password. Leave the User Name box blank. In all future attempts to access the configuration program, you'll be asked to enter your password (see Figure 8-6).

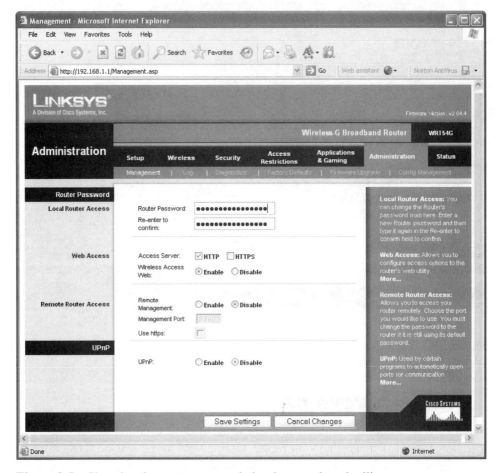

Figure 8-5 Changing the router password via a browser-based utility

Figure 8-6 Enter a password to access the router's configuration utility.

TIP You can configure your AP/router using the interactive software on the CD that came with your home gateway, or you can use the AP/router's built-in browser-based utility. Either approach should work, but it has been my experience that the interactive software will occasionally not recognize a properly installed network device. For this reason, I recommend using the utility that links you directly to the home gateway's built-in software. The interactive software on the CD works with the gateway indirectly through separate software, and sometimes, communications are misinterpreted.

The Initial Setup Screen

Completing the information in the initial setup screen may be all that is needed to configure the AP/router to get it working properly. Figure 8-7 shows a setup screen for a Linksys gateway that is representative of similar browser-based utilities for net gear from other companies. The Linksys setup screen has two parts: Internet Setup and Network Setup. Each is divided into logical sections. In the Internet Setup portion of Figure 8-7, you will need to define the Internet connection type and, possibly, some optional settings.

- **Internet connection type**   In the setup screen, a drop-down menu lets you pick Automatic Configuration – DHCP, static IP, PPPoE (Point-to-Point Protocol over Internet), PPTP (Point-to-Point Tunneling Protocol), and others you are not likely to use. Most of us will select Automatic Configuration – DHCP.

- **Optional settings**   You are given an opportunity to name the router. Usually, the model numbers for network gear are descriptive, so I suggest you simply adopt the name for a network device. For example, the Linksys Wireless-G Broadband Router (an all-in-one wireless gateway) in the example of Figure 8-7 is tagged as WRT54G. The *W* indicates wireless, the *RT* stands for router, and the *54G* is the transmission speed. Your ISP may require that you enter a host name and a domain name (both provided by the ISP). For MTU (Maximum Transmission Unit), the largest packet size permitted for Internet transmission, it's best to stay with "auto" or the manufacturer's default setting.

The Network Setup portion of the setup screen in Figure 8-7 has three parts.

- **Router IP**   The two entries here are the IP address of the router and the subnet mask. Typically, you would accept the default settings, which often are those shown here (192.168.1.1 and 255.255.255.0). A *subnet* is those network devices whose IP addresses have the same prefix (for example, 255.255.255). The *subnet mask* identifies which portions of the IP address correspond to the network (the first three numbers in the example) and which is the host (the last number).

Figure 8-7   Initial setup screen for configuring a Linksys Wireless-G broadband router via a browser-based utility

● **Network Address Server Setting (DHCP)**   Typically, you would enable the DHCP server function so that your router can manage IP addresses within the home network. The only time you would disable the server would be if you already have a DHCP server on the network. It is a good idea to accept the default starting IP address (192.168.1.100 in the example). The same is true for the maximum number of DHCP users (50 in the example). In a home network, there is no reason to limit the number of PCs you expect to have on the network. The client lease time is just the amount of time a network user will be allowed a connection to the router with the current dynamic IP address (0 indicates one day). Typically, you would not need to enter anything in the static domain name system (DNS) boxes, because your ISP will provide you with at least one DNS server IP address. Typically, the Windows Internet Naming Service (WINS) box is not applicable in a home networking environment and is left blank.

Time Setting Choose your time zone from the drop-down box and then check the box to automatically adjust the time (via the Internet) and you will not have to worry about setting the network clock again.

The Basic Wireless Settings

If your home network has a wireless component, you might wish to customize your wireless gateway's AP. Figure 8-8 shows the wireless settings that are common to all AP/routers and to stand-alone APs. If you have a stand-alone AP connected to a gateway, the settings are the same (see Figure 8-8). For the Linksys all-in-one wireless gateway and the Linksys access point in the examples, these are accessed via the device's browser-based utilities.

- **Wireless networking mode** The drop-down box allows you to choose whether you wish the gateway to service only Wireless-G clients, only Wireless-B clients, or both Wireless-B and Wireless-G. Another option is

Figure 8-8 Basic wireless settings for a Linksys Wireless-G Broadband Router and a Linksys Wireless-G Access Point (at the bottom under Wireless)

to disable the wireless feature. The Wireless-G or Wireless-B Only selection excludes connectivity by other than Wireless-G or Wireless-B devices, respectively. Usually, the best choice is both or mixed.

- **Wireless network name (SSID)**   The SSID, or Service Set Identifier, is a name shared among all nodes in a wireless network. Each node must be associated with this case-sensitive name, which can be 32 characters in length. The default SSID for Linksys network gear is "linksys." For security reasons, I recommend you change the SSID. If you do, be sure to change it on all network devices.

- **Wireless channel**   In North America, you can choose one of 11 channels. This is so that you can change the channel to one that won't conflict with the neighbors' AP channels. Also, having multiple channels from which to choose gives you the flexibility to assign each AP in the network its own channel. Avoid using the same channel if you have more than one AP in your home network.

- **Wireless SSID broadcast**   The way Windows works is that it chooses an AP that is broadcasting its SSID over one that is not, regardless of the order of the networks on the Preferred Networks list. It's best to enable SSID broadcast in a home network.

Once your PCs are configured with wireless adapters and you have entered your router settings, you're ready to set up your wireless PCs.

Security Settings

At this point, I suggest you accept the default settings relating to network security. Let's hold off on the security settings until all PCs are working with the gateway (router/AP). Security issues and configuration settings are addressed in Chapter 10.

Run the Wireless Network Setup Wizard

Wireless networking support is integrated into Windows XP. If your home network includes wireless network adapters that link to an AP, run the Windows XP Wireless Network Setup Wizard (see Figure 8-9) and enter the requested information for all wireless PCs on the network. To run the wizard, click Start | All Programs | Accessories | Communications | Wireless Network Setup Wizard.

Enter the name of the network (the SSID), the same name you enter during the AP/router setup procedure ("linksys" in the example). Normally, you would choose to automatically assign a network key. Leave the WPA check box blank. You are

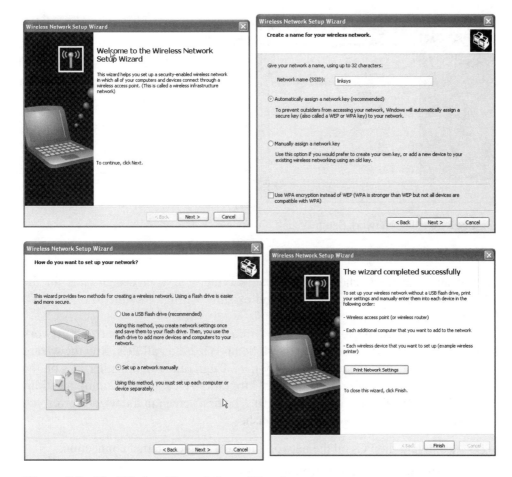

Figure 8-9 The Wireless Network Setup Wizard

given the option to employ a USB flash drive, if you have one. You can use the flash drive to transport these settings to other wireless PCs; however, it may be just as easy to repeat the manual entry process for each wireless PC.

Make All Connections and Run the Network Setup Wizard

If your network design calls for wired Ethernet links and you have completed the required cabling, it's time to make those Catx Ethernet cabling connections. Most of these connections link the Ethernet ports on the gateway to network adapters

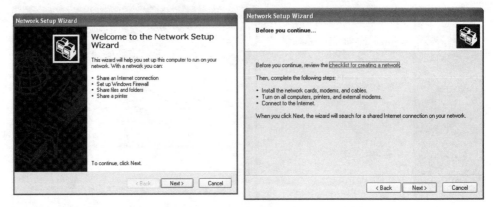

Figure 8-10 The Network Setup Wizard: Overview

and, if applicable, switches and/or network bridges. If your design calls for the HomePNA or HomePlug technology and existing wiring, it's time to make those cabling connections.

Once you have connected the PCs via wired or wireless links as per your network design, you will need to run the Network Setup Wizard on all PCs. Run the wizard on the PC attached to the home gateway first. Then, run it on the other PCs on the network. To run the wizard, click Start|All Programs|Accessories|Communications | Network Setup Wizard (see Figure 8-10). The first screen in the wizard gives you an overview of what the wizard accomplishes.

- Configure the PCs on the network to use a single Internet connection.
- Assign a name and description to each PC.
- Enable file and printer sharing.
- Set up the Windows firewall.

The second screen of Figure 8-10 reminds you to review the checklist for creating a network (in the Windows Help and Support); to confirm that the installation of all devices and cables is complete; to turn on all PCs, printers, and modems; and to make the connection to the Internet.

The third screen in the Network Setup Wizard (see Figure 8-11) addresses the Internet connection method and asks you to choose whether you plan to connect using the Windows Internet Connection Sharing (ICS) feature or a home/residential gateway. As explained earlier in Chapter 5, using the home gateway has emerged as the overwhelming choice for home networking. If this is the case, check the radio button to indicate that the computer connects through a home/residential gateway.

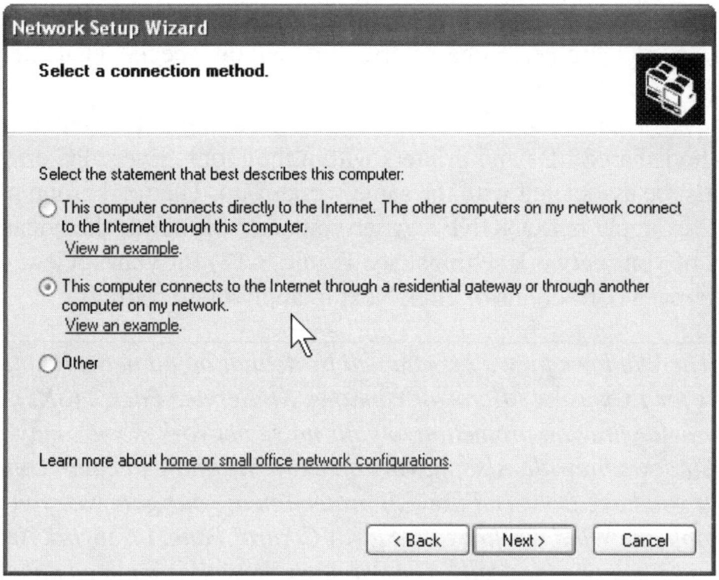

Figure 8-11   The Network Setup Wizard: connection method

If not, I highly recommend you reconsider the substantial benefits of a relatively inexpensive gateway.

Now it's time to name the PC and the network (see Figure 8-12). Although optional, I recommend you enter a short explanation in the computer description ("Larry's Computer" in the example) that serves to clarify the computer name. Each PC on the network must have a unique name. Typically, you give each a short,

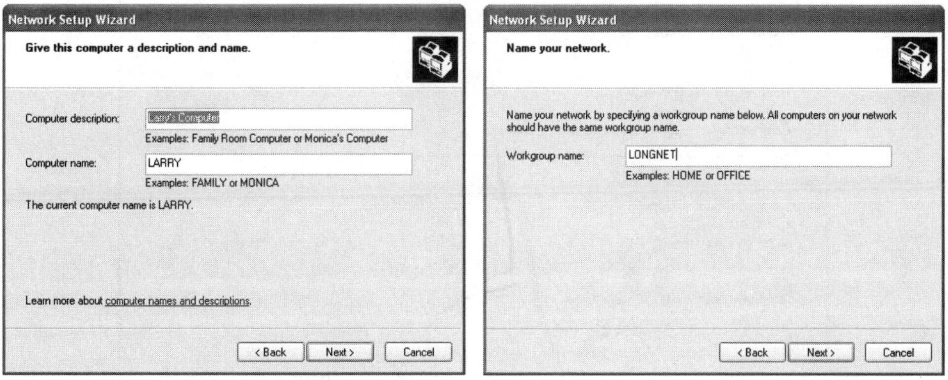

Figure 8-12   The Network Setup Wizard: naming the PC and the network

simple name that associates it with an individual, location, or function. The name is limited to 15 alphanumeric characters, and certain special characters are not permitted (; : " < > * + = \ | ? ,).

In Windows, a named workgroup is a logical grouping of PCs that is intended to help users find shared files and printers within the group. Every PC on your home network must be associated with the same workgroup. The workgroup name in the Figure 8-12 example is LONGNET. After you enter the name, the wizard presents a summary of your network settings (see Figure 8-13) for your review. Go back if you need to make corrections or click Next to apply these settings.

CAUTION *The Windows firewall is enabled by default on all network and Internet connections for PCs using Microsoft Windows XP Service Pack 2 (SP2). All gateways provide firewall protection to your home network, so you may not need an active Windows firewall. Also, having an extra firewall can cause connectivity problems. If you have front-end firewall protection at your gateway, you might wish to disable the Windows firewall (Start | Control Panel | Network And Internet Connections | Windows Firewall). The Windows firewall is enabled on a PC each time you run the Network Setup Wizard, so if you rerun the wizard, be aware that the firewall is enabled for that PC.*

The next option presented by the Network Setup Wizard gives you the option to turn on or turn off file and printer sharing (see Figure 8-14). In the home networking

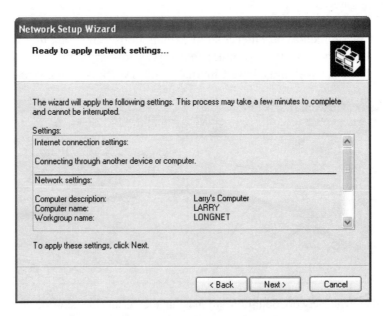

Figure 8-13   The Network Setup Wizard: summary of settings

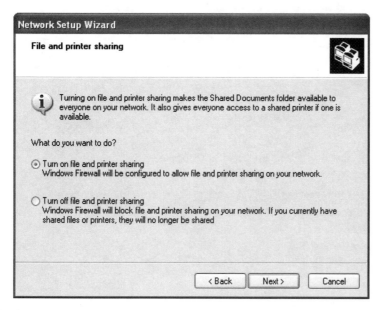

Figure 8-14   The Network Setup Wizard: file and printer sharing

environment, you would normally select the "Turn on" option to make the Shared Documents folder on the PC available to other network users. Selecting this option also enables sharing of the printer connected to the PC (if applicable); that is, anyone on the network can print directly to the printer.

NOTE   When you turn on file and printer sharing, only those files in the Shared Documents folder are made available to other users. All other files are protected unless you specifically choose to share those files. This procedure is discussed in Chapter 9.

When you click Next, an animated screen appears while your network settings are being applied to the PC and then you are given an option to create a network setup disk (see Figure 8-15). Normally, you would click either Create A Network Setup Disk or Just Finish The Wizard. If you choose the former, you're presented with an additional screen that allows you to save the Network Setup Wizard settings (except PC name) to a floppy disk. The disk can then be used to copy the network settings to the other PCs in the network. The PC is now configured for networking, and if you wish to change these settings, you'll have to rerun the Network Setup Wizard. Click Finish to complete the Network Setup Wizard (see Figure 8-16).

Home Networking Demystified

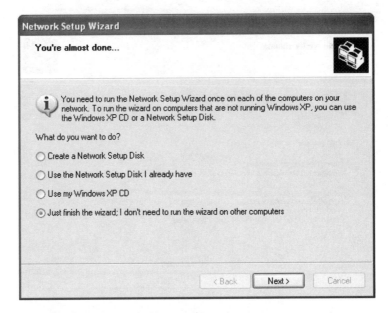

Figure 8-15   The Network Setup Wizard: create setup disk

Once you have run the Network Setup Wizard on all PCs, you should have an operational home network. Use your "status" option in your browser-based AP/ router utility to view active PCs on the network (see Figure 8-17). Alternatively, enter command mode (Start | Run | **cmd**) and enter **net view** at the prompt (see Figure 8-17).

Figure 8-16   The Network Setup Wizard: finish setup

Figure 8-17   View active PCs on the network via the browser-based utility or by entering "net view" in command mode

Can You Hear Me Now?

The cell phone tester on the ubiquitous TV commercials has a good idea. If you're creating a wireless network, you should test its effectiveness. Do a walkaround with a wireless notebook; if you have one, that is. Use a portable wireless PC to test signal strength and speed at various locations in and around the house. Instead of saying "Can you hear me now?", just open the Wireless Network Connection Status dialog box on a notebook PC (see Figure 8-18). To do this, double-click the network connection icon in the notification area of the taskbar.

Figure 8-18   The Wireless Network Connection Status dialog box and its properties box

To perform the walkaround survey of your network's hot spot, move carefully about the house and note the signal strength and connection speed in the portion of each room in the house and at places outside the house where you expect to be using a wireless PC. Keep in mind that the strength of the signal is not nearly as important as the transmission speed. If the transmission speed is less than maximum, try alternative positions within a room or about the house to achieve a higher transmission speed. If you are not getting the transmission speed you want, you might try repositioning the access point and repeating the walkaround survey. Sometimes moving the AP just a few feet can make a difference. Table 8-1, presented earlier in this chapter, includes hints for improving wireless communication speeds.

It's possible your wireless PCs will detect more than one wireless LAN. If you are receiving one or more signals from your neighbors' wireless networks, you will need to put your network at the top of the Preferred Networks list in the Wireless Network Connection Properties dialog box (see Figure 8-18). The Windows XP *Wireless Zero Configuration (WZC)* service dynamically selects the wireless network to which your computer connects according to your default settings or your preferences.

Step 7: Upgrade the Gateway's Firmware

Your all-in-one home gateway is actually a single-function computer that runs firmware. *Firmware* is just software stored in rewritable flash memory. I have included "upgrade the Gateway's firmware" as a separate step to emphasize the importance of keeping up with the manufacturer's continual string of new releases for its gateway's firmware. The same is true of any other network devices with upgradable firmware.

Historically, network gear manufacturers release new versions of the firmware for their "intelligent" devices every three to six months. The upgrades are needed to keep up with ever-changing security issues, compatibility with evolving wireless standards, and innovations in their product line. There is a good chance you will need to upgrade the firmware even if you purchased the gateway yesterday.

To find out if you need an upgrade, use your browser-based utility to determine the current version of your firmware (such as v3.04). Then, navigate to the manufacturer's web site, find the support page for your gateway, and view the version of the current firmware release. If applicable, download the file to your PC. In the browser-based utility, find the upgrade page and choose the path of the downloaded file (see Figure 8-19). You'll need to press the gateway's reset button (or turn the power off, then on) after the upgrade is complete.

For decades, automobile manufacturers have asked us to change the oil every 3000 miles. Now, our net gear vendors are asking us to change our firmware every few months. You can get away without changing your oil for a long time, but eventually,

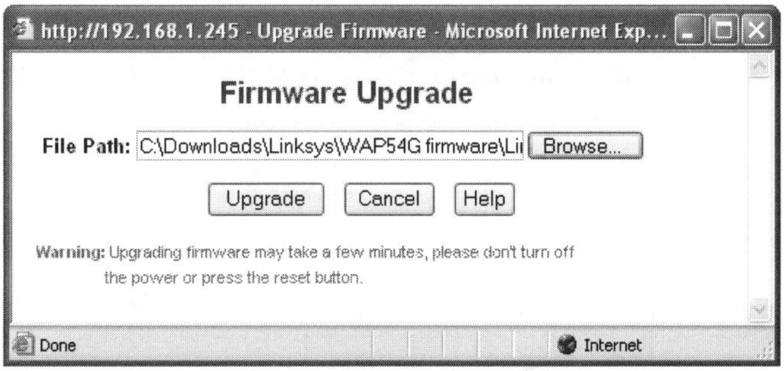

Figure 8-19   Periodically upgrade the home gateway's firmware

your engine will begin to make strange noises. If you get behind with your firmware upgrades, you may not hear noises, but in time, strange happenings are inevitable. Change your oil and upgrade your firmware to keep your car and network happy.

Setting Up an Ad Hoc Network

The two modes of wireless network operation, infrastructure and ad hoc, are introduced and illustrated in Chapter 4. Most of this book is devoted to infrastructure mode, the foundation of home networking. However, the ad hoc network can be helpful when you take your notebook PC to the corporate office or to a customer location. In ad hoc mode, employees, customers, or everyone else with a wireless-ready notebook PC can form a spontaneous network without the use of an AP.

The first step in creating an ad hoc network is to set up a host computer. Open the Wireless Network Connection Properties box (Start | Control Panel | choose the wireless adapter) and click Add to open the Wireless Network Properties box (see Figure 8-20). Click the Advanced button and choose "Computer to computer (ad hoc) networks only." Click the Properties button and enter a unique SSID for the ad hoc network, "HomeOff" in the Figure 8-20 example.

The other wireless PCs in the vicinity should see the HomeOff host PC in the available wireless networks list (view in the Wireless Network Connections Properties box). Each person wishing to participate in the ad hoc network would need to configure his or her client PC to join the ad hoc network. This would involve choosing the "Computer to computer (ad hoc) networks only" setting and entering configuration information (click Add), as needed, to link up and participate in the ad hoc network. The Wireless Network Connection Status box in Figure 8-21 shows a link to the HomeOff network. If you want to a form a wireless network and you don't have an access point, the ad hoc mode is a quick and easy solution.

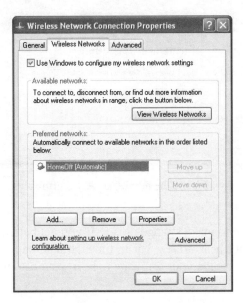

Figure 8-20 Wireless Network Connection Properties dialog box

Figure 8-21 Wireless Network Connection Status dialog box

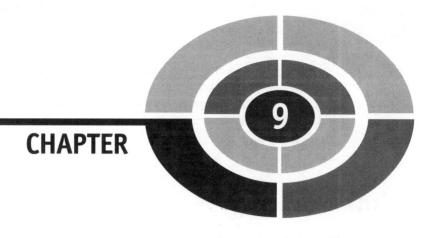

Sharing Printers, Files, and an Internet Connection

Networks are about sharing resources. Once the PCs throughout your home are linked via wired or wireless connections in a LAN, you can share anything that can be reduced to bits and bytes. Home networks, however, often are justified solely on their ability to share an Internet connection, printers, and files. In fact, the savings resulting from sharing any one of these resources can more than offset the cost of implementing a home network.

It's helpful to view file and printer sharing separate from Internet access sharing. File and printer sharing is built into the Windows operating system and involves

sharing among PCs and other networked devices within the confines of the home network. In contrast, Internet access sharing is facilitated by the home network but is controlled by the router, usually a home gateway function. The router provides a bridge between the Internet, which is sent/received via a modem (usually DSL or cable), and your home network.

Printer Sharing

When you have a home network, one good printer will suffice, even for an electronically active family. We have two printers on the Longnet, but only because my office is 200 feet from the house. The printer at the house easily handles the printing needs of my wife and two teenage sons, all of whom would be considered heavy users.

If you have a bunch of old printers scattered throughout the house, now is a great time to consider upgrading to a state-of-the-art network printer. If you have only one printer, you may as well have one with all of the modern features. Modern printers are networkable, faster, higher resolution for photo printing, more energy efficient, and possibly, multifunction (copy, fax, scan).

Printer sharing is one of the handiest applications for home networking. There are two ways to share a printer on a LAN:

- **Sharing a PC-based printer** A printer connected to a particular PC on the network can be shared with other PCs on the home network. In fact, all attached printers can be shared with the other networked PCs.

- **Sharing a network printer** A printer can be connected directly to the network via a print server through a wired or wireless link, enabling it to be shared with all PCs on the LAN.

Each approach has its advantages and disadvantages. The one big disadvantage of sharing a printer attached to a PC is that the host PC must be on and connected to the network before the other PCs on the LAN can print to it. By contrast, the network printer's best asset is that it is a network device like the other PCs and is always ready to accept print jobs from throughout the LAN. Sharing printers attached to Windows-based PCs is the least expensive approach because a network device called a *print server,* which can cost from $50 to $150, is required to link a printer directly to a network. An attached printer can be monitored by its host PC (for example, low-cartridge or out-of-paper notification), but this feature is disabled for networked printers. Also, the host PC of an attached printer is able to "spool" any number of print jobs, whereas the spooling capability of a networked printer is limited to the size of the printer's memory. When jobs sent to the printer are "spooled" to storage, they are printed on a first received, first printed basis.

Sharing a Printer Attached to a PC

The easiest and least expensive way to share a printer on the home network is to use the Windows printer sharing feature. Typically, printer sharing is enabled when you run the Network Setup Wizard (discussed in Chapter 8). When the wizard gives you the opportunity, select Turn On File And Printer Sharing. If you add a printer to a PC and wish to share it, then you would follow these three steps:

1. Open the Printer And Faxes window in the Control Panel. The hand under the highlighted printer indicates that this printer already is shared.

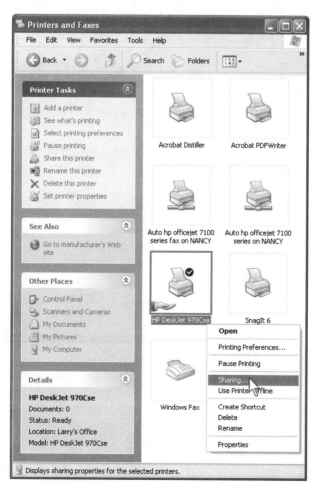

2. Right-click the printer you wish to share to open that printer's properties box at the Sharing tab. Click the Share This Printer radio button to share the printer. To disable sharing, click Do Not Share This Printer.

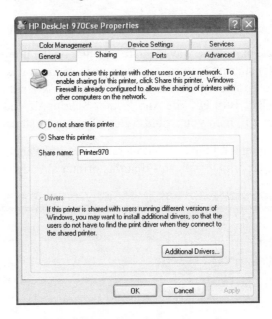

3. Click the General tab. Enter descriptive information in the location and comment boxes.

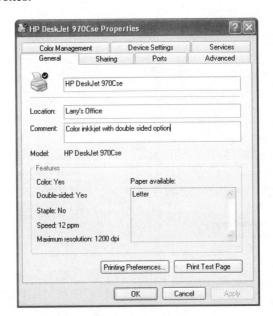

After you close the properties dialog box, the printer is made available on the network. However, the printer must be added to the list of available printers on each networked PC.

TIP *The USB ports on some older PCs run at speeds set by the original USB standard. If you choose to share a PC-based printer, I recommend you attach it to a PC with the much faster USB 2.0 ports so that your printer can operate at full capacity.*

Sharing a Network Printer

Like a PC, a printer can be a device on the network. To enable this, however, you must have a print server. A print server is to a printer as a network adapter is to a PC. It's the device that enables the printer to be connected directly to the home network. Print servers can be wired (Ethernet), wireless (Wireless-G/B), or both. They can be stand-alone units, or they can be built into the printer. The stand-alone print server shown in Figure 9-1 supports both Ethernet and Wireless-G connections. That is, the unit can be connected directly to a home gateway, switch, or Ethernet bridge via an Ethernet cable. Alternatively, the unit can establish a wireless link from anywhere within the range of the AP. In either case, the printer is simply plugged into the USB port (the one in Figure 9-1 has a parallel port, too) on the back of the print server to complete the link to the network.

(Photo courtesy of Cisco Systems, Inc.)

Figure 9-1 Print server that supports Ethernet and Wireless-G connectivity

---

TIP *If your home network design calls for a networked printer, you may be able to save a little money by purchasing a home gateway with a built-in print server capability. If you choose this approach, be aware that you must place the printer near the gateway.*

The trend in midrange to high-end consumer printers is to build and sell them with integrated print servers to accommodate the growing number of home networks. Ethernet/Wireless-G networking is built into the all-in-one printer in Figure 9-2. The embedded print server can be connected via an Ethernet cable or via a wireless link. If your plans call for a stationary printer near a gateway or switch, a hardwired Ethernet cable is preferred. If you anticipate some printer mobility or wish to locate the printer away from Ethernet connectors, wireless is preferred.

To install a print server or network printer, you must have a working network. Connect the print server to the home gateway or a network switch via an Ethernet cable and then connect the printer to the print server via a USB or parallel cable. Power on the printer and the print server and proceed with the configuration process. As with other net gear, this process varies between manufacturers. Typically, use the print server's step-by-step installation CD (see Figure 9-3) or the browser interface (see Figure 9-4). If you use the latter, you will need the IP address of the print server. Find the print server's IP address in a listing of networked devices (see network status information in the home gateway's browser interface). During installation, you accept most of the manufacturer's default settings, such as "Obtain an IP address automatically," but if you have a wireless print server, you may need to enter the SSID and WEP encryption information for your home network (see Figure 9-4).

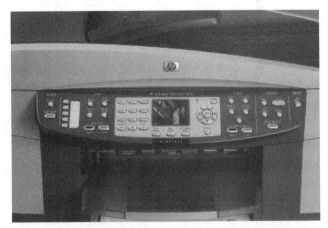

(Photo courtesy of Hewlett-Packard)

Figure 9-2   Network-ready printer with a built-in Ethernet and Wireless-G print server

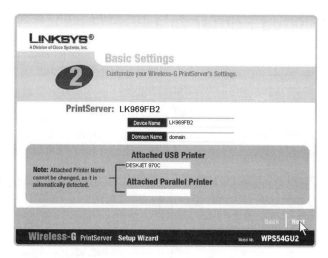

Figure 9-3   Linksys print server installation CD

NOTE *At this time, printers with built-in print servers can cost up to $75 more than similar printers without the server feature. However, I would expect that virtually all midrange and high-end home printers will come with print servers, most with wireless capabilities, by 2010 to accommodate the explosion of home networks.*

CAUTION *On any network printer, you will need to coordinate print activities. For example, suppose sister inserts a stack of premium photo paper ($0.50 a sheet) and forgets to replace it with regular printer paper. The next print job might be brother's glossy and unnecessarily expensive term paper.*

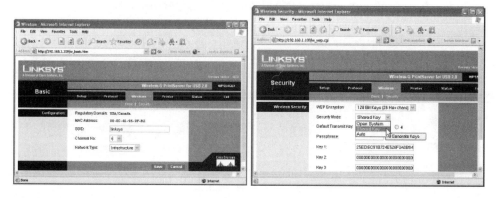

Figure 9-4   Linsys print server browser interface (SSID and WEP information)

Adding a Shared Printer to a PC

Once the printer(s) is installed on the home network, either as an attached printer or a network printer, you will still need to add the printer to each of the PCs on the LAN. To add a shared printer, follow these steps:

1. Open the Printer And Faxes window in the Control Panel, and then choose Add A Printer in the Printer Tasks pane to open the Add Printer Wizard. Indicate whether you are adding a network printer or a local attached printer.

 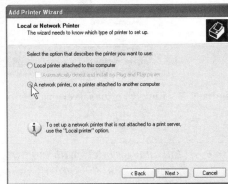

2. Click Browse For A Printer to view a list of available printers and choose the shared printer you wish to add to the PC.

NOTE Any list of printers will include all installed printers on the network. Even though you have only one physical printer, you may see others in the list. Typically, the list will include the printer's fax feature separately, and it will include a list of software programs capable of producing print files.

 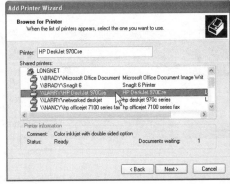

3. Finally, choose whether or not you wish to make the newly added printer the default printer and complete the wizard.

When you add a shared printer to a PC, Windows XP automatically downloads and installs the printer driver from the printer's host PC.

Adding a Networked Printer to a PC

The Add Printer Wizard is used for adding a networked printer to a PC, too. However, the procedure for adding a printer that is connected directly to the network via a print server is slightly different.

1. Open the Printer And Faxes window in the Control Panel, and then choose Add A Printer in the Printer Tasks pane to open the Add Printer Wizard. Logic tells us to select "Network printer…," but Windows treats a networked printer as a local printer. Anyway, you select Local Printer Attached to This Computer.

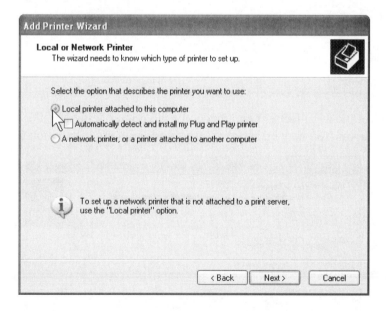

2. Choose the port from the drop-down list that you want your networked printer to use.

NOTE If the port for the print server is not listed in the Select A Printer Port screen in the Add Printer Wizard, you will need to create a new port. To do so, choose Standard TCP/IP Port from the Create New Port options in the illustration and click Next to display the Add Standard TCP/IP Printer Port Wizard. You may need to open the print server's browser-based interface and assign a fixed IP address to the print server before running this wizard.

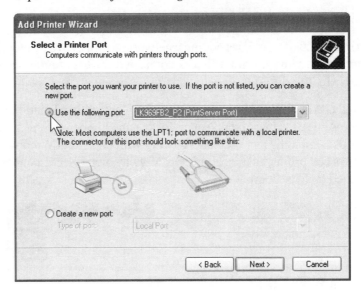

3. Select the manufacturer and model for the printer being installed and install the driver. You may be asked to insert your printer's installation CD.

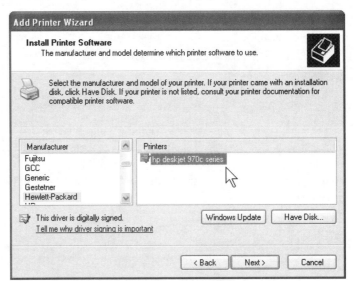

4. Remember, the printer is set up as a network printer and is, by function, shared. Therefore, choose Do Not Share This Printer. Complete the wizard to add the network printer to the PC.

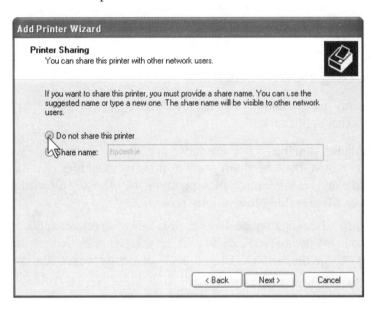

Once you have run this wizard on all PCs, the PCs throughout the LAN are ready for printing.

File Sharing

File sharing is one of the main reasons people install home networks. The network file sharing feature built into Windows XP enables network users to share and use files stored on other PCs. Every PC has a lot of files—songs, reports, images, programs, and so on. Invariably, there will be files on your PC that have value to someone else on your home network and vice versa.

With so many files on your PC and throughout the network, files must be organized into logical *folders* and *subfolders*. Windows uses the folder metaphor to refer to a named group of files. We use the same familiar Windows Explorer interface to work with files on networked PCs that we use for local file management.

TIP *It takes a little extra planning, but having a well-organized hierarchy of files can save you a lot of time. Not only will you be able to navigate quickly to the files you need, but others on your LAN will be able to find shared files easily, too.*

NOTE Window XP Professional has file sharing features not available on Windows XP Home Edition. Because our emphasis is the home networking, the features discussed and illustrated in this section apply to the Home Edition. If you have Windows XP Professional, you can learn more about the software's user-level access control features by searching for "file sharing" in Help and Support.

File Sharing Applications

There are many reasons and occasions for file sharing on a LAN. These are among the more popular applications:

- **Simple file sharing**   If you're active in personal computing, I would expect that you will be sharing and using networked files on a daily basis. These could be MP3 music files, photo image files, downloaded program files, or files resulting from family projects.

- **Backup**   Backup may be network file sharing's premier application. Home networks make it easy to back up personal files to one or more of the other PCs on the network. Even though your daily/weekly backup is to a hard drive on a network PC, it's still a good idea to do monthly backups to rewritable CD or DVD discs that can be stored in off-site locations.

- **Mobile computing**   The primary computer for each of the four people in my family is a desktop PC; however, each of us routinely uses the family notebook when personal computing calls for mobility. When we use the notebook, we have ready access to the files on our desktop PCs when operating within the range of the APs. Many people routinely synchronize files between their home-based desktops and their office notebook PCs.

- **Media hub**   The media hub, perhaps in a home theater setting, can recall and play media server–based images, songs, and/or videos.

Security Issues

Any type of file sharing raises the security flag. As a rule of thumb, it's good policy to avoid making your personal files available to other network users. Those files that you wish to share, such as those that make up your music library, can be placed in the Shared Documents folder. Windows created this folder specifically to facilitate file sharing on a network. All files that you place in this special folder will be made available to other PCs on the network if you choose Turn On File And Printer Sharing when you run the Network Setup Wizard (see Chapter 8). All other folders are protected unless you specifically choose to share them.

To view the Shared Documents folder, open My Computer and choose Shared Documents. Windows has set up three topical folders that are the counterparts of those in My Documents: Shared Music, Shared Pictures, and Shared Video (see Figure 9-5). Place any songs, images, or videos that you wish to share in these folders. You can create as many subfolders as you wish under the Shared Documents folder. I have a "Manuscripts" folder where I place chapter files (text and images) when they are ready for review by my wife. My sons place school projects, reports, and so on they want me look over in the "Schoolwork" folder. My wife puts her current backup files in "Nancy backup," and then I move them to a protected area of my PC's hard disk. When I go on the road, I'll transfer appropriate folders to the notebook PC via the "Notebook" folder, and then I do the reverse action when I return home with modified files. Depending on your mix of software, one of your applications may create a folder in Shared Documents.

Sharing Folders and Files

The files and folders within the Shared Documents folder are, by definition, made available for sharing and use among network users when you choose this option in the Network Setup Wizard. All other files and folders, including those in the My Documents folder, are not shared by default. However, if you wish, you can designate specific folders to be shared on the home network.

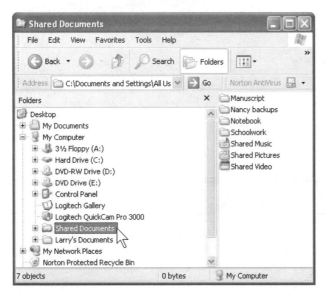

Figure 9-5   Shared Documents folder

To share a folder, along with its subfolders and files, open the Windows Explorer and right-click the folder to be shared (see Figure 9-6). Choose Sharing And Security from the pop-up menu to display the properties box for the highlighted folder (see Figure 9-7).

In the Network Sharing And Security portion of the folder properties box in Figure 9-7, check Share This Folder On The Network to share the folder. The folder name is inserted automatically into the Share Name box, but you also can change the name of the folder on the network. The folder name on your PC is unchanged. If you wish to allow other users to change the files in the shared folder, check Allow Network User To Change My Files.

CAUTION When you share a folder or disk, you make its contents available to other network users and you make it more accessible to successful hackers. It's important to understand that sharing a file means that others on the network can read, copy, and modify those files you are willing to share. These files are not as protected when shared, so share personal folders with great care.

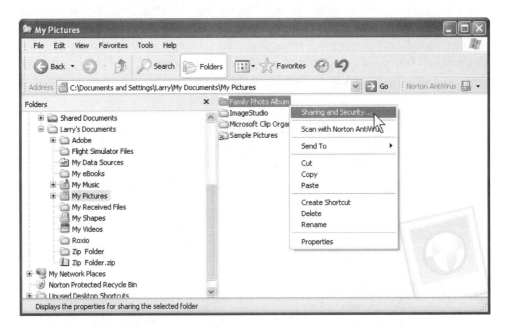

Figure 9-6 Sharing folders via the Windows Explorer

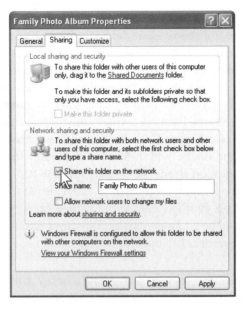

Figure 9-7   Sharing options in the folder properties box

Sharing a Disk

You can share your entire hard disk on a LAN, but when you attempt to do so, Windows displays this warning: "To protect your computer from unauthorized access, sharing the root of the drive is not recommended." I, too, would not recommend that you share your C: drive, but there may be circumstances where you might wish to share a second hard drive. For example, one of the networked PCs may have a second hard disk that is dedicated exclusively to backup storage. If you do share a disk drive, I would encourage you to leave the box permitting others to change your files as unchecked.

Using Shared Files

You can access shared files directly from any Windows application (File | Open), just as you would local files, except you would need to go to My Network Places and the appropriate "SharedDocs" folder or other shared folder. Alternatively, you can use Windows Explorer. Simply navigate to the desired folder via My Network Places and then open, move, copy, rename, or perform whatever operation you want on the file.

To display My Network Places within the Windows Explorer, click Start | My Network Places. Figure 9-8 shows all of the SharedDocs folders and shared disks for Brady's PC on the Longnet. Each of these SharedDocs folders was added to My Network Place list by running the Add Network Places Wizard (choose Add A Network Place in the task pane). Clicking the "SharedDocs on Larry's Computer (Larry)" folder displays available folders, including the three standard media folders (see Figure 9-8). Choosing Shared Pictures displays the folders and images stored in this folder on Larry's PC (see Figure 9-9). Double-clicking the "Brady and Larry on Baldy" image opens the image within Microsoft Digital Image Pro, the program assigned to JPEG images, on Brady's PC (see Figure 9-10).

Any authorized file operation (copy, delete, move, rename, open, and so on) that you might do locally on your PC can be performed on files in shared folders, as well. File operations can be completed in the Windows Explorer or within any other Windows facility that permits file operations (for example, File | Open).

CAUTION *You can open images, play songs, and display a Word document from files on another networked PC, but you can't run programs from another PC. When you install software, such as Excel, to a PC, the installation process involves copying files to a variety of folders and making changes to the PC's registry. Consequently, the program file runs only on the PC on which it is installed.*

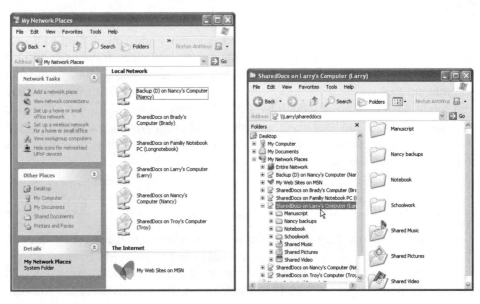

Figure 9-8   Windows Explorer displaying the contents of the SharedDocs folder on Larry's PC

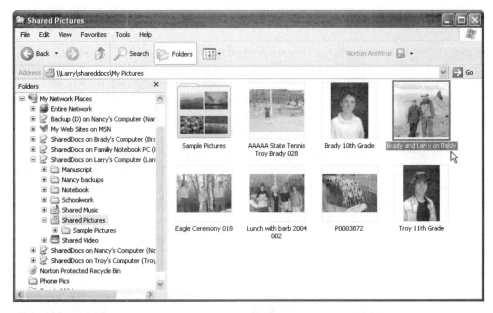

Figure 9-9   Windows Explorer displaying the images in the Shared Pictures folder on Larry's PC

Figure 9-10   An image from Shared Pictures on Larry PC's opened on Brady's PC

Mapping Network Drives

If you regularly work with files from a shared folder on another PC, you might wish to assign a drive letter to the folder. Mapping a network folder to a drive letter gives you access to the folder from My Computer rather than having to go to My Network Places. For example, My Computer on the Family Notebook PC has mapped the SharedDocs folder on Nancy's PC and the SharedDocs folder on Brady's PC to drives Y: and Z:, respectively (see Figure 9-11).

To open the Map Network Drive dialog box, open the Windows Explorer and right-click either My Computer or My Network Places. This option also is available in the Windows Explorer Tools menu. In Figure 9-12, choose Browse to view shared resources and select the desired shared folder. The information entered in the Map Network Drive dialog box in Figure 9-12 will map the shared documents folder on Brady's PC to drive letter Z:. Having frequently used network folders displayed within My Computer can be a real convenience.

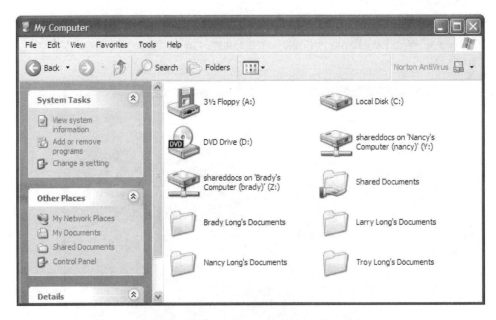

Figure 9-11   Shared Document folders mapped to drives Y: and Z:

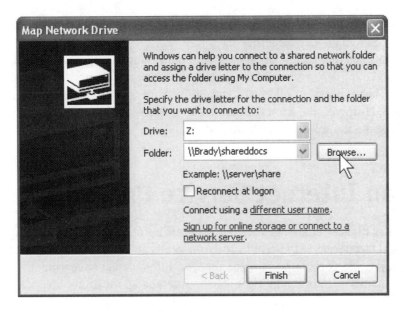

Figure 9-12 Map Network Drive dialog box

Internet Access Sharing

In all likelihood, you probably have or soon will have multiple PCs in your home. Through the 1990s, the vast majority of us had dial-up Internet access, whether we had one or four PCs. Family members in multiple-PC homes with dial-up access learned about patience and waiting their turn on the Internet. Many households installed a "data line" to take the pressure off the telephone line, but the extra line didn't help much with the queue for the Internet. Internet access became the point of family conflict. Mom, Dad, and the kids wanted on the Internet, and they wanted on now.

Three things came together in the late 1990s with the potential to make everyone happy:

- The advent of broadband Internet access at prices families could afford
- Economically priced consumer-oriented communications equipment for home networks
- Windows support for Internet connection sharing

A single broadband line feeding a home network can give everyone in the family his or her own high-speed Internet access.

To enable Internet access sharing on your home network, you need to set up your modem and configure your PCs and your home gateway's router for Internet access sharing. This process is relatively straightforward and is described in detail in Chapter 8. However, the most difficult task in setting up Internet access sharing is not technical—it's selecting a broadband ISP.

Choosing an Internet Service Provider

One of the biggest challenges in setting up a home network is deciding which broadband Net access is the best fit for your needs and circumstances. Because the selection process is an important precursor to Internet access sharing, this topic is covered in this resource sharing chapter. Internet applications are presented in Chapter 12.

There are literally thousands of Internet service providers, most of which are local and several of which are national/international. Our focus is popular broadband options (cable-modem, DSL, and satellite). When you begin your search for an Internet service provider or ISP, you may see other options listed, including dial-up, ISDN, T-1, and T-3. ISDN is a dial-up service (128 Kbps) that is being phased out. T-1 and T-3 are expensive, high-speed services designed for businesses.

ISP Service Options

At least 90 percent of the ISPs offer dial-up service at 56 Kbps, and most of them offer ISDN at 128 Kbps. About half of the ISPs offer DSL service. A few are DSL-only ISPs, but that number will continue to rise as people migrate from dial-up to broadband service. Your ISP for cable-modem access and your cable TV company probably are the same. However, even if you have cable TV and a terrestrial telephone service, there is no guarantee that you will have cable-modem and/or DSL service.

There are plenty of satellite ISPs that cater to those people who are "rural and underserved." That means you don't have access to DSL or cable-modem because, if you did, you would not be considering satellite. Although satellite offers comparable service, the monthly service charges can be double or triple those of cable-modem or DSL. My home is somewhat rural, so satellite service was my only option for several years. It worked well; however, I switched to DSL at the first opportunity and cut my monthly Internet service cost in half.

Anyone with a terrestrial telephone line can subscribe to dial-up access. If you live in America and have a southern exposure to the sky, you can get broadband satellite. This means that the vast majority of people will have a choice between slow and fast Internet access.

Choosing a Type of Internet Access

When you are ready to subscribe to an Internet service through an ISP, your choices probably will be dial-up (slow) or broadband (fast); however, the overwhelming choice of people with home networks is broadband. Although dial-up service can be shared, it's slow (especially in a LAN) and cumbersome to use. Your choices, however, may be limited by availability of certain types of service and your financial circumstances. You can expect to pay $X for dial-up access and from $2X to $4X for broadband access, depending on where you live. The classic decision process for people seeking a broadband ISP for a home network is illustrated in Figure 9-13.

The extra cost for high-speed broadband service is well worth the money, especially in a home network where everyone can enjoy broadband—all of the time. Always-on broadband access offers a completely different experience than dial-up. Your will to surf, to download, to send images, and to participate in real-time applications is markedly subdued when you must continually wait for web pages to build, or watch download-completion bars that seem stuck in time. Numerous studies have shown that broadband users are more willing to explore and take full advantage of cyberspace when they don't have to wait for pages to build. You may pay a little more for broadband, but you get up to 50 times the access speed. If you do any work at home, the extra capacity will pay for itself in a single day of use. If you need help justifying the extra expense of broadband, just consider that you won't need an extra "data line" for dial-up access. Many people with dial-up access choose to have an extra phone line so that their main voice line is available for incoming and outgoing calls.

Figure 9-13 shows that if you want broadband and neither DSL nor cable is available, your only choice is satellite. The problem with satellite is that it can be very expensive (possibly in excess of $1200 per year), and to some people, broadband just isn't worth that much money. If this is the case, then click-and-wait dial-up is clearly better than no Internet access.

Although it may not be a choice during the currency of this book, I would be remiss not to mention what appears to be the inevitability of widespread wireless broadband. Industry forecasters are telling us that wireless broadband based on a cell phone technology called *EV-DO* (Evolution-Data Optimized) will be available to most of us as early as 2006. This is different than today's very limited wireless broadband in "hot spots," such as coffee shops and airport waiting areas. The new

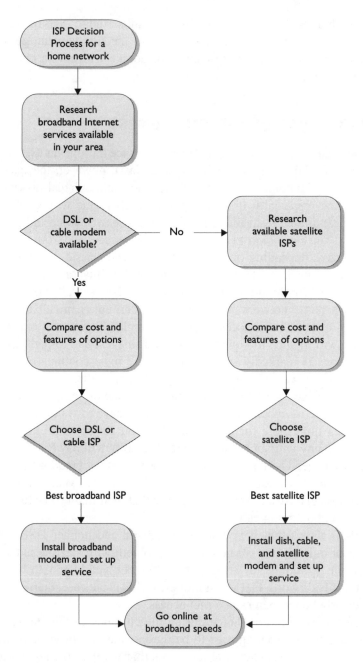

Figure 9-13 The ISP decision process

wireless broadband will provide broadband access for your home network at DSL/cable-modem speeds, and it will offer the same speeds for your mobile devices (notebook PC, PDA, or cell phone) from any location in any metropolitan area in the United States.

DSL Considerations

For most of us seeking broadband Internet access, the question is "Do I choose DSL or cable-modem?" One of DSL's advantages and disadvantages is that it is distance sensitive; that is, the longer the DSL run between the house and a telecom office or a DSLAM (Digital Subscriber Line Access Multiplexer) booster station, the less the capacity of the line. If you're lucky enough to live close to the phone company office or a remote DSLAM, the access speed you experience will be superior to those unlucky souls at the end of the line (about three miles). The DSLAM at the office or a remote facility links a number of DSL customers to a single very high speed communications channel, usually fiber optic cable. The DSLAM for my DSL service is about 1000 feet from my home, so I routinely enjoy the maximum available capacity from my ISP. If you're considering DSL, you might wish to research your location relative to the nearest DSLAM or chat with your neighbors about their bandwidth speed. A number of web sites offer a free "bandwidth speed test" service.

With DSL, you need only one telephone line for voice and data. Because they use different frequency bands, the digital DSL signal can be transmitted at the same time you are holding an analog voice conversation. When you subscribe to DSL, you will receive a certain number of line filters that are designed to eliminate "data noise" during voice conversations. The small pass-through filters are placed in-line between your voice phone jack and telephone line. If you have a lot of phones and hear a hissing sound on the lines without filters, you may need to purchase more of them.

Cable-Modem Considerations

Cable-modem offers a "shared neighborhood" style of connection that potentially can reach hundreds of people in a single neighborhood. Having cable-modem access is like being on a network where all people share the Internet capacity of a single cable. A digital TV cable is a "really big pipe" with an enormous transmission capacity, but it can be seriously diluted for an individual when hundreds of your neighbors choose to surf the Internet during the peak personal hours of 5:00 to 11:00 in the evening. Cable-modem is more people sensitive, so the more people on the network, the slower the transmission rate. Your best source of information regarding the level of service in your neighborhood is your neighbors. An experienced subscriber to your cable-modem ISP can give you examples of speeds that you can expect at various times during the day.

Choosing an ISP

On the scale of importance in setting up a home network, choosing the right ISP ranks up there with choosing the right communications equipment. In terms of cost, this decision may top that of the net gear. An ISP can be a mom-and-pop shop or a multinational conglomerate. It can offer basic Internet access and nothing else, or it can offer a range of Internet access services and a laundry list of additional services. The following is a list of things you should be looking for in an ISP, with the most important first:

- **Quality of the ISP**   Every company has a reputation. Pick a good one.

- **Internet access**   Unlimited service is widely available and the most desirable service. Unfortunately, high-volume users, namely those who are continually downloading/uploading movies and music, have forced some ISPs to limit the amount of information that can be transmitted per day for a given account.

- **Internet service speeds**   Broadband ISPs can limit downstream and upstream speeds. Several web sites, such as Broadband Reports (www.dslreports.com), routinely test the actual (versus advertised) bandwidth speeds for major ISPs and then report their findings.

- **Number of e-mail accounts**   The ISP should provide enough e-mail accounts (the main account plus subaccounts) for each person in your family to have his or her own e-mail address.

- **Support hardware**   Many ISPs will provide the hardware needed to enable broadband Net service (modem, home gateway, Ethernet NIC, and so on) for free or at a substantially reduced cost. If you accept their free hardware (worth as much as $200), they probably will ask for a one- to two-year contract.

- **Storage space**   An ISP may provide online storage space in which you can store files, photos, or whatever can be accessed from any Internet-ready PC. This is a good way to share photos and videos with family and friends. The amount of space offered may vary from 5MB to over 100MB.

- **Personal web page**   Some ISPs will host your personal web page (size may be limited to around 10MB).

- **Technical support**   If everything goes smoothly, you can be up and running in five minutes and you may not need technical support for years. If it doesn't go smoothly, technical support is critical. Give a company that offers 24/7 support a few extra points.

- **Additional services**   The additional services that can be offered by an ISP are many and varied. For example, an ISP can offer parental controls, firewall software (Internet protection), Internet radio, an online encyclopedia, a gaming package, newsgroups, instant messaging, free classified ad listings, free *Consumer Reports* information, securities market research and analysis, and many other possibilities. On my personalized "home page," my ISP lists news and sports of interest to me, show times for all the local movie theaters, and the local weather.

Frequently there is a "come on" price for three months or so. Be sure to look past that price and know exactly what you will be paying up front and each month over the term of the contract. It pays to read the small print, as telecoms are notorious for tacking on mysterious charges over and above the advertised rate. It's not unusual for these charges (not counting taxes) to be in excess of $10 a month.

Another important consideration is the number of PC users permitted on a single account by the ISP. Some ISPs are now limiting the number of PCs, often to two or three, that can tap into the Internet access for a single account. ISPs initiated this restriction because families/individuals in adjoining apartments would subscribe to broadband access and then share the line via a wireless network. Make sure that the limit will handle your home networking needs over the next couple of years.

American Online: AOL

Another very popular approach to gaining Internet access is to subscribe to a commercial information service, such as America Online or CompuServe. Approximately one in four Internet-ready homes subscribes to America Online. That percentage is lower for homes with home networks. When you log in to AOL, you are on the AOL network, not the Internet. Once on AOL, you have a *gateway* to the Internet through its software and network. CompuServe is a subsidiary of America Online, Inc. Both offer Internet access and a variety of online services, but CompuServe may be more oriented to adults and their information and entertainment needs.

AOL is sometimes called "the Internet with training wheels." The "training wheels," however, may be AOL's greatest asset. AOL has a user-friendly proprietary interface with numerous easily accessible online services (see Figure 9-14). The many services, which include personal finance, instant messaging, news, Internet radio, travel, shopping, and many others, are easily customized for a personalized online experience. AOL maintains an army of technical support people who are used to working with people who are beginning their online experience or installing home networks.

Figure 9-14   America Online (AOL)

Virtually everything on AOL is available on the Internet in one form or another. AOL is not for everyone, but it offers a nonthreatening approach to the online experience that can be very appealing to both the novice user and the experienced user who has become comfortable within the cocoon of AOL services.

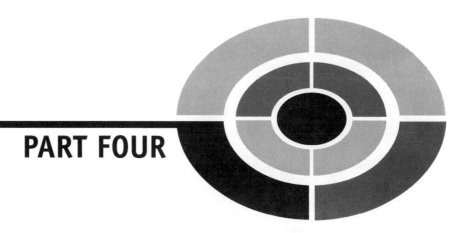

PART FOUR

Protecting and Operating a Home Network

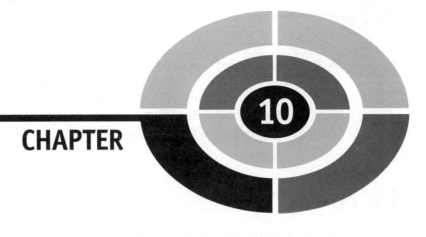

CHAPTER

Privacy and Security

There are organizations charged with maintaining some semblance of order in cyberspace, but the cybercops are ill-equipped and existing laws often are ambiguous and difficult to enforce. For the most part, it is up to you to protect yourself, your home network and its PCs, and your valuable information from the continual threats and annoyances streaming over the Internet.

The Internet opens the door to the wonders of global sharing, but it also opens doors for people whose interests are scams and malicious destruction. Crackers are continually "cracking" through Internet security at the server and the PC levels to disrupt the flow of information and, in general, wreaking havoc. Hate mongers, stalkers, and the like have found a home on the Internet, too. Cyberthieves will even steal your identity by surreptitiously gathering enough personal information about you (without your knowledge) to assume your identity.

DSL, cable-modem, and satellite connections are "always on," so the risk of unauthorized access to your home network and PCs is ever present and must be addressed. This chapter is intended to raise your awareness of the dark side of the Internet and introduce you to the tools that can help you feel more secure in your continuously linked home networking environment.

NOTE I want to remind you again how important it is that you keep your Windows operating system current with the latest releases from Microsoft. Having the latest Windows updates installed will give your system the best available protection from Internet intruders. To install the latest Windows XP updates, click Start | Help And Support | Windows Update.

The Firewall

An estimated 5 percent of all transactions on the Internet are fraudulent or an attempt at theft. Scary, isn't it? Unfortunately, we are forced by these Internet realities to build a wall around our PCs and home networks, an electronic wall called a firewall. A *firewall* is software that sets up a protective "wall" between a home network or a particular PC (the private side) and the rest of cyberspace (the public side). Having a firewall is a good starting point for the implementation of a personal computing plan for Internet security.

A firewall is a system that enforces access control policy between your home network (or PC) and the Internet. All home gateways have built-in firewalls. In fact, firewall protection is built into the Window operating system. However, the front-end protection provided by your home gateway's (router/AP/modem) built-in firewall is preferable to the PC-level firewall within Windows.

Firewalls differ widely in methods and levels of sophistication, but all of them have essentially two tasks—to block traffic and to permit traffic. A firewall's access control policy can be set up to screen electronic traffic in both directions. It restricts unwanted access to a home network or a PC, and it can block certain types of outgoing communications. Most firewalls automatically block unsolicited attempts at communication from the public side of the electronic "wall" that stands between your LAN and the Internet. They do this according to control policies set forth as a group of rules for access. For example, one rule might be to permit e-mail traffic and another might be to deny unauthenticated logins from the public side.

The screening process can be adjusted to the desired level of security. A high security setting may block all e-mail with attachments or embedded graphics. Most people choose a lower firewall setting to permit the flow of legitimate traffic. Of course, this small opening is enough for some undesirable transmissions to pierce your PC's armor. I would suggest that you choose nothing less than a medium level of security.

Crackers and hackers use *port scanner* software to search the Internet for unprotected networks and PCs so that they can hijack and use them to distribute pornography, send spam, gather personal information, or carry out some other illicit activity. Port scanners comb the Net 24/7 at electronic speeds seeking servers or home gateways with public IP addresses that respond to connection requests to specific ports of entry to a network.

Port numbers are assigned to each packet of information traveling the Internet. The packet's port number associates it with a type of traffic. For example, port 80 is for browser traffic (HTTP services) and port 25 is for e-mails (SMTP services). Windows file sharing is done through port 139, which is always a target for crackers. Xbox Live uses ports 88 and 3074. The unique IP address and the port number embedded in an Internet packet compose a *socket* that directs communication between specific applications (Web Wide Web or e-mail) that run on specific host computers.

Firewalls have a *port filtering* capability that selectively enables or disables Transmission Control Protocol (TCP) ports and User Datagram Protocol (UDP) ports (the latter used for messaging applications). Port filtering serves to insulate home gateways and their networks from cracker/hacker attacks by blocking entry to certain ports.

Your gateway has a firewall (see Figure 10-1). Windows has a firewall. And, you probably will have Internet security software that offers firewall protection, too.

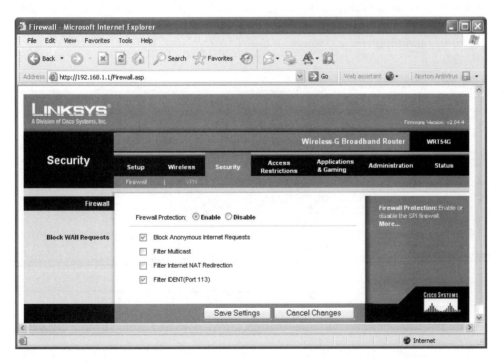

Figure 10-1   Firewall options for a Linksys wireless home gateway

Your gateway's firewall sets up a protective wall between the public Internet and your private LAN. The gateway firewall will be enabled by default. Windows and commercial Internet protection software provide protection at the PC level.

Commercial Net security products, such as Symantec's Norton Internet Security Professional and McAfee Security's Personal Firewall Plus or Internet Security Suite, offer excellent PC-level firewalls. So does Windows. These, plus your gateway, offer a solid line of defense against unauthorized access, but you probably don't need all of that redundant protection in a home network environment. Your gateway's firewall should be sufficient. PC-level protection is easily enabled or disabled. The Windows firewall (see Figure 10-2) is enabled by default. To enable/disable the Windows firewall, click Start | Control Panel | Network And Internet Connections | Windows Firewall. To enable/disable the firewall that comes with your Net security software, turn it on/off in the software's main menu (see Figure 10-2).

CAUTION *Having a gateway with a firewall does not mean you are fully protected from the bad stuff on the Internet. The firewall, with the help of NAT (Network Address Translation), which is discussed in Chapter 3, does a good job of selectively permitting authorized traffic flow between your home network and the Internet. It does not, however, evaluate the content of that traffic. For example, all firewalls let you send and receive e-mails, even those with attachments containing viruses. For protection from viruses, you need antivirus software.*

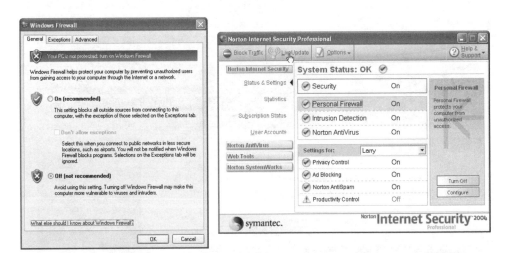

Figure 10-2 Enabling/disabling the firewalls for Windows and Norton Internet Security Professional

Security for Wireless Home Networks

Most home network security threats come from Internet hackers, but to get to your network, they must find a way to get past your firewall—not an easy task. With the rapid acceptance of wireless home networking, a new breed of hackers has emerged. Wireless hackers tap directly into your wireless network, thus bypassing the firewall. Wireless LANs are installed on the private side of the firewall, so the firewall offers no protection from wireless hackers. Wireless hackers can tap into your home network from the house next door or from a car parked at curbside in front of your house. Unless you are constantly checking the status of the LAN, you are probably unaware that your network is being violated. Once online, the wireless hacker's PC becomes just another peer node on your LAN.

WEP and WPA Encryption

Virtually all network gear supports a security feature called *Wired Equivalent Privacy,* or simply *WEP.* WEP uses data encryption techniques to scramble information passed between wireless devices. A hacker attempting to tap into your WEP-enabled wireless network would find only meaningless bits. The AP and client device on the home network shares an *encryption key* that is used to scramble and unscramble the encrypted information sent via wireless links.

Wi-Fi Protected Access, or *WPA,* is an enhanced encryption technique that is available on most modern network gear (after 2004). WPA employs authentication via user ID and password and uses more sophisticated encryption. Once the authorized client PC is authenticated, the AP sends a temporary encryption key that is valid only during the current communications session.

WEP is not as secure as WPA, but having any encryption method in place is a major deterrent to hackers. However, most systems are set up such that you must activate WEP or WPA to enable wireless protection. Because WEP and WPA are turned off by default, many, perhaps most, home networks are vulnerable to intruders. WEP is not perfect, but with so many unprotected networks in your neighborhood, simply having it enabled is enough to send hackers down the street (or hall in an apartment building) to an easier target.

The primary difference between WEP and WPA is the handling of the encryption key. WEP uses the same encryption key, whereas WPA constantly changes the encryption key. With WPA, the hacker has very little time to break the key.

To turn on WEP or WPA encryption, navigate to the wireless setup screen on your gateway and choose an encryption method. WPA has a higher overhead and may slow the network more than the more straightforward WEP; however, WPA encryption offers a higher level of security. For WEP, you may need to choose between levels of WEP security, either 64-bit or 128-bit. The 128-bit option provides better security, but network speed is sacrificed at the higher bit level.

The information you enter to enable WEP or WPA encryption is similar but may vary slightly among gateway vendors. The Linksys gateway's wireless setup screen lets you generate keys by entering an alphanumeric passphrase (see Figure 10-3). I suggest doing this rather than entering a long string of hexadecimal numbers. For WPA encryption, you must enter a shared key password (see Figure 10-4). I encourage you to enable one of these encryption methods, but if you do, be advised that each device in your wireless LAN must use the same encryption method and encryption key.

NOTE: *Hexadecimal is a base-16 numbering system that uses 0 through 9 plus A through F for its numbers. Because a hex number can represent four bits (binary numbers), "hex" has evolved as shorthand for representing bits. For example, a hex A is a binary 1010 (or a decimal 10).*

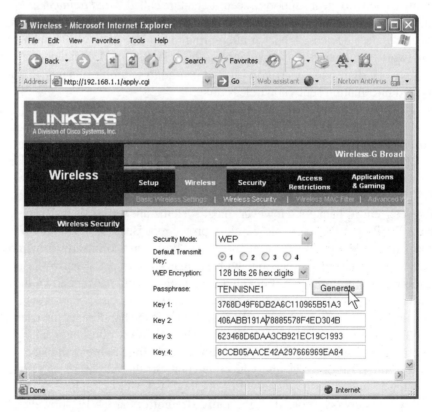

Figure 10-3 WEP wireless security setup screen for a Linksys gateway

Figure 10-4   WPA wireless security setup screen for a Linksys gateway

Other Wireless Security Precautions

Enable WEP or WPA encryption and follow these guidelines, and your private
home network should remain private:

- *Change the default administrator password for access to the gateway.* All
  hackers know the manufacturers' default passwords, and they routinely hack
  into home networks via this password. Once in, they can change important
  network settings, including the SSID and security keys. Change this password
  to something of your choosing, preferably one that has both letters and
  numbers and cannot in any way be associated with you. A password made
  up of random characters, such as "8cexb43", is superior to one formed from
  your last name with address, "jones1583".

- *Change the wireless network name (SSID).* Change the SSID (Service Set Identifier) from the manufacturer's default (for example, "linksys" for Linksys products). Each network node must be associated with this case-sensitive name, so be sure to change it on all network devices by running the Windows XP Wireless Network Setup Wizard (click Start | All Programs | Accessories | Communications | Wireless Network Setup Wizard). It's a good practice to change the SSID every month or so.

- *Disable SSID broadcast.* When a wireless PC begins seeking a signal from a wireless network, it detects the SSID broadcast by the gateway's AP. Router/gateways give you the option to enable or disable wireless SSID broadcast. There is a convenience in permitting SSID broadcast, but doing so makes it easier for hackers to log into your system. My recommendation is to disable SSID broadcast in your gateway's setup. This will thwart attempts by the vast majority of wireless hackers, but the persistent, hard-core hackers can still capture the SSID.

- *Change the passphrase for WEP.* If you use WEP wireless security, you can increase your level of security by changing the WEP encryption key periodically on the AP and its client PCs. This involves changing the passphrase that generates the encryption key.

- *Change your workgroup name.* It's a good idea to change your workgroup name from the system default because it sets up one more hurdle for any would-be hackers.

Internet Threats

Before the Internet, people who do dastardly deeds were limited by geography. The Internet has lifted that constraint, and the seedier elements of our society are free to traverse the globe at electronic speeds planting malware wherever they go. *Malware* is short for malicious software, that is, software that is designed to damage your PC, disrupt its operation, or in some way violate its security. Malware refers to a host of hostile software, such as viruses, Trojan horses, worms, spyware, and so on.

Computer Viruses

The *computer virus* is a program or portion of a program that causes something (usually something bad) to occur in your PC. A computer virus can cause anything from a minor inconvenience to major devastation. A virus can take over your computer and cause a range of events to occur. Some viruses destroy the contents of your hard disk. Others grow like a cancer, eating away at your files. Some are virtual bombs that "explode" at a preset time (for example, Friday the thirteenth). One strain of virus causes the Internet to be flooded with e-mail, each message with an attached program that causes more infected e-mail to be sent out over the Internet. This type of assault is referred to as a *denial of service* attack. Some viruses are relatively benign. For example, the Cookie Monster virus displays "I want a cookie" and then locks your PC until you enter "Fig Newton."

Over 50,000 viruses flow freely through the Internet. Most are spread as attachments to e-mails. However, they also can be passed by shared interchangeable disks/discs and via PCs on a home network.

Types of Viruses

The two main types of virus are the macro virus and the worm virus. The *macro virus* is a small program that might be embedded in an application document, such as a Microsoft Word or PowerPoint file. This type of virus is spread via e-mail attachments. The macro program is executed when the e-mail recipient opens an infected attached file. A *worm* is a parasitic program that makes copies of itself. Worms are separate entities and don't attach themselves to programs, files, or documents.

The Trojan horse isn't actually a virus, because it doesn't replicate itself. The Trojan horse appears as a seemingly useful program. For example, one Trojan horse announces that your PC is vulnerable and invites you to click OK if you want to make your system more secure. When executed, it plants a malicious program in your system. Many Trojan horses are "dialers" that use your dial-up modem and phone line to make international calls or fee-based 900-number calls.

Virus Protection

The firewall and a good antivirus program are your best protection against the malicious people who hang out on the Internet. Modern *antivirus programs* do a good job of keeping our PCs free from virus. However, they are not perfect but are only as good as their list of *virus definitions*. The two biggest names in virus protection are the Norton AntiVirus program (Symantec Corporation), shown in Figure 10-5, and the VirusScan program (McAfee Security). Most new PCs have one of these programs installed or offer them as supplemental software. If you have any networked PCs that do not have antivirus protection, I would recommend that you get it at your earliest convenience. A PC without virus protection is a point of vulnerability that could cause serious problems for other PCs on the network.

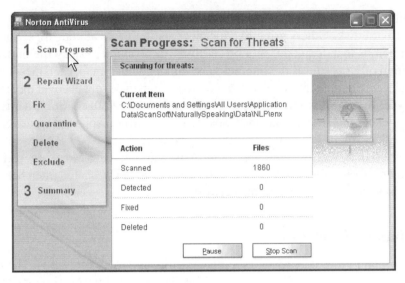

Figure 10-5   Scanning for viruses: Norton AntiVirus

Antivirus software is used in conjunction with a virus protection subscription service that lets you download protection for recent viruses, including the virus du jour. My software is preset to update virus definitions daily. Antivirus software and protection service can cost from $25 to $50 (software included) a year. That cost is small relative to the cost of a single fling with a virus-infected home network.

An antivirus program protects you against all kinds of viruses by checking all material that streams into your PC from the Internet. It also checks for viruses when you open a document file and when you insert any type of removable media. The antivirus software also monitors your computer for indications that a virus may be present. Table 10-1 lists some virus protection tips.

Tip *If your PC is without virus protection but you have Internet access, several Internet security companies offer a free security check that includes a scan of your PC for viruses. To check your PC for viruses, navigate to the Symantec (www. symantec.com) or McAfee (www.mcafee.com) web sites and start the free scan. Usually the free scan is available on the home/home office page.*

Tip	Description
Delete suspicious e-mails.	Be suspicious of any e-mail from an unknown source, especially e-mail with an attached file.
Confirm the source of attached files.	If you're not absolutely sure that the sender and his/her attached file are legitimate, confirm the e-mail with the sender, even if he/she is a trusted friend.
Be careful what you download.	Download files from the Internet only from legitimate and reputable sources—and *never* from a stranger.
Choose the option to list and not view e-mail content.	Choose the e-mail client option to see only a list of sources and subjects of received e-mail and avoid the option that includes viewing the content of the highlighted e-mail. The latter automatically opens the e-mail, which could contain a virus.
Never share your C: drive (hard disk).	Your C: hard drive normally contains the operating system and critical security information and should not be made available to external sources, even other PCs on a home network.
Keep antivirus software up-to-date.	Each month, over 500 new viruses are fed into the Internet.
Avoid common passwords.	Create passwords that are meaningless and impossible to guess (for example, "w12xutr9" instead of "wildcats").
Back up your files.	Your chances of surviving a virus attack are greatly improved if you have a backup procedure in place.
Disconnect from the Internet.	Whenever you are online, your system is vulnerable to a persistent hacker.

Table 10-1   Virus Protection Tips

Spyware

Electronic spy programs, called *spyware,* may be lurking around your PC, especially those PCs on home networks with "always-on" Internet access. Spyware is loaded and installed on your PC without your consent. Shortly after spyware began floating around the Internet, I used a crude antispyware program to delete over a hundred clandestine programs, each of which was gathering and reporting personal information about my family.

Spyware is doubly annoying in that it steals processing and Internet capacity. If your PC is running slowly, there is a good chance that the various pieces of spyware on your PC are launching and running unwanted programs. If your Internet access is unusually slow, your spyware is probably having a conversation with its host— about you.

Once installed, spyware can monitor your Internet activity and transmit collected information back to another computer. Spyware can take many forms. Many spyware programs monitor your web surfing habits and then report your web surfing tendencies to another computer. As you might expect, these reports trigger an avalanche of targeted e-mail spam and *pop-up ads* that stream down over the Internet and "pop up" on your desktop. One particularly malicious type of spyware plays to your fear, with pop-ups that look like Windows system messages that announce your vulnerability to viruses and give you a web link to a corrective patch. Spyware can include *key-loggers* that secretly record and report your keystrokes, even during logins (your passwords) and when you enter your credit card numbers. Spyware can hijack your Internet browser and change the default home and your favorites such that no matter what you do you can't change them back.

With over 80,000 spyware programs on the loose, you must protect your PC and yourself. Ad-aware (see Figure 10-6) and Spy Sweeper are popular *antispyware* programs. The best way to protect yourself against spyware is to run antispyware on a regular basis. Spyware protection works like antivirus protection in that these programs find and remove only those programs on a spyware definitions list, so be sure to update your list before scanning for spyware.

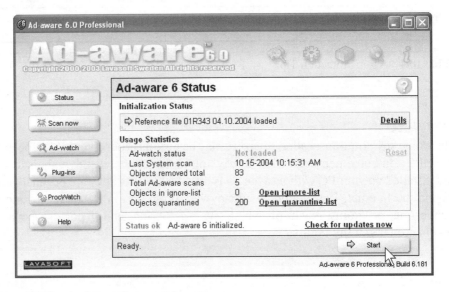

Figure 10-6   Antispy software: Ad-aware

Adware

Some people don't distinguish adware from spyware, as they both gather and report personal information; however, most people would suggest that adware does not offer the same level of threat as spyware. *Adware* is software that prompts targeted pop-up ads to display when you surf the Web. Adware is not always bad, in that it might alert you when a product or service of interest becomes available. Often, adware companies offer something you get for free, perhaps a program or an Internet service. They tell you about the adware in the fine print, but you probably missed it. Adware protection is built into antispyware software.

Cookies

As you surf the Net, you pick up cookies. The web server being accessed often will leave a cookie on your hard disk that describes, in some way, your interaction with the server. The *cookie* is a message that takes the form of a text file (.txt extension). The information in the cookie is sent back to the server each time the browser requests a page from the server. A cookie might contain your name, e-mail address, interests, and personal preferences. When you enter personal information at a web site, chances are your browser is storing it in a cookie.

Cookies can personalize your interaction with a web site such that the server presents you with a customized web page, perhaps one with your name at the top of the page. A good cookie can make your interaction with an often-visited web site more efficient and effective. For example, an auction web site might provide links to the items you viewed during your last session.

There are three basic types of cookies. *Temporary cookies* are deleted at the end of the current browser session. *Persistent cookies* remain on the hard disk. *Third-party cookies* originate from or are sent to a web site other than the one you are viewing. In any case, Windows gives you the flexibility to choose how cookies are treated. In your Internet Explorer browser, choose Tools | Internet Options, and click the Privacy tab to set preferences for handling cookies (see Figure 10-7). Possible settings range from blocking all cookies to allowing all cookies. The medium setting offers a good compromise, leaving the good cookies and protecting against the bad ones.

To view and delete cookies, choose Tools | Internet Options, click the General tab, click Settings, and then click View Files. You may need to scroll through the files to the filenames that begin with "cookie." I routinely cull cookies from my system, but I leave those from the trustworthy web sites I visit often so that I won't have to reenter information. If I don't recognize the site associated with a cookie, I delete it. These probably are third-party cookies generated by companies that want as much information as possible about my computer settings, web surfing habits, preferences, and anything else they can get.

Figure 10-7 Setting preferences for handling cookies

Spam and Spim

The cyberworld's version of junk mail, called *spam,* is among the most annoying of all annoyances. Spam is unsolicited e-mail that bombards us with advertising for mostly worthless, deceptive, and/or fraudulent products or services. "Quit your day job," "Is your health important?," "Lose that weight while you are still alive," and "Want to play," form a typical mix of spam. Occasionally, a spam will provide information on legitimate services, but most are scams.

It's virtually impossible to avoid the spammers' lists. Many web sites and spammers sell their "hit list," the e-mails of the people who visit their sites. Especially prized are the response lists, the e-mails of those who actually respond to spam. Often, spammers will give you the opportunity to "opt out" of receiving further messages, but as any veteran cybernaut can attest, clicking "opt out" simply confirms that the spammer has a valid e-mail address. Some spammers ask you to call them to opt out—at $2 a minute! My personal strategy is to tap the DELETE key on any suspicious e-mails that make it through my spam filter, typically from one to five a day.

Each day, over two billion spam messages are sent to our electronic mailboxes—without our consent or invitation. In contrast, the instant messaging (IM) version of spam, called *spim,* arrives at the rate of around two million spim messages a day. Most forecasters are predicting that spim will spin out of control as soon as spimmers find a way to abscond with large numbers of IM screen names, which are not as readily available as e-mail addresses.

To me, spam and spim are particularly irritating because they invade my personal cyberspace, wasting my time and my resources. So how do you get rid of them? Well, you don't. You control them, primarily by practicing responsible Internet surfing habits and by the judicious use of *spam filters* that filter out obvious spam.

Popular e-mail client software, such as Microsoft Outlook 2003, has filters that do a pretty good job of detecting and isolating junk e-mail, especially pornography-related spam. Keep the Outlook filter up-to-date by periodically choosing Help | Check For Updates. Client filters don't block specific senders but are based more on content. For example, the client filters send spam to a junk e-mail folder if certain keywords or phrases are found in the subject or message ("100%," "guaranteed," "Viagra," "best mortgage," "refinance," "FREE," "!!!," and so on). They also use analytical techniques to determine the probability of a message being junk e-mail. Commercial antispam software programs, often called *spam blockers,* have more sophisticated, continuously updated filters that do a much better job. For example, they often can catch spam messages even when spammers use tactics to evade filters, such as deliberately misspelling words ("garanteed" and "FREEE"). Norton AntiSpam (Symantec), shown in integration with Microsoft Outlook in Figure 10-8, does an excellent job, as does SpamKiller (McAfee Security).

CAUTION   *Your PC could be a zombie. Zombies are PCs taken over by spammers who use them to send their spam. Of course, the owners are unaware that their PCs have become slaves to spam makers. It is estimated that 40 percent of all spam is sent by hundreds of thousands of zombie PCs.*

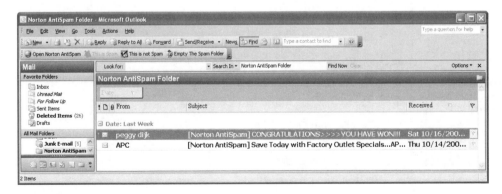

Figure 10-8   Norton AntiSpam integrated with Microsoft Outlook

Transaction Security on the Internet

Most of the bits that travel the Net are unsecured and vulnerable to being intercepted en route between computers. This is a concern, especially for financial transactions and those that involve personal data. A byproduct of an explosion in e-commerce is that Internet security is maturing and is better prepared to handle these transactions. Web site security may not be perfectly secure, but I'm a lot more comfortable entering my credit card number for an online transaction than I am handing my credit card to a waiter in a restaurant.

Secure web sites use the *Secure Sockets Layer (SSL)* protocol and encryption technology to encrypt data that are transferred over SSL links. Reputable e-commerce sites use this protocol to ensure secure transmission of sensitive information, such as credit card numbers, between web client (your PC) and web server computers. You'll know it's a secure site if the "http" in the browser's URL address bar changes to "https" (the added "s" for secure) and/or a padlock icon appears in the status bar at the bottom of the browser (see Figure 10-9).

Although the PCs or our home network sit safely in the confines of our homes and offices, their online links to the Internet expose them to the unsavory elements of the virtual world. The Internet community is employing SSL and other tools to ensure Internet security, but all their security measures go for naught if we netizens don't do our part, too. This chapter identifies points of vulnerability and presents specific approaches that can be implemented to create a secure personal computing and home networking environment. The threats are real, so I encourage you to adopt these suggestions and build an envelope of security around your home network and the information on its PCs.

The https and the padlock icon denote an SSL-secured server

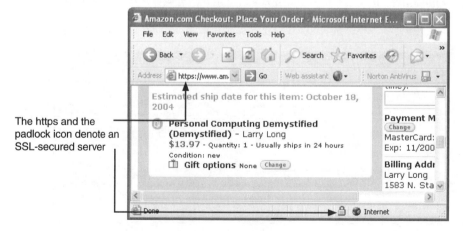

Figure 10-9   SSL-secured web server indicated by https and the padlock icon

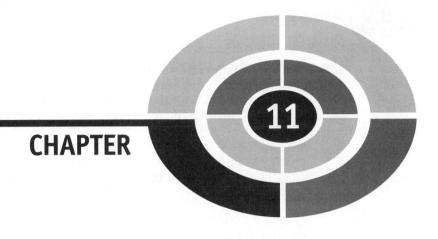

Maintenance and Troubleshooting

When you purchase a new air conditioner, an installation crew comes to your house, installs it, tests it, and thanks you for your business. When you purchase net gear for a home network, *you* unpack the boxes, *you* connect the devices, *you* flip the on switch, and *you* hope everything works. Also, *you* are responsible for network maintenance and troubleshooting duties. This chapter contains tips and hints that can help make your network administration duties go smoothly.

Maintaining a Home Network

One of the easiest ways to enhance your home networking experience is to commit to proper maintenance of your PCs and your network. Good maintenance begins when you unpack the equipment.

Unpacking the Net Gear

When you purchase network devices, they will come in separate boxes. These recommendations can save you time and money:

- *Save all sales documentation.* Keep all shipping invoices, sales receipts, delivery information, credit-card statements, and other documents that relate to the sale. You might need them for rebates, warranty work, or returns.

- *Promptly register each network device (online or by mail).* Product registration may be important for warranty protection and for long-term access to technical support. Be sure to write down the product serial numbers on the inside covers of the user's manuals and/or the support CD-ROM covers. You will need these if you reinstall the software, or you may need them if you seek technical assistance from the vendor.

- *Keep the shipping material.* If you have the space, keep all boxes and packing materials for a few months. If a piece of net gear fails during the warranty period, chances are it will do so during the first month or so.

Upgrading the Network

We routinely upgrade our PCs' electronic components and peripheral devices to take advantage of new innovations in technology. Part of maintaining a home network is growing the network gear and communications links to meet your ever-changing needs. We also grow our networks so that we can enjoy the functionality afforded by the latest technology. Counting modems and network adapters, I would imagine that the various incarnations of the Longnet have encompassed at least 100 devices over the past 20 years. The current version of the Longnet has 17 network devices. Fortunately, it's surprisingly easy to upgrade an existing home network.

LANs are upgraded by adding new units and replacing old ones. For example, many people are upgrading to a new printer that can be connected directly to the network via a print server. You might need to add a wireless signal booster to expand the range to the upstairs bedrooms. When you decide to bridge your home network to your entertainment center, you will need to add a multimedia hub. You might need a larger switch for bigger gaming parties. A new state-of-the-art gateway might offer superior firewall protection.

Home networking devices are building blocks that allow you to create and grow the network to meet your family's changing needs. Mostly, they are easily added and replaced, especially if they are within a particular manufacturer's family of communications equipment. Net gear costs and functionality vary little between the major manufacturers, so it's relatively easy to commit to a particular manufacturer. The major manufacturers are easily identified, as they are the ones with the most extensive selections at Best Buy, Circuit City, and hardware/software e-tailers.

TIP *If at all possible, I would encourage you to build and grow your network with devices from a single manufacturer. You might be able to save a few dollars by mixing and matching, but is it worth opening the door for manufacturers to play the blame game where each blames the other's equipment for the malfunction?*

Software Maintenance

Software maintenance is an ongoing task that involves installing *updates* to firmware and software in support of network devices. It also involves purchasing software *upgrades,* the most recent versions of installed software. The focus of software maintenance in home networking is the firmware and driver software for the network devices and the Microsoft Windows operating system.

Firmware Upgrades

The last step in the home network design process presented in Chapter 8 is to upgrade the gateway's firmware, the software stored in its rewritable flash memory. Home networking technology is constantly changing. The vendors routinely publish new versions of firmware to reflect these changes. Upgrading the firmware in net gear is a bit more involved than upgrading Windows or Microsoft Office, where you simply click Check For Update in the Help menu to automatically download and install the new software.

Most of your network's intelligent devices have upgradable firmware. These might include the gateway, a router, an AP, an Ethernet bridge, and a print server. The only way to know whether you're due for an upgrade is to find out which version of firmware the device is currently running and then go to the manufacturer's web site and check the version number of the latest release. To check which version is currently running on the device, open the device's browser-based interface. The version number may be noted on every screen, or it can be found in the status information. The Linksys print server interface in Figure 11-1 displays the version number in the corner of every screen, and it is included with the server's detailed information.

TIP *If you don't know the IP address of the device you wish to upgrade, go to the gateway's user interface and request a list of DHCP clients. This list will include the device's IP address.*

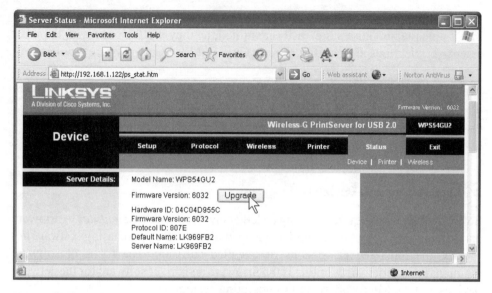

Figure 11-1   Print server browser interface: firmware information

To upgrade net gear firmware, follow these steps:

1. Go the manufacturer's web site and navigate to the support page for the device. Click Downloads or Firmware and download the firmware file to your PC. Some manufacturers provide a user-friendly setup wizard to help with the firmware upgrade.

2. Using either the upgrade feature within the device's browser interface (see Figure 11-2) or the downloaded setup wizard, install the new version of the firmware.

3. Press Reset or flip the power off and then on to complete the upgrade.

TIP *Wait a few weeks after the firmware's release date before downloading and installing the latest version. This gives the company a little time to fine-tune the firmware and remove the bugs that often surface after a new release.*

Updating Windows and Net Gear Drivers

One of the hacker's ongoing quests is to find holes in Windows that will enable him or her to get into a system or a network. Hackers find holes and Microsoft plugs them. This cat-and-mouse game has been going on since the first release of Windows. Each

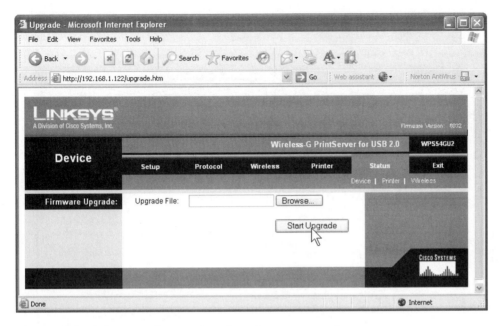

Figure 11-2 Print server browser interface: firmware upgrade screen

counter by Microsoft results in a "critical" Windows update, which Microsoft makes available free to registered users via downloads over the Internet. To retrieve an update from the Microsoft web site, click Start | Help And Support | Windows Update (Figure 11-3). When you begin the Windows update procedure, Windows scans your system to determine which updates are needed. Each update is described, and you are asked to choose those you wish to install. Always install "critical" updates, as these updates may do something like plug a hole in Windows' online security.

For each PC on the network, I recommend that you do the online Windows Update automatically or no less often than once a month if done manually. To set Windows update options, click Start | Control Panel | System | Automatic Updates (tab). If you choose to "Keep my computer up-to-date," Windows automatically determines which updates you need and delivers them directly to your PC via the Internet. An icon and message appear in the notification area when an automatic update is complete.

***TIP** A workable strategy for small nonvolatile LANs is, "If it ain't broke, don't fix it." If your home network is simple, perhaps two or three PCs on a wireless LAN, and it's working well, you may wish to wait until something goes wrong before updating the network device drivers. That could well be the life of the LAN. For larger, more complex LANs, it's good policy to keep up with the driver updates.*

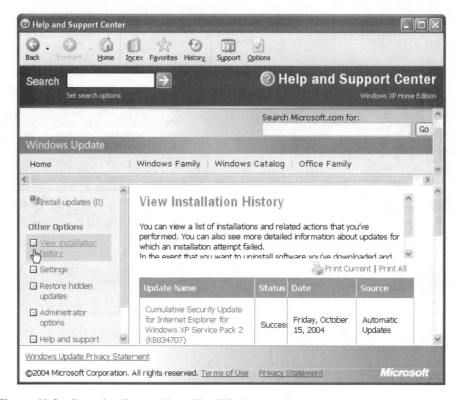

Figure 11-3 Downloading and installing Windows updates

PC input/output devices and some communications equipment, including network adapters, come with their own *device driver software.* The device driver provides instructions needed by Windows to communicate with the peripheral or network device. Net gear drivers are installed during the device installation process. Technology marches on, and these drivers must be updated periodically to keep pace. As with firmware, manufacturers post new releases for drivers to their web sites that can be downloaded and installed. However, the quickest way to update a device driver is to open the Device Manager. To do this, click Start | Control Panel | System | Device Manager (in the Hardware tab). Then expand the entries, as needed, and double-click the device to open the device's properties dialog box. Click the Driver tab and then the Update Driver button to open the Hardware Update Wizard. From there, follow the wizard's directions.

TIP *Occasionally, updating a network device driver can upset the delicate balance in a working network. Fortunately, one of the Windows features is the Driver Rollback, which lets you restore the previous driver. To do this, click the Roll Back Driver button found in the Driver tab of the device's properties box.*

Upgrading Windows

Upgrading Windows is major surgery for your PC. I'm reluctant to advise you to upgrade Windows unless you purchased a PC system at the tail end of your Windows version's life, that is, within a few months of the introduction of a release of Windows. At this writing, the current version of Windows is Windows XP. Microsoft has scheduled the next release for 2006, about the time the next edition of this book hits the shelf.

In theory, installing a new version of Windows over an old one should be painless and flawless. In truth, it seldom is and can be a real mess. If you have a truly compelling reason to upgrade your Windows operating system and are willing to put up with several days of conversion headaches, be my guest. If not, take comfort in the fact that your existing operating system will probably do 99.2 percent of what you wish to do.

Preventive Maintenance

Simple preventive maintenance can make a big difference in the longevity of your home network. For example, network devices should be cleaned on the same schedule as other computing devices. Mostly, the electronics within network devices is sealed, so the main concern is that dust bunnies don't collect in or near the ports. However, the most important preventive maintenance for network devices involves protecting them from power aberrations and from careless people.

Power Protection

I would not plug in a PC or a network device without minimal protection from AC power disturbances, such as "dirty" power (sags and surges in power output), brownouts (low power), or power outages. Power surges, in particular, are a serious problem for PCs and communications equipment.

Dirty power is an enemy of personal computing and networking. It can be delivered directly from your power company, or it can surface when your computing and networking hardware share a circuit with a power-hungry appliance, such as a toaster oven or a washing machine. Dirty power and brownouts can cause network transmission and program execution errors.

There are several levels of protection you can adopt to protect nodes on your LAN from electrical problems that result in loss of data or damage to electronics. These devices also offer protection from surges that can come through telephone lines and TV cables that link to modems.

Surge Suppressors

The relatively inexpensive *surge suppressor* ($20 to $50), considered the most basic level of protection, will protect your PCs and net gear from most lightning hits and other electrical aberrations. The surge suppressor (see Figure 11-4), sometimes called a *power strip,* is placed in line with your PC system's and your net gear's power supply so that it can absorb the shock of voltage spikes and surges. Having lost several system components, I learned the hard way that having just any type of surge suppressor does not guarantee protection from serious surges in electrical current. You must have a good one.

The better surge suppressors are more likely to thwart a damaging electrical surge over your power source and over your phone line (DSL) or TV/data cable (cable modem). The quality of surge suppressors is proportional to cost, with those on the low end being virtually useless. Surge suppressors are rated in joules, the energy they can absorb. Six hundred joules is basic protection, and 1000-plus joules is superior protection. I plug my peripheral devices, such as printers, speaker systems, scanners, and Webcams, into a surge suppressor. Also, I plug network devices that are isolated from any PC into surge suppressors.

Uninterruptible Power Sources

If your finances will allow, spend another $60 to $150 and buy an *uninterruptible power source* or *universal power supply (UPS)* for protection for each PC's system unit (see Figure 11-5). Then, use these UPS units to protect nearby net gear, too.

Courtesy APC Corporation

Figure 11-4   Surge suppressor (AC and communication channels)

Courtesy APC Corporation

Figure 11-5 An uninterruptible power source (UPS)

Network devices draw relatively small amounts of power and will have little impact on power available to your PC in case of a power outage.

The function of a UPS unit is to provide uninterruptible power by offering a secondary source of power. The UPS has a big battery, which is continuously recharged by AC power. Upon detecting any type of power disturbances, the UPS unit beeps a warning and instantaneously switches to battery power to provide clean, continuous power for several minutes. This time cushion allows you to complete network transmissions and "shut down" each PC normally.

If you experience regular power flickers that force you to reset digital clocks, then you should consider a UPS. Those power flickers reset your PC and network gear. Of course, any changes to unsaved files and network transmissions are lost, too.

TIP *The manufacturers of the better surge suppressors and UPS units will replace your computer or network device if their unit fails to protect it from power disturbances. This insurance costs a little more, but it's well worth the investment.*

Everything on the Longnet is near a UPS serving a PC except the range extender and the Ethernet bridge linking the media hub in the home theater. These devices are protected by surge suppressors. When I have a power outage, I lose access to the media hub and the extra wireless area made available by the range extender. All PCs and the rest of the network remain operational for at least ten minutes.

You will need to match your system's power requirements and your desired run time (the amount of time your system will run on the battery) with the rated output of the UPS unit. For example, to get ten minutes run time for a desktop PC system

unit with a Pentium 4 processor, you might need a 500 VA (voltage-ampere) UPS unit. The low-power net gear has little impact on run time.

Protecting Net Gear from People Mishaps

Believe it or not, one of the biggest problems with networking is the ill-advised placement of cabling. Most cabling is hidden within walls or ceilings, but ultimately, some of it can become an invitation to an accidental mishap. Position your cabling to eliminate the possibility that someone might trip over it or get entangled with a cable that is hanging. I mention this because people seem to latch onto and pull network cabling far more frequently than you would expect.

All kinds of bad things can happen when cables are inadvertently yanked. Connectors and ports can be broken. Loops in the cabling can be turned into kinks that can cause connection problems. Expensive devices can be pulled off shelves or desks onto a hard floor. Network devices are not nearly as drop-proof as cellular phones. Just place wires away from foot traffic, wandering arms, and curious animals, and you should be okay.

Security Maintenance

All good network maintenance programs include routinely changing the elements of the network that serve to keep intruders at bay. I recommend you change the passwords that enable access to the browser-based interfaces of the home gateway, access point, and other intelligent devices in the network. If you have a wireless network, I would encourage you to change the SSID and WEP encryption keys at least once a month, especially if you live in an apartment or a densely populated area. Remember, you will need to make these changes on all PCs and network devices that require these settings (see Chapter 10).

Troubleshooting

Trouble is part of the home networking adventure, so everyone with a LAN at home becomes a troubleshooter at one time or another. The typical reaction to a seemingly serious problem is panic, then anger. There's no reason to panic. Just take a deep breath and remind yourself that other people with home networks have their share of network problems, too. This section is about demystifying LAN troubleshooting.

It's easy to turn your anger toward your network, your PC, Bill Gates, the manufacturers, or whoever sold you the stuff in the first place. In truth, your network, your PC, Mr. Gates and his colleagues, and the various vendors and manufacturers are your friends. They have done a great deal to help you in time of need. Millions of people have home networks much like yours, so there's a good chance others have experienced a similar problem. Moreover, there is probably a carefully documented description of your problem and what you have to do to solve it. Your challenge is to find the solution and implement it.

Okay, so troubleshooting isn't your thing, not with the washing machine, the car, or the home network. Well, you can always mortgage your house and call a networking specialist. However, I heartily encourage you to try basic troubleshooting first, arguably the quickest and least expensive approach to fixing the vast majority of networking problems. Networking problems can be frustrating, but with a little thought, research, and confidence, you can take care of most of them.

Network Troubleshooting Strategies

Potential network problems span the gamut of hardware, software, connective media, and firmware. The problem could be inconsistency in settings across network devices. A network adapter might be accidentally disabled. Incompatibilities may surface because of the presence of an older version of Windows. An Ethernet cable may not be fully seated in its port. The always-on Internet connection might disconnect without notice. The two PCs and the printer connected to an Ethernet switch located in the master bedroom are no longer accessible to other PCs on the network.

There are literally hundreds of things that can go wrong in a home network. Sometimes a solution to the problem surfaces quickly and the fix is easy. Other times, it is well camouflaged and tough to find, much less fix. Fortunately, virtually all network gaffes have happened before, so it's likely that someone has felt your pain and documented a solution.

The objective of troubleshooting a home network is to find and isolate whatever is causing the problem so that you can fix it. I suggest you consider this network troubleshooting strategy when a problem occurs:

- *Attempt the universal solution.* The "universal solution" to network problems, which is described in the next section, involves doing the easy stuff: resetting critical network devices, checking the connections, and/or rebooting PCs.

- *Isolate the problem.* If the cause of the problem is not apparent, you will need to go into sleuth mode. Use available diagnostic tools and your investigative skills to isolate the trouble spot.

- *Derive a solution.* Once you understand the problem and what is causing it, use myriad resources to help you find a solution.

- *Fix the problem.* Implement the solution and fix the problem.

The Universal Solution to Most PC/Network Problems

The number and variety of potential PC and networking problems boggles the mind. These aggravating problems are commonplace on a home network: the printer isn't responding, the web browser or e-mail client doesn't recognize the broadband connection, the PC in the home office doesn't recognize the PC in the den, and so on. Although these could be symptoms of serious problems, most of the time these and other common problems are simple annoyances that are easily solved with a universal troubleshooting solution that may involve both PCs and network devices.

It has been my experience that resetting the PC or PCs having connection problems and/or the modem/gateway/router will solve most network problems. In most situations, perform this simple nine-step procedure to get back online:

1. Reset the DSL/cable modem, if separate from the gateway (press the reset button or turn it off, then on). The initialization process may take a minute or two.

2. Test the network. If the problem persists, continue with the next step.

3. Reset the home gateway/router (press the reset button or turn it off, then on). If the unit does not have a reset button or an on/off switch, just unplug the power briefly, either at the wall plug or the unit. The initialization process may take from one to five minutes.

4. Test the network. If the problem persists, continue with the next step.

5. Go through the normal system shutdown procedure (not restart) such that the PC or PCs in question are shut down and the power is off.

6. Check that all network connections between network components are secured and in the proper ports. Also, confirm that the power is on for all non-PC network devices.

NOTE *Network devices have visual indicators. What is indicated by these lights varies among devices (indicator lights are described in the device manuals). Most devices have* Link *and* Activity *lights. When the Link light is on, there is a connection to another network device. However, the light is not a confirmation that the link is properly configured and that traffic is flowing normally. Typically, the Activity light blinks when traffic is flowing.*

7. Confirm that all network adapters are firmly seated in their PCI, CardBus, or PC card slots. Ensure that USB cables for USB adapters are fully engaged in their ports.

8. Turn on the PC(s) and reboot the system.

9. Test the network. If the problem persists, then use the Windows network troubleshooters to solve the problem. These are discussed in the next section.

Windows Network Troubleshooting Support

The Windows *Help and Support* feature includes a number of "troubleshooters" that use interactive questioning (see Figure 11-6) to walk you through the troubleshooting process. Think of an electronic troubleshooter as a friendly expert who wants to work with you to solve your problem. The Windows troubleshooters home in on a suggested solution by asking you to select the most appropriate description from several options or to respond with a yes or no to a specific question. During this interactive process, the troubleshooter may ask you to perform specific corrective actions. Ultimately, the troubleshooter may make very specific suggestions that lead to a solution to your problem. If the "universal solution" doesn't fix the problem, chances are, you and your troubleshooting partner will be able to home in on a solution.

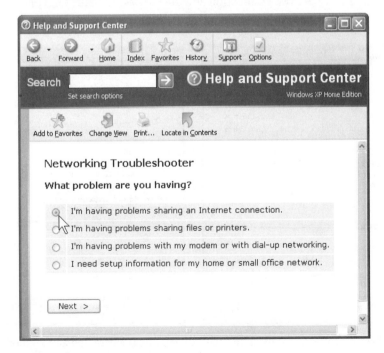

Figure 11-6   The Windows network troubleshooter

To view or use available Windows troubleshooters that address networking problems, choose Start | Help And Support | Fixing The Problem | Networking problems. The list of troubleshooters includes the following:

- Modem Troubleshooter (modem connection, setup, configuration, and detection problems)
- Internet Connection Sharing Troubleshooter (ISP problems)
- Home and Small Office Networking Troubleshooter (setup, Internet connection, and file/printer sharing problems)
- File and Printer Troubleshooter (network file/printer sharing problems)

Several other network troubleshooters deal with connection problems associated with Bluetooth devices (network devices, such as some PDAs, that use the Bluetooth standard for wireless communication).

The Windows network troubleshooters can lead you down any number of paths to a solution. For example, the troubleshooter might ask you to open the Local Area Connection Status dialog box to view the connection status, determine the IP address of the connected PC, or initiate the connection repair option (see Figure 11-7). To view this dialog box, click Start | Control Panel | Network Connections. Then, highlight the LAN network connection and choose View Status Of This Connection in the Network Tasks pane.

Figure 11-7   Local Area Connection Status dialog box (General tab and Support tab)

The Windows troubleshooters may also ask you to ensure that Windows recognizes a particular network adapter and that it is working properly. To do this, open the Local Area Connection Status dialog box as just described. Then, click Properties to view the Local Area Connection Properties box (see Figure 11-8) and the connectivity information on its three tabs. Click the Configure button on the General tab to view the [name of adapter] Network Connection Properties box. This box contains information related to the adapter, including whether or not the adapter is working properly (see Figure 11-9). Click the Troubleshoot button on the General tab to start a device troubleshooter.

The Windows troubleshooters will occasionally ask that you verify IP-level connectivity between the PCs and net devices on the home network. This involves using a *ping* command at the *command prompt*. To open the command prompt, click Start | All Programs | Accessories | Command Prompt. Entering **ping** with an IP address causes an echo message to be sent to the designated IP address. The receipt of the corresponding echo reply message is displayed along with the elapsed time for the message's round-trip.

In Figure 11-10, the command *ipconfig* is entered to display the IP addresses of the PC and the home gateway. This information is also available in the Local Area Connection Status dialog box. The command "ping 192.168.1.1" (the IP address of the gateway) is entered to verify connectivity between the PC at 192.168.1.105 and the gateway. Note that the elapsed time for the four echo replies from the home gateway is 2 ms (milliseconds), 1 ms, 1 ms, and 1 ms.

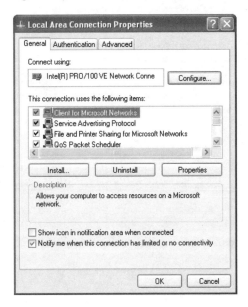

Figure 11-8   Local Area Connection Properties dialog box

Figure 11-9 Network Connection dialog box for a network adapter

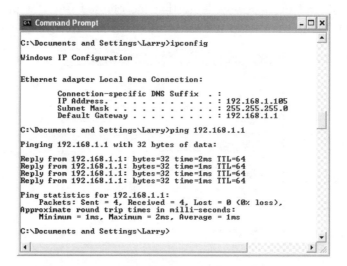

Figure 11-10 Using the ping command to verify connectivity

Troubleshooting wireless communication often involves a search to find configuration settings that are incorrect on one or more devices. The Windows troubleshooters will invariably ask that you confirm configuration compatibility for key settings. For example, the SSID setting must be the same for all network devices. All devices must be using the same WEP key(s) and either 64-bit or 128-bit encryption. The channel setting must be the same for all devices, too. Another important fix that may be suggested during troubleshooting is the Windows *System Restore* feature. Often, a current problem is a result of a software package or driver software being installed, with or without your knowledge. When attempts to troubleshoot the problem are futile, you can use the Windows System Restore feature to return your PC to its state before the problem-causing software/driver installation. Windows automatically creates *restore points* each day and at the time of significant changes to your PC, perhaps the accidental deletion of a critical file or a virus attack. Restore points go back up to three weeks, depending on the amount of activity on your PC. You can restore your system to any of these restore points. To reset your PC to an earlier restore point, click Start | Help And Support | System Restore (under Pick A Task). The system restore process does not affect your personal data files, including Microsoft Office documents, passwords, and e-mail.

Vendor/Manufacturer Troubleshooting Assistance

If both the universal fix and the Windows troubleshooters fail to solve the problem, there's plenty of help in the form of reference manuals, technical support web sites, and call-in technical support.

Reference Manuals

Most hardware products are accompanied by some type of reference manual. The trend with communications devices is to build manual content into the software, often within the Help facility, or to present it as a separate electronic document that can be viewed with word processing software, Adobe Reader (PDF format), or an Internet browser. Typically, these *e-manuals* are files on the network device's installation CD-ROM, or they are made available when you install the product. If you can't find the CD, no problem. Virtually all manuals are available at the manufacturer's web site under support for the device in question.

Most reference manuals, whether hardcopy or electronic, will have a troubleshooting section that includes step-by-step solutions to common problems. The troubleshooting section for a Linksys wireless home gateway (see Figure 11-11) includes solutions to a wide range of problems, including the following:

- I can't get the Internet game, server, or application to work.
- The firmware upgrade failed and/or the power LED is flashing.
- My DSL service's PPPoE is always disconnecting.
- My Wireless-G speed seems to be slow.

If the troubleshooting guide does not give you the information you need to solve the problem, your next step is to go to the manufacturer for insight. You can either visit the manufacturer's technical support web site or call the manufacturer's technical support hotline (find the telephone numbers listed in product documen-tation). If you're comfortable fixing problems on your own, I would recommend the former. It's usually faster.

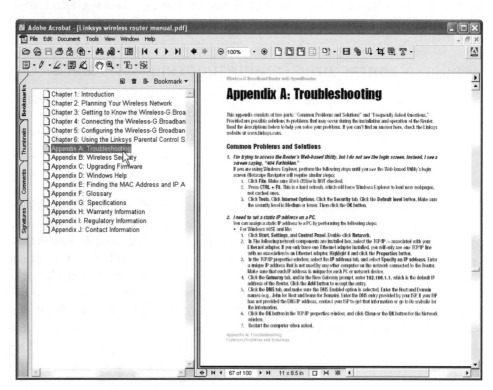

Figure 11-11 The troubleshooting section of a wireless home gateway manual (PDF format)

Technical Support Web Sites

It's to the advantage of the manufacturer to have a comprehensive, easy-to-use technical support web site. An hour's worth of personalized technical support can cost the company up to $100 an hour. The cost to the company of helping a customer solve a problem via an interactive tech support web site is considerably less than one dollar. The company wants you to go to their web site first, and most major vendors are making every effort to give you the information you need to solve your own problems. The typical PC/network device manufacturer will have most or all of the following technical support aids:

- **A knowledge base**   In the knowledge-based tool, you simply enter keywords relating to your problem and/or enter the question directly. For example, the D-Link knowledge base could help you with disabling SSID broadcast (see Figure 11-12). Occasionally, the system might ask you to refine your question by entering more detailed information.

- **Tutorials**   A tech support web site may offer a variety of tutorials, each designed to walk you through some facet of the operation and application of a product. Or, the site might include step-by-step tutorials on how to complete a particular procedure, such as upgrading the firmware on a home gateway.

- **Frequently asked questions**   Depending on the size of the tech support web site, the FAQs may be categorized and placed in a hierarchical menu so that you can easily find those that relate to your concern. Companies that sell millions of products get millions of questions. Chances are someone else has asked your question before. A good tech support web site has clear resolutions to these common problems.

- **Tips and hints**   The manufacturer may provide tips and hints to help you get the most out of your home network, plus one of them may pertain to your particular problem.

- **Contacts**   This section of the online technical support web site normally will allow you to submit a written description of your problem within an online form. Technical support personnel usually respond to these types of inquiries within 24–48 hours, often sooner. The contacts page may not list tech support telephone numbers, but they will be included with your product documentation.

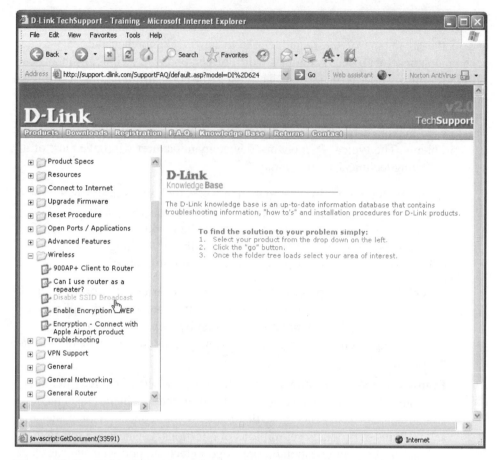

Figure 11-12   D-Link Knowledge Base for a wireless home gateway

Call-in Technical Support

The manufacturer would prefer that call-in technical support be your last choice, because it is their most expensive support service. The major network communications device manufacturers have hundreds of technical support personnel, some of whom are good and know what they're doing. Many, however, are rookies and may not be very helpful for difficult problems. Most of my interactions with these people have been positive, but some conversations have been overly time-consuming, sometimes expensive (not all are toll-free), and of little help. Nowadays, however, online support is so comprehensive that I seldom call tech support. To save time and possibly money, I will always check the support web site first. Most of the time, I find a detailed solution to my problem within minutes.

If you have exhausted your options and feel a need to talk with a real person, be aware that there may be costs involved. Look over your warranty and/or a description of your telephone-based technical support options so that you understand the costs, if any. However, if you are out of your warranty or support, a per-problem fee ($15 and up) or a per-minute fee ($1 and up) may apply. Your product documentation or the web site details these costs.

When you call tech support, be prepared. Remember, the call might be on your dime. Have all the information you need to describe your network and the problem. I would suggest that you write this information down so that you can relate it clearly to the tech rep:

- A description of the problem, noting what the network is doing now that it should not be doing and/or what the network isn't doing that it should be doing

- A description of the circumstances under which the problem occurs

- The text and number of any error messages (note whether these are Windows or application software error messages)

- What you might have done to attempt to fix the problem

- A description of any hardware or software changes you have made to your PC system just before and during the occurrence of the problem (for example, changing network preferences or the installation of a new modem)

Regarding the last point, if you suspect that the change(s) you made may be causing the problem, you might try reversing the change(s). This will involve removing devices and/or software from the system or changing settings back to what they were before the problem occurred. Once everything is working again, reinstall the hardware and software and/or repeat the changes you made to the settings. This time, however, do it with extreme care.

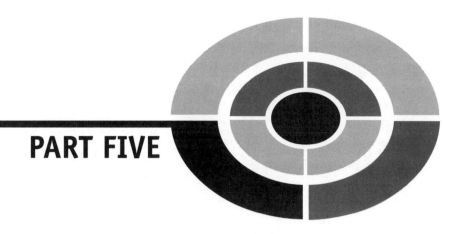

PART FIVE

The Internet, Entertainment, and Telework on a Home Network

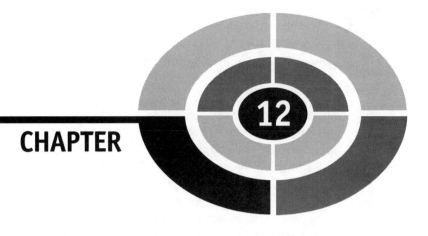

CHAPTER

12

Internet Applications: Cruising the Internet

To me, the single most significant benefit of having a home network is having high-speed Internet access all the time on all of the PCs (and game controllers) in the house. This means that my wife, my two boys, and I can send/receive e-mail at any time, upload or download files at any time, cruise any corner of the Net at any time, play online songs at any time, go e-shopping at any time, or interact with the Net in any way we want, whenever we want. Every person in my family has been shocked, overwhelmed, amazed, enlightened, and appalled by the Internet. This chapter offers an overview of the Internet's maze of applications and resources that can help

you and your family take full advantage one of home networking best features—broadband Internet access sharing.

Perhaps someday the term *Internet* will emerge as a new word to describe anything that is really big. Colossal, gigantic, and massive simply are not adequate to describe the size and scope of the Internet. The Internet includes literally billions of constantly updated pages of information and a growing number of applications, all accessible by anyone with a PC and Internet access. When you have a home network, that usually includes everyone in the family.

To a newbie, navigating the Internet is like trying to get around in a foreign megalopolis, like Tokyo or Budapest. Once you are able to speak a little Japanese or Hungarian, as the case may be, and know a little about the layout of the city, you can begin to explore. The more you explore, the more comfortable you become with navigating about the city and understanding its many points of interest. It's the same with the Internet. As you gain experience with this electronic behemoth, you will want to veer off the main roads and check out the side streets, as well. Table 12-1 summarizes many of the Internet's broad spectrum of applications and resources.

PERSONAL COMMUNICATIONS	
E-mail	Send/receive electronic mail.
Instant messaging	Communicate via real-time text, audio, and/or video communication.
Chat	Have virtual text-based chats among groups of people.
Internet telephony	Hold telephone conversations over the Internet.
GROUP COMMUNICATIONS	
Mailing lists	Share e-mail (all e-mail goes to all members on a distribution list).
Newsgroups	Post messages to the Internet version of a bulletin board (newsgroups are topical).
Blogs (web logs)	Create topical online journals that invite feedback.
INFORMATION	
News	Newspapers, magazines, television stations, Internet portals, and other sites provide continuously updated news.
Weather	Up-to-the-minute weather and weather forecasting is available for any city or region.
Sports	All professional leagues and teams, as well as all colleges, provide sports information and, sometimes, real-time statistics.
Research for school or job	Billions of pages of information are available on almost any subject.

Table 12-1   Popular Internet Applications and Resources

Travel information	Cities, states, resorts, hotels, national parks, and thousands more destinations offer a breadth of travel information.
Medical information	Medical data, advice, and information on virtually any condition can be found.
DOWNLOADING AND FILE SHARING	
Images and video	Still images of great variety, from NASA space shots to family photos, and brief videos, from music videos to family clips, are shared across cyberspace.
Music	Millions of songs are downloaded and shared, both legally and illegally, each day.
Movies	Commercial and private movies, both legal and illegal, are freely distributed throughout the Internet.
STREAMING MEDIA	
Video clips	News events, movie trailers, sports highlights, and so on are offered at a variety of sites.
Audio	Speeches, radio station broadcasts, and so on are streamed over the Internet.
Movies	On-demand movies may someday threaten the existence of the video store.
ONLINE TRANSACTIONS	
Online shopping	Shop and buy almost anything on the Internet, from diamonds to airplanes.
Online auctions	Bid on any of millions of new and used items on the virtual auction block or place your own items up for auction.
Online banking	Most banking transactions can be done online.
Making reservations	All types of travel reservations, including airline, train, hotel, auto rental, and so on, can be made online.
Stock trading	Stocks can be bought and sold online.
Gambling	Visit virtual casinos and win/lose real money.
ENTERTAINMENT	
Multiplayer gaming	Play bridge or fight galactic battles with other Internet-based gamers.
Serendipitous browsing	Surf the Internet just for fun to see where it leads you.
Adult content	Adult entertainment is a major dot-com industry.
Hobbyist	All popular hobbies have sites that include information and related activities.

Table 12-1   Popular Internet Applications and Resources (*continued*)

The World Wide Web

"The Internet" and "the Web" are used interchangeably, but actually, the World Wide Web is the Internet's dominant application for accessing information and services. The Web got its name because it is an interconnecting "web" of servers and linked multimedia documents. The beauty of the Web is that the linked relationships are independent of physical location. These are the main attributes of web sites and pages:

- They are user-friendly.

- They can contain any or all multimedia elements (graphics, audio, video, text, and animation).

- They can be interactive, enabling interactivity between users and servers.

- They are linked via hyperlinks.

- They can be composed in frames, enabling several independent sections to be displayed on a single web page.

Figure 12-1 takes you on a brief tour of the Web to show you a few of the stops along this stretch of the information highway. The operative word here is "few." These don't illustrate how you can do comparison shopping between dozens of e-tailers in seconds. They don't include the fastest-growing application on the Internet, the matching of people in pursuit of romance. For a complete tour, log on and enjoy.

The Internet may not become a "way of life" for you and your family as it has for so many others, but when everyone in the house has broadband access, all the time, the Internet tends to take on an increasingly significant role in family life. For those of us who have been using the Internet for a while, it's difficult to pinpoint an activity that does not in some way overlap with Internet-based information or services. For me, a good example is shopping. When I wanted to buy something in 1995, I drove from store to store until I found what I wanted at an acceptable price. Now, I do most of my shopping online because I'm confident that I'm getting the best available price and that I will find the right shoe in my size, the exact audio/video component I need, a specific out-of-print book, and a hard-to-find part for the dishwasher. Convenience, price, and selection are the most important reasons why Internet sales are growing at about 40 percent a year.

File Transfer Protocol: FTP

Through the 1990s, FTPing was a popular Internet activity. *FTP (File Transfer Protocol)* servers on the Internet let you download and upload files in much the same way you work with files and folders on your PC. Thousands of FTP sites let netizens download music, art, games, clip art, published and unpublished books,

Buy and sell almost anything at an Internet auction site.

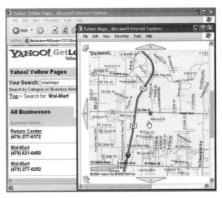

Find and get directions to any business in the United States.

Send musical, animated, and interactive greeting cards.

Enjoy Leonardo da Vinci's painting *The Mona Lisa* at the Louvre Museum in Paris.

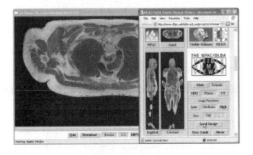

Select and view two-dimensional slices from any part of the human body.

Search for a job with the help of an automatic agent.

Figure 12-1 Cruising the World Wide Web

Learn how stuff works at HowStuffWorks.

Get real-time financial information.

Read and see news as it happens.

Visit pages devoted to virtually every hobby and special interest.

Scan the ultimate travel brochure to learn about points of interest and destinations throughout the world.

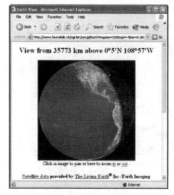

View what is happening at any of thousands of locations on earth and beyond via webcams.

Figure 12-1   Cruising the World Wide Web *(continued)*

maps, software, and anything else that can be digitized and is not copyright protected. Some FTP sites are password-protected, but most are "anonymous"—you can just enter "anonymous" for the user ID and your e-mail address for the password if prompted to do so. To find a topical FTP site, just search on any portal for FTP and the topic (for example, "FTP clip art").

Much of what used to be on FTP servers has been moved to more user-friendly web servers with similar file management capabilities. However, FTP servers continue to perform a valuable function and can be accessed directly from any Net browser. For example, all the files created, revised, and prepared for this book, about 500 in all, are stored on a common password-protected FTP site. The files at the site are viewed on the Windows Explorer and treated similarly to local files (see Figure 12-2). In the address box of Figure 12-2, note the ftp:// prefix in the URL. All files at this FTP site are available to me and others around the country that do editing, art, layout, composition, indexing, printing, and project management.

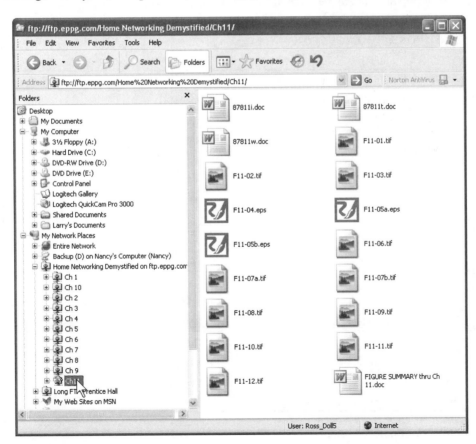

Figure 12-2   FTP site at McGraw-Hill for the files associated with this book

Communicating with People via the Internet

The Internet is a wonderful tool for all kinds of communications, but Internet communications are different in that most of what we say over the Internet is via text and not spoken words. In this section, you learn about the more popular Internet-based methods for personal and group communications.

When we speak, our conversation is enhanced with eye contact, voice inflection, and body English—none of which is possible in a text message. Recognizing the shortcomings of text communication, ever-inventive netizens have created *emoticons* (emotion icons), often called *smileys*, to show emotion in keyed-in text and an Internet shorthand to speed text entry. Some of the more popular emoticons and keyboard shortcuts are shown in Table 12-2. As you might imagine, it was inevitable that pop art would evolve from these text glyphs. Table 12-3 shows a few of the hundreds of pieces of pop art that can be created from the characters on your keyboard.

EMOTICONS: EMOTION ICONS			
:-)	Smiling	:-~)	User with a cold
(-:	Left-handed smile	(@_@)	Stunned
:-}	Mischievous smile	)-::-(	Married
:'-)	Crying (happy)	:-&	Tongue-tied
:-(	Sad	:-Q	Smoker
:-((	Very sad	,':-)	A really interesting idea
:'-(	Crying (sad)	O :-)	Angel
(:-*	Kiss	;-)	Wink
:-/	Skeptical	:c)	Pigheaded
:-l	Bored	8-)	Wearing sunglasses
:-D	Laughing	::-)	Wearing glasses
<:(	Dunce	#-)	Partied all night
:-o	Amazed	>:)	Little devil
:-I	Indifferent	%-6	Brain-dead
%-(	Confused	[[[***]]]	Hugs and kisses
~ :-(	Steaming mad	^5	High five
#:-o	Shocked	:-l :-l	Déjà vu
(:&	Angry	-,-	Sleepy

Table 12-2 Emoticons and Keyboard Shortcuts

:-@	Screaming angry	(I	Asleep
(:-#	Wearing braces	<^O^>	Laughing loudly
(:-...	Broken heart	:-C	Unhappy; really bummed
KEYBOARD SHORTCUTS			
AFAIK	As far as I know	KUTGW	Keep up the good work
AFJ	April fool's joke	L8R	Later
AFK	Away from keyboard	LOL	Laughing out loud
BRB	Be right back	MYOB	Mind your own business
BTW	By the way...	ROTFL	Rolling on the floor laughing
CU	See you	SPST	Same place, same time
CUL (8R)	See you later	THX	Thanks, thank you
F2F	Face-to-face	TIA	Thanks in advance
FAQs	Frequently asked questions	TPTB	The powers that be
GR8	Great	TTFN	Ta-ta for now or goodbye
HAND	Have a nice day	TTYL	Talk to you later
HTH	Hope this helps	<VBG>	Very big grin
IGU	I give up	WAG	A guess
IMHO	In my humble opinion	Wizard	A gifted or experienced user
IRL	In real life	YKYBHTLW	You know you've been hacking too long when

Table 12-2   Emoticons and Keyboard Shortcuts *(continued)*

@-->->-	A rose	|://	George Bush
= =):-)=	Abe Lincoln	/:-)	Gumby
~8-)	Alfalfa	=(_8^(1)	Homer Simpson
0:-)	Angel or saint	>>:-1	Klingon
~:o	Baby	)P-(	Long John Silver
q:-#	Baseball catcher	@@@@@@@@:)	Marge Simpson
]B-)	Batman	(:-(|	Mick Jagger

Table 12-3   Keyboard Pop Art

*:o)	Bozo the Clown	(8-o	Mr. Bill
IIIII8^)X	Cat in the Hat	(Z(:^P	Napoleon
=l:=)X	Charlie Chaplin	(OvO)	Owl
Q:-)	College graduate	:----}	Pinocchio
;-)}<////>	Corporate guy with tie	([(	Robocop
C):-)	Cowboy	7:-)	Ronald Reagan
==:-D	Don King	*<(:-{o{{{{	Santa Claus
@;^D	Elvis	*!#*!^*&:-)	Schizophrenic
[8-]	Frankenstein	(:=<	Star Wars stormtrooper
*<(:')	Frosty the Snowman	(-l---(: -)	The Pope

Table 12-3   Keyboard Pop Art *(continued)*

The following are some basic rules of Internet etiquette, called *netiquette*, which, if followed, will minimize the possibility of your message being misinterpreted or your recipient being offended:

- Don't send spam, the ultimate Internet faux pas.

- Use capital letters only if you wish to shout.

- Be sensitive to your recipients' values and be very selective when sending Internet content.

- Honor someone's private communication with you and keep it private.

- Be patient with newbies.

- Accept any style and say nothing. Some people may never insert a capital letter or correct a misspelling.

- Never forward a virus warning without confirming it with reliable sources, because most virus warnings are hoaxes.

- Never forward pyramid messages ("Send this to ten friends and...")

- Use antivirus software to maintain a virus-free environment, as most viruses are passed via e-mail.

E-Mail

E-mail has transformed the way we communicate with one another. We send/receive e-mail through either *e-mail client software*, such as Microsoft Outlook, or via *web-based e-mail*, such as Hotmail.com. If you're installing a home network, you're probably familiar with the e-mail application. Well, the settings and the way you interact with e-mail on a home network are the same as they are for e-mail on a stand-alone dial-up PC.

The primary advantage of e-mail client software is that the received e-mails and their attachments are stored on your PC. Being stored locally allows the e-mail client to be more responsive to keyword searches and the e-mail application to be more easily integrated with other, related applications, such as a calendar and a task list. Web-based e-mail's big advantage is that the received e-mails and their attachments are stored at the e-mail server site, so you can check your e-mail from any Internet-connected PC in the world. This type of e-mail is handled through interaction with a web site, such as Yahoo.com. Figure 12-3 illustrates an e-mail message that is received and viewed in both Microsoft Outlook and Yahoo! Mail. It also shows an Outlook reply to the e-mail.

Your online identification is your e-mail address, which is in two parts separated by an @ symbol. In the e-mail address Heather_Hill@aol.com, *Heather_Hill* is the username and *aol.com* is the domain name for the Internet host/network, sometimes called the e-mail server.

If you wish, you can add graphics and use fancy formatting to enhance the appearance of your e-mails. Just click the paper clip icon to attach any type of file or files to an e-mail. The *attached file(s)* is sent with the message when you click the Send button.

Instant Messaging

Instant messaging may be the fastest-growing application on the Internet, especially with the explosion of home networks. Our teenagers sign on to instant messaging whenever they are home. *Instant messaging* differs from e-mail in that messages are sent and displayed in real time (instantly). Although most instant messaging is text-based, the Windows Messenger example in Figure 12-4 shows that it also allows voice or video conversations.

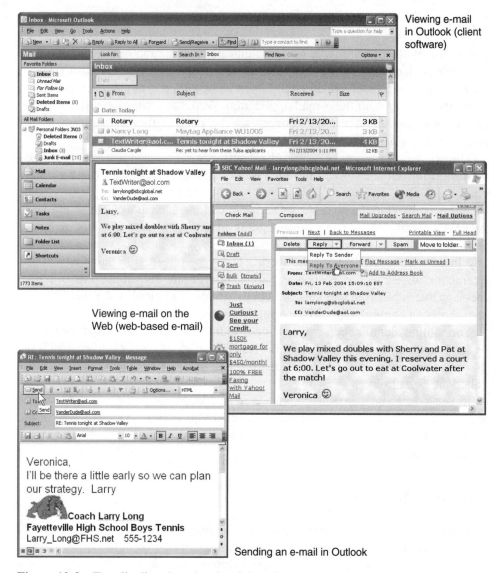

Viewing e-mail in Outlook (client software)

Viewing e-mail on the Web (web-based e-mail)

Sending an e-mail in Outlook

Figure 12-3   E-mail: client-based and web-based

America Online popularized instant messaging, and it quickly became a vehicle for casual conversations. Now, instant messaging is available from several companies, including Microsoft, America Online, Yahoo, ICQ, and others. Each offers instant messaging along with some very enticing services such as file sharing, simultaneous viewing of programs, *whiteboarding* (using a common workspace for drawing), wireless-pager messages, and text messaging to cell phones. Instant messaging is

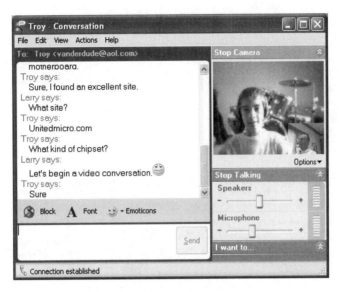

Figure 12-4   Instant messaging: text, voice, and video

rapidly becoming a viable way to communicate. In some companies, instant messaging is emerging as an essential communications tool because it eliminates telephone tag. Telecommuters who work at home, often on home networks, love instant messaging because it gives them the look and feel of being there.

All you have to do to begin instant messaging is sign up with one of the instant messaging services and install its client software. Some companies support a web-based version of instant messaging, as well. Then, you create a contact list with the online identities of those people you wish to track for instant messaging. When you go online, the people in your list, your "buddies" or "colleagues," are notified. People are added and deleted from your real-time list when they sign on or sign off.

Chat

Thousands of topic-specific virtual *chat rooms* are filled with people talking about a broad array of subjects, from personal computers to sailboats. Figure 12-5 shows a conversation in an AOL Harley (Davidson) rider chat room. AOL has a number of organizations that sponsor chat rooms. Most chat rooms are free, such as those on Yahoo and Microsoft Network (MSN), but others may charge an annual fee. The people in the room "talk" to one another by keying in messages that are immediately displayed on the screens of everyone else in the cyberspace room. Chatting has emerged as a favorite pastime of many cybernauts.

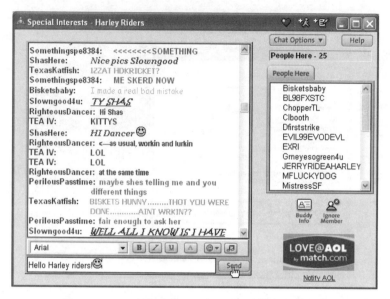

Figure 12-5 A chat room

Chat rooms can be a great pastime if you're willing to accept that participants may not stay on topic. Actually, many chat rooms are pure drivel, no matter what the topic. The chat room shown in Figure 12-5 is typical. You may have to check out several chat rooms before you find one to join that has compatible participants and acceptable language.

Mailing Lists

I subscribe to a *mailing list*, which generates roughly half of all my e-mails. One of my volunteer Rotarian duties is to help place American exchange students to locations throughout the world. The mailing list is a very helpful tool in accomplishing these exchanges. Here is how it works: My international Rotarian counterparts and I subscribe to the Rotary youth exchange mailing list. When I or any of my fellow youth exchange leaders send an e-mail to the list, it is distributed to all mailing list subscribers. When a Rotarian in Japan sends an e-mail to the mailing list that states he has six students who would like to spend a year abroad in Western Europe, his e-mail is viewed by everyone, including those leaders in Portugal, Spain, Belgium, France, Germany, and so on. The response from a leader in France would probably be an e-mail sent directly to the Japanese leader and not through the mailing list.

This mailing list is restricted to youth exchange leaders, but there are thousands of mailing lists on myriad topics that are open to the public. If you wish, you can create one of your own, usually through your ISP's *mailing list server*. To find a topical mailing list, key in the topic and "**mailing list**" in any portal's search box (for example, "**environment**" and "**mailing list**"). The mailing list will have an address similar to your e-mail address (for example, RotaryYE@yahoogroups.com).

Subscribing to a mailing list can be simultaneously informative and overwhelming. Over the years, I've subscribed to a number of interesting mailing lists only to unsubscribe within a short time because of the massive amount of e-mail generated by the list.

Newsgroups

The *newsgroup*, which is analogous to the hallway bulletin board, is another group communications tool. Messages are posted by individuals to a particular newsgroup on a *news server computer*, which may host thousands of newsgroups. There are tens of thousands of newsgroups on almost any imaginable topic, from Elvis Presley sightings (alt.elvis.sighting) to European politics (alt.politics.europe). Some newsgroups have a moderator who owns the newsgroup and regularly reviews postings and, if needed, deletes inappropriate messages. Others are created and have a life of their own. Newsgroups, generally, are open to whoever wants to participate. Major newsgroup topic areas include *alt* (alternative), *news*, *rec* (recreation), *soc* (society), *sci* (science), and *comp* (computers). For example, comp.hardware is the name of a hardware-oriented newsgroup in the computers topic area.

To read and post messages to newsgroups, you use *newsreader client software*, which is built into most Internet browser clients. Some newsgroups are maintained within the Web and newsreader software is not needed. The newsreader lets you read previous postings, respond to them, or add your own messages (see Figure 12-6). The original message and any posted replies to that message are a *thread*.

Blogs and Blogging

The *blog*, short for *web log*, is one of the newest methods of Net-based communication. The blog is simply an online journal that includes the writings of a *blogger*, with the most recent entry at the top of the list. Most of the blog communication is one way, but bloggers always invite and often respond to feedback.

The focus of a blog can be anything. For example, an expectant mother might use a blog, which is simply a web site, to chronicle her thoughts and emotions during

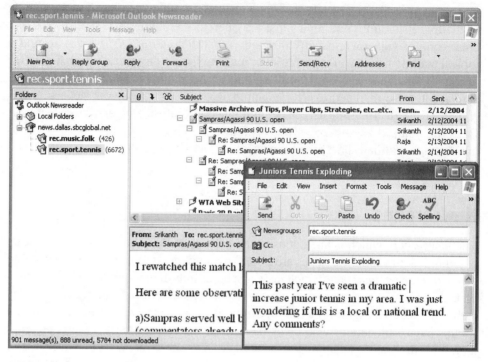

Figure 12-6   Newsgroups

pregnancy. There are blogs on careers, education, cooking, fitness, sports, politics, and everything in between. Political pundits tell us that blogs may have played a significant role in the voting for the 2004 election. You can find thousands of blogs on hobbies from amateur radio to winemaking. To find a topical blog, just key in the topic and "**blog**" in any portal's search box (for example, "**health care**" and "**blog**").

Internet Telephony, or VoIP

Internet telephony has been around for a while. The problem is that the quality of service has not been nearly as good as that which we enjoy on public switched telephone networks that use dedicated voice circuits. Sometimes referred to as voice over IP (VoIP), Internet telephony voice transmissions are sent in the same way everything else traverses the Net—in packets. The obvious advantage to VoIP is that long-distance charges are avoided. Generally, Internet telephony requires that the parties speaking to one another be online and registered with the same directory server. There are, however, services that, for a small charge, will connect you to any phone in the world.

In time, VoIP has the potential to redefine remote voice communication. Certainly, the proliferation of home networks is sure to have an impact on the speed at which VoIP is implemented in homes. The implementation of VoIP on a home network is discussed in Chapter 14.

Webcasting

The Web is based on *pull technology*, where information is delivered to your PC only when you request or "pull" information from a particular site. A number of organizations use *push technology* to *webcast*, or automatically broadcast, news, weather, sports, and other information in real time without being prompted by the user. For example, you can sign up to receive news on a particular topic (information technology, politics, and so on) or from a particular country, weather for your area, stock quotes for selected companies, business news for selected industries, sports news relating to a particular sport (even specific to your teams), and so on. Webcasting organizations, which include some major newspapers, The Weather Channel, sports news services, and brokerage houses, to mention a few, periodically scan available Net sources and then deliver information automatically to your PC for viewing. The always-online PCs on the home network are made to order for webcasting applications.

The Personal Home Page

It might surprise you to find out how easy it is to create your own web page and be a part of cyberspace. A *personal home page* might include personal and family history, an ancestral tree, historical and current photos, vacation summaries (with photos, of course), a holiday newsletter, personal news and/or commentary, links to areas of personal interest, a résumé, and so on. Or, perhaps you might wish to create a presence on the Internet for your child's Boy/Girl Scout troop, the Parent Teacher Organization, or your civic service club. Some people use the Internet to showcase their artistic work (paintings, e-art, original music, and so on).

When content is placed online for public viewing via Internet browsers, the web site is said to have been *published*. Within minutes, you can publish a simple, but informative web page whose content is available to billions of people. There are two common approaches to creating and publishing a simple personal home page:

- **The "free" web site**   Most ISPs, including America Online, allow you to post a personal home page of limited size as part of your usage fee. The "free" means that you probably will have advertisements peppering your home page. All you have to do is select one of the ISP's templates and complete a user-friendly fill-in-the-blank form (see Figure 12-7).

- **The minimal fee–based web site**   A number of *web hosting services* would be delighted to host your web page and keep it free of ads, for a fee, of course. The amount charged varies significantly, depending on expected activity, disk space required, and quality of service needed (from as little as $5 per month). Each of these host sites will have specific instructions as to where and to whom you would send your web content for publishing.

Figure 12-7   A "free" personal home page

Follow these tips and you will present yourself, your club, or whatever in an attractive, informative web page:

- Have a purpose for your web page(s).

- Keep it simple.

- Minimize download time (remember, much of your audience has slow dial-up access).

- Be honest, be courteous, and, most important, be yourself.

- Maintain your web site (once on the Net, it's your obligation to keep your site current).

If you would prefer a more sophisticated web page, you might wish to use *web page design software*, such as Microsoft FrontPage or Adobe GoLive. Or, if you're reluctant to learn another software package, the content for a single page can be created easily with a word processing program, such as Microsoft Word, and then saved as an HTML document. Other office suite programs, such as spreadsheet and presentation software, can export directly to HTML as well. Any HTML document can be posted directly to the Net. All you need to become a player in cyberspace is a few colorful digital images, a little imagination in design, and something to say. If you have these ingredients, you're ten minutes away from a URL and virtual fame in cyberspace.

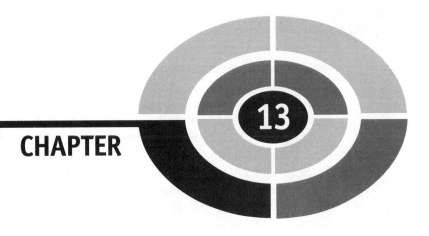

Growing the Network: Entertainment and Beyond

For most of my professional life, networks were made up of computers, PCs/ workstations, and supporting communications equipment. Now, networks are taking on new, exciting roles in the workplace and, especially, at home. The home network is emerging as the nerve center for the *e-home* (electronic home). E-home has displaced smart home as the preferred descriptor.

In the e-home, intelligent electronic devices communicate and cooperate to make our lives easier, safer, less expensive, and more enjoyable. The most popular add-on

application for home networks falls under the umbrella of home entertainment. Many other applications, however, are possible, and in time, security, telephony, lighting, heating/air conditioning, video surveillance, and a host of other applications will be integrated into what we now call a home network.

As digital convergence of computing and consumer electronics marches into our lives, the home network will take on expanded functionality, and eventually, it may be called something else. Perhaps, it will take on some exotic moniker like multifaceted domestic intelligent systems network, or it may just remain a plain old home network. Time will tell. This chapter is intended to expand the scope of your thinking regarding what you can do with home networking.

Networking Entertainment

The home network is redefining our view of the home entertainment center. For decades, the ultimate in a home entertainment center has been a fancy cabinet in the den that houses a TV, the component audio system, and, possibly, a game console. In the future, families with home networks may not have a focal point for their audio/visual entertainment. The home network makes it possible to pipe entertainment in many forms throughout the house via wired and wireless links. The rapid pace of changes in home networking technology is slow compared to the pace of innovations in *digital entertainment,* the umbrella term that is used to describe the ability to manipulate and play digital media over a home network.

This section talks about how computers, home networks, a variety of special-function network devices, and a plethora of entertainment services are changing our concept of home entertainment. Home digital entertainment implies using the LAN to enhance the multimedia experience and enable online gaming. For now, home networking multimedia encompasses television, radio, audio (mainly music), images, and video.

Our television experience is on course for radical change. For example, we'll be able to watch our favorite shows at our convenience—without commercials. The new radio is delivered over the Internet and includes stations from all over the world. Of course, you can still play your CDs on a CD player, but you may prefer playing songs stored on PCs around the house, where they are conveniently organized by song, genre, and artist. The family photos and videos will be online and readily accessible for viewing from any PC, the home theater, or a portable wireless device. Gamers can match skills against each other on the home network and others on the Internet.

Home Digital Entertainment in Practice

Sometimes I believe that digital entertainment applications have grown out of control at the Long place. It's not so much that we're audio/visual/gaming freaks, it's more that our collective interests span the gamut of A/V and gaming gadgetry. When something new hits the market, one of us wants to try it. The result of this curiosity is that we have plenty of places to play the movies, listen to music, and view images/video. Each family member's PC is on the Longnet, our home network, and has one or two large flat panel monitors suitable for viewing movies or anything else. We have plenty of TVs, but usually only the home theater's media hub has a link to the home network. However, the media hub is small and wireless and is easily moved to enable playing of multimedia files stored on the home network on A/V equipment in other rooms. All PCs and the home theater have 5.1, 6.1, or 7.1 sound systems with powered subwoofers—3000 watts of sound in all.

Do we take advantage of all of these entertainment resources? Amazingly, yes. On any given evening, Brady might be in his room watching a movie downloaded the night before from Starz (a subscription movie service), Troy might be in the home theater playing Halo 2 with friends from around town, Nancy might be reviewing the photos from last weekend's getaway in the Ozark Mountains, and I might be finishing my workday while listening to songs from our online music library. We no longer have an entertainment center. We have a home that's filled with entertainment options in many different places, all made possible by the Longnet.

Digital Entertainment Technology

Some day in the not-too-distant future, all digital media—photos, videos, radio, music, and television—will flow through our PCs and over our home networks. The source of much of these media is an every-growing number of entertainment services being packaged for delivery over the Internet. The universal availability of broadband Internet access at reasonable prices and the growing popularity of home networks are prompting an avalanche of innovation and offerings in digital entertainment.

There are a variety of solutions to integrating digital entertainment applications, including TV, radio, still and video imagery, and movies, with home networks. Each solution offers different capabilities and features, and each requires additional hardware and software. The media hub, TiVo and DVRs, Windows XP Media Center Edition 2005 and the Media Center PC, and other related hardware/software options are introduced in the following section to show you some of the currently available ways you can leverage your home network to open new vistas in whole home entertainment.

NOTE *We truly are in the embryonic stages of home digital entertainment. The demand and the technology are in place; however, there is some reluctance on the part of content producers (primarily the movie and recording industries) to open the flood gates before all copyright issues are resolved. This ideological tug of war between content producers and consumers is being debated publicly and in court rooms throughout the land.*

The Media Hub

The *media hub* is a network device that serves as an interface between a home network and consumer devices, such as TVs and stereos, that play music, display images, and show video/movies. As is the case with so many network devices, the industry has yet to adopt a common name for this device. Some companies call it an *entertainment gateway.* Here are the names that some companies give their media hubs: Media Center Extender (Linksys and Hewlett-Packard), PRISMIQ MediaPlayer (PRISMIQ), MediaLounge (D-Link), Media Adapter (Linksys), and Connected DVD Player (Gateway). The last of these, which doubles as a DVD player, links our family media files on our media server (Brady's PC) to the Longnet.

The media hub connects to the LAN via Ethernet or Wireless-G/B, and it connects to the audio/visual devices using standard audio/visual cables (composite, component, S-video, fiber optic, and coaxial). In a nutshell, the media hub enables the streaming of digital media files stored on PCs in your home network to play on your TVs, audio systems, and/or home theaters.

Once you have a home network in place, setting up a media hub will normally involve these four steps:

1. Connect the hub to the home network. The media hub will have a wireless network adapter, an Ethernet adapter, or both. If the connection is wireless, then you will need to enter the appropriate settings (IP address, WEP, and so on) in step 2.

2. Install the software that accompanies the media hub on the PC that you designate to be the media server (the PC that contains the media files). The media server program normally will load automatically when the media server PC boots up.

3. Use the media server program to import the media files (pictures, music, and video) that you wish to make available to the media hub. These shared files are presented on the TV's/home theater's onscreen menu.

4. Connect the media hub to the audio/video system (TV, stereo system, home theater, and so on).

Figure 13-1 illustrates the relationship between the server PC, the media hub, and the home theater. When we are ready to play media on the Longnet to the home theater, we select the media hub as the input device on the A/V multichannel receiver and the media hub's onscreen menu interface is projected onto the screen (Figure 13-1). All media hubs have remote controls that let you navigate through menu options displayed on the TV/home theater screen (My Music, My Pictures, and My Video). A representative stack of home theater A/V equipment is shown in Figure 13-1, including an Internet-linked Xbox game console (via Ethernet bridge), VCR with a TV tuner, a media hub, and an A/V multichannel receiver. All A/V input and output (speakers and TV/projector) are connected to the multichannel receiver.

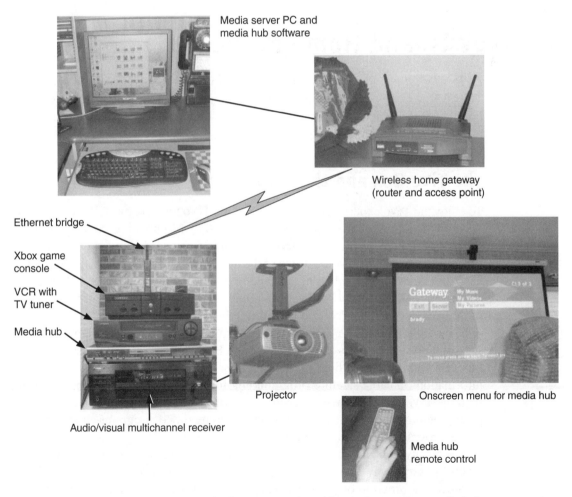

Figure 13-1   Wireless link between the home network and home theater via a media hub

The media hub can give new life to media files, which usually require people to crowd around a PC with its small monitor or listen to music on speakers set up for a single listener. Over the years, our family has taken thousands of digital photographs, including about 300 on a backpacking trek in the Rocky Mountains. Showing these images on the seven-foot screen in the home theater gives us that feeling that we're back in the Rockies.

Some media hubs enable the streaming of premium subscription services over the Internet, as well as local media files. For example, MediaLouge gives you the capability to stream Radio@AOL (commercial free radio), Napster (one million tracks of music), or Rhapsody (radio and music).

TiVo, DVRs, and Home Networks

DVRs (digital video recorders) are slowly redefining the way we watch television. The DVR, which is just a special-function computer with a hard disk, was developed by TiVo. TiVo, which was founded in 1997, isn't the only DVR company, but it has had the greatest influence on the way we watch television.

The TiVo Box and the TiVo Service

To enjoy the TiVo experience, you will need the TiVo box and the TiVo service. The TiVo box is a DVR that lets you record from 40 to 140 hours of your favorite TV shows (see Figure 13-2). The number of hours of recorded programming that can be stored to disk depends on the size of the hard disk. The TiVo box with the smaller hard disk sells for around $100, and the one with the high-capacity disk sells for about $300. As the cost of hardware continues to dive, I would imagine that the cost of these devices will be reduced accordingly.

The second part of the TiVo experience is the TiVo service. At this writing, the subscription service costs about $13 a month. Each day, the TiVo box uses a dial-up link (via your telephone line) or your home network's Internet access to download information on cable/satellite programming to the hard disk. Subscribers interact with the TiVo box's onscreen user interface via a remote control to watch live TV, pick programs they wish to record, select prerecorded programs, and view the online programming guide (see Figure 13-3).

The beauty of having a DVR is that you have the capability to view television in much the same way you do a DVD. You can pause, fast-forward, or rewind any recorded TV program on the hard disk. You can play the program in slow motion. You can also pause and replay portions of live programming. This is particularly

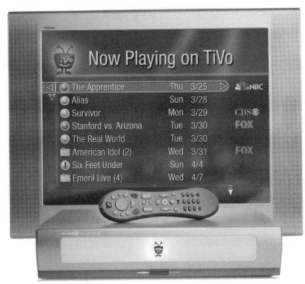

Courtesy of TiVo

Figure 13-2   The TiVo box and its remote control

handy if you enjoy watching sports. After pausing and/or replaying video segments, you can play what you have missed or jump to the live broadcast.

TiVo on the Home Network

The TiVo box can be linked to a home network for expanded functionality. For example, the online scheduling feature lets you search the programming guide and

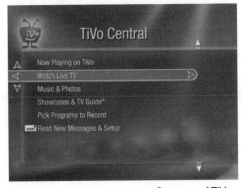

Courtesy of TiVo

Figure 13-3   The main menu for TiVo

schedule programs to be recorded from any PC with an Internet connection. Also, the TiVo box can double as a media hub, giving subscribers the flexibility to view more than live or recorded TV. To link a TiVo box to a LAN, connect either a wired or wireless network adapter to one of its USB ports. From there, the setup is similar to that of media hubs. Once online, you can use your TiVo remote control to share photos (see Figure 13-4) and music through your TV, audio system, and/or home theater.

In the future, TiVo plans to expand its services to encompass Internet-based entertainment and the use of home networks. For example, TiVo users can download movies and music over the Internet from content partners. Another feature is TiVoToGo, which lets you upload recorded programs from the TiVo box to a notebook PC on the home network. The transfer of an hour of programming takes only a few minutes at Wireless-G and Fast Ethernet speeds.

Hacking TiVos

As I mentioned earlier, the TiVo box is a computer. "Hacking TiVo" has emerged as a popular pastime for this Linux-based (the operating system) computer. Hacking is the term used by those people who modify TiVo to enhance its capabilities. The most popular "hack" is to increase the amount of disk storage. For example, hackers can add a 100GB hard disk to get an additional 100-plus hours of TV programming storage. Other hacks include software that extends TV content to other PCs on a home network.

TiVo neither encourages nor discourages hacking. TiVo is reluctant to add some features that hackers enjoy because of copyright issues, but the company recognizes that some customers will go to great lengths to get expanded functionality. They

Courtesy of TiVo

Figure 13-4   Viewing photos on a network via TiVo

also recognize that hackers may be blazing the trail for the future of home entertainment.

CAUTION *When you open your TiVo box to hack it, you void the warranty. Make sure you're fully aware of the risk before you attempt to add some unauthorized features to your TiVo box.*

Windows XP Media Center 2005

You don't have to own a TiVo box to enjoy TiVo-like capabilities. Microsoft and several other companies are offering unprecedented choices for digital entertainment in the home. Let's talk first about the Microsoft solution, the *Windows XP Media Center Edition 2005* operating system, which is abbreviated as *Windows XP MCE.* This newest version of Windows is essentially Windows XP Professional with an additional application called *Media Center,* which gives you the capability to consolidate all of your digital entertainment. The Media Center application gives a modern multimedia-ready PC the ability to let people choose how and where they enjoy their digital media. It also gives them the flexibility to customize their digital entertainment experiences, which can include viewing videos, photos, recorded TV, and live TV, as well as listening to locally stored and Internet-based music (see Figure 13-5).

Courtesy of Microsoft

Figure 13-5   The Start menu for multimedia applications on a Media Center PC

The Media Center PC

I would imagine that all successors to Windows XP will have the Media Center capabilities of Windows XP MCE. For now, however, if you want these capabilities, you will have to purchase a new *Media Center PC,* which comes with the new operating system. This version of Windows is not available as an upgrade to Windows XP Home Edition or Windows XP Professional.

The Media Center PC, which is available from most major PC vendors (see Figure 13-6), is configured with the hardware needed to run all forms of home digital entertainment. That means it has a high-capacity hard disk to record many hours of television programming, a powerful processor to handle multimedia tasks, a high-end graphics card for the best possible visual presentation of the media, a quality sound card, and a TV tuner card. The piece of hardware, however, that sets it apart from the rest of the PCs in the store is the remote control that allows you to navigate through onscreen menus from the comfort of your favorite living room chair.

NOTE *The reason Windows XP Media Center Edition 2005 is available only on Media Center PCs is its stringent hardware requirements. By limiting the use of the software to PCs that meet all hardware requirements, Microsoft can avoid the nightmare that might ensue if millions of people upgraded their current version of Windows only to find that their systems fell short of the very exacting hardware requirements. I expect these hardware requirements to emerge as the de facto standards for off-the-shelf multimedia PCs in the near future.*

Courtesy of Hewlett-Packard

Figure 13-6   A Media Center PC with a remote control

An alternative to the Media Center PC is the Digital Entertainment Center (see Figure 13-7). The Digital Entertainment Center is essentially a Media Center PC that is packaged to fit within an existing entertainment system (amplifier/tuner, DVD player, VCR, Xbox, and so on). The system's monitor is the connected TV or home theater screen.

CAUTION   Not all Media Center PCs do it all. Some low-end Media Center PCs (around the $1000 price tag) may not have a TV tuner. If you want TV and DVR capabilities, you will need the TV tuner.

The Media Center Extender

The Media Center Extender (see Figure 13-8) is the media hub for Media Center PCs. The network device lets you take advantage of your home network's connectivity to extend the Media Center PC experience to televisions throughout the house or to a home theater. It lets you enjoy digital entertainment where, when, and how you want it. You don't have to have a PC in the living room to enjoy access to a plethora of media resources.

NOTE   The link between the Media Center PC and the Media Center Extender must be fast enough to handle video and recorded TV. This is true for all media hubs. Wireless-G at 54 Mbps and Fast Ethernet at 100 Mbps are fine. Wireless-B and basic Ethernet will work for pictures and music, but they don't have enough capacity for video or TV. For example, 22 Mbps is needed to transmit the signal stream for high definition television (HDTV). If a wireless network device has Microsoft's Windows XP Media Center Edition Logo Certification, you can be confident that it will handle TV and other transmissions that require high-speed links.

Courtesy of Hewlett-Packard

Figure 13-7   A Digital Entertainment Center

Courtesy of Linksys

Figure 13-8 Media Center Extender used with a Media Center PC on a home network

The Media Center Extender works like any media hub, except it works only with Media Center PCs. Connect it to your audio/visual equipment using standard A/V cables. Use the remote control to interact with the unit via the onscreen menu to play any multimedia files stored on the Media Center PC, including pictures, music, videos, and recorded TV programs. Someone on the Media Center PC can browse through the family music library while the rest of the family watches a movie using the Media Center Extender.

NOTE *If you already have an Xbox console in your home theater and you were planning on purchasing a Media Center Extender, please wait. You can save a bunch of money by purchasing a Media Center Extender for Xbox, a packaged software product that runs as a game on an Xbox. The software, which is sold with a remote control, gives the Xbox full Media Center Extender functionality.*

Digital Entertainment Around the Home

Ideally, people want to choose how and where they are able to enjoy the various forms of digital entertainment. And, they want the experience to be readily accessible and simple to achieve. The Media Center PC and its operating system coupled with a home network give you TiVo-like capabilities and all of the features of any media hub. With one or more Media Center PCs on a LAN, you have the power to reinvent home entertainment.

My Music

The My Music feature of Windows XP MCE gives you the ability to organize songs into an easily accessible music library that can be played on your stereo system, your home theater, portable wireless devices (a PDA or a notebook PC), and even your car MP3 player. Use the remote control to play a music CD or copy its content to your music library. You can also download digital music, create customized playlists (see Figure 13-9), and, of course, play songs on your audio systems. You can also edit music album details.

My Music picks up live FM or Internet radio, too. Use Media Center to tune into local FM radio stations, or you can find just about whatever you want on Internet radio stations from around the world—talk shows, comedy, rock, classical, alternative jazz, and much more. If you wish, you can pause, rewind, and fast forward through FM broadcasts (the last of these assumes you have paused or rewound a transmission).

My Pictures

Digital cameras have created a new era in photography. The crisp, vibrant pictures that result are essentially free and can be viewed on any type of electronic display. Moreover, they are instantly available for viewing—no developing or printing required. Our family's photography habits changed dramatically when we purchased our first digital camera. They changed again when we integrated our home theater into the home network. Now, we routinely take a couple dozen photos at events—a tennis match, an awards ceremony, a party, or whatever. Then, we upload them to the media server PC and relive the event on the big screen in the home theater, often on the same day.

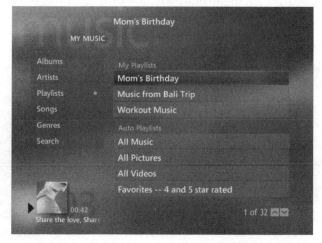

Courtesy of Microsoft

Figure 13-9   My Music: My Playlist

Windows XP MCE's My Picture feature gives you the capability to organize and view images stored on your Media Center PC on your TV or home theater (see Figure 13-10). If you have a wireless home network, the pictures are also available for viewing on portable devices, such as PDAs and notebook PCs.

My Videos

The My Videos feature is the Windows XP MCE response to the growing legion of families who now own and use digital video cameras. Digital videos are easily uploaded to a PC's hard disk. My Video lets you recall and play videos stored on hard disk or DVD on your PC or home theater. If your home network has a wireless access point, video can be played on portable wireless devices, such as notebook PCs and PDAs. This feature can also be used to view a live video feed from a home webcam or security camera. The My Videos interface is shown in Figure 13-11. Use My Videos to play downloaded HD (high definition) videos and enjoy amazingly clear resolutions.

My TV

The integration of TV into personal computing and home networking is the last step and, possibly, the most important step in spreading digital entertainment throughout the home. Already, people in 5 percent of the 120 million homes in America watch TV on their PCs.

It's not unusual for each member of a family of four to watch 25 or more hours of TV each week, or 100 collective hours of TV. Are they watching what they want,

Courtesy of Microsoft

Figure 13-10 My Pictures: menu and an image being displayed while a song is playing

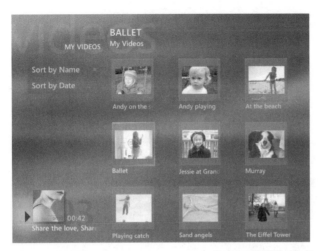

Courtesy of Microsoft

Figure 13-11   My Videos: menu and selection screen

when they want, and where they want? Probably not. My TV can give each family member the flexibility to watch TV exactly the way he or she wants it. The My TV feature has the potential to have a tremendous impact on how we spend our home entertainment hours, and the people at Microsoft (and other companies) are keenly aware of this. The General Manager of Microsoft's Windows eHome Division, Joe Belfiore, said that "As far as we're concerned, TV watching is the new mission critical application for Windows."

My TV gives the Media Center PC TiVo-like capabilities (see the earlier discussion on TiVo). Essentially, your PC becomes a DVR that can record TV programs on your command. Some people use the term *personal video recorder (PVR)* to refer to a PC with DVR capabilities. One big difference between TiVo and My TV is that, with My TV, you don't have to pay for a subscription service. The onscreen program guide (see Figure 13-12) is made available to Windows MCE users at no charge. Watch, pause, replay, or record live TV. It's relatively easy to set My TV to record a program for an entire season. You can even set My TV to record movies that include your favorite actors. Watch one TV show while recording another. If you are at the office and forget to record the big game, you can do so from any PC with Internet access. Once you've recorded shows, play them on any PC on the home network, or if you have a Media Center Extender, you can play them on any TV or the home theater.

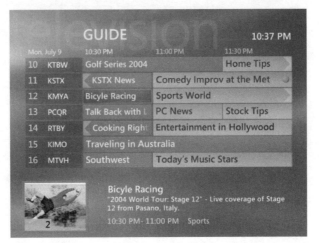

Courtesy of Microsoft

Figure 13-12   My TV: onscreen program guide

Microsoft has partnered with a number of third-party services that deliver premium digital media over the Internet via Media Center. For example, use My Music to play music from Napster. My TV handles video-on-demand services such as MovieLink and Cinemanow. As Media Center PC gains momentum, expect the number and variety of third-party services to grow rapidly.

Media Center Applications Without Windows MCE

With the trend toward digital convergence in music, photography, video, and television, PCs have emerged as warehouses for digital media. In 2004, about one million homes have some level of integration between digital entertainment and personal computers/ home networks. By 2010, analysts are projecting this number will be between 20 and 30 million. Microsoft and other companies recognize this trend and have made e-home entertainment a priority. Now, several companies are developing hardware and software that can turn any PC into an entertainment device and a home network into a vehicle for distributing entertainment throughout the home.

If you're not ready to spring for a new Media Center PC, but you want its neat digital entertainment applications on your home network, you now have several very workable alternatives. SnapStream Media, Pinnacle Systems, and ATI offer integrated home entertainment solutions with features that are similar to those of Windows MCE and the Media Center Extender. Any one of these companies offers a family of products that can leverage the entertainment value of your PCs and home network (see Figure 13-13). For a few hundred dollars, you can have live or recorded television throughout your home and a music jukebox wherever you have audio equipment. Your home videos and photos can be accessed from any PC and the home theater. The solutions also rely on an Internet-based TV programming guide and can interface with third-party movie and music services.

There are several major differences between the Windows MCE/Media Center PC e-home solution and non-Microsoft solutions. The most important difference is that the latter do not require a Media Center PC, which includes all the necessary software (Windows MCE) and the required hardware. To implement a Pinnacle Systems or SnapStream Media solution, you will probably need to install a quality TV tuner, either an external USB 2.0 device or a PCI card, which includes a remote control. You may need to upgrade your video card as well, to meet the software's minimum hardware requirements. Because the Media Center Extender works only with Window MCE, you will need to purchase a compatible media hub, sometimes called a *remote media player*, if you wish to extend the media resources on your PC to rooms without PCs. The media player is connected to the home network via a wired or wireless line.

The winds of home digital entertainment are continually shifting, but you can bet that, in time, Microsoft will emerge as a major player in the software that drives this killer app. Only the fickle IT gods know whether Microsoft, TiVo, SnapStream, Pinnacle Systems, ATI, or some other company will survive the scrutiny of the digital entertainment marketplace.

Courtesy of SnapStream

Figure 13-13   SnapStream Media's Beyond TV 3: Onscreen programming guide and live TV in-home theater

Gaming and the Home Network

It's not unusual to see more retail shelf space devoted to gaming software for PCs and game controllers, such as Xbox, GameCube, or Playstation 2, than to all other software combined. Gaming is not just a hobby or activity to gaming enthusiasts, it is an experience. That's why online gaming has emerged as one of the fastest-growing applications for home networking. No longer is the game limited to how many controllers can be attached to a PC or game console or to the size of the display. Now, gamers can play against others in the house over the home network or can play against *netizens* (citizens of the Internet) from around the globe.

What You Need for Internet Gaming

What you need to enjoy Internet gaming depends on whether you are doing PC-based gaming or using a game console, such as Xbox. For PC-based gaming, you need the software for a multiplayer game, such as Warcraft, and broadband Internet access. If you have a home network, you and your friends can play the game locally, with each person setting up play at one of the PCs on the LAN.

NOTE *Realistically, the lag time resulting from slow dial-up access puts the player at too great a disadvantage to be competitive, so virtually all online play is at broadband speeds. Lag is not good when you're trying to block an opponent's blow to your character's head with a sword.*

Let's use Xbox Live, the most popular online gaming console, as an example to discuss what you need for console-base multiplayer gaming. To enjoy Xbox gaming with gamers in cyberspace, you need the following:

- **The Xbox video game system**   The game console, which can double as a DVD player, is relatively inexpensive for what you get (the expense of online gaming is in the cost of the games).

- **Broadband Internet access**   Split-second timing is critical during online gaming, so Broadband service is a requirement to play Xbox games.

- **Ethernet link to the Internet**   The Xbox has a built-in Ethernet adapter that enables a link to a home network. Many gamers just plug their Xbox directly into an extra Ethernet port on the home gateway/router. Others connect it to an available port on an Ethernet switch. The wireless connection is made possible by a *wireless game adapter,* which is just an Ethernet bridge by another name (see Figure 13-14).

Figure 13-14   An Xbox game console is linked to the home network via a wireless Ethernet bridge (middle top)

- **A multiplayer online game**   Games such as Halo and Halo 2 are designed for multiplayer gaming over the Internet.

- **A subscription to the gaming service**   Gamers purchase an annual subscription to Xbox Live, which lets them log on to the Xbox Live hosting service. There, gamers can find tens of thousands of people playing any of over 100 multiplayer games—all day, every day.

Playing the Game

Nearly all video games have a *single-player* feature. This is where you play against or with the computer. The trend in gaming, however, is to have *multiplayer games* where the gamer plays with or against other players. Players can have multiple controllers on a PC or a game console, but increasingly, gamers are playing online with people on a home network or people in cyberspace (see Figure 13-15). You can play games with netizens you've never met before, or you can limit the game to your friends, who may be playing at their homes. Sometimes, gamers have "LAN parties," where players bring their PCs (or game consoles) to one location so that they can enjoy higher connection speeds and personal camaraderie.

Many multiplayer gamers choose to game from their own home over the Internet. In Internet games, you can join a game, host a game, or just play on your own with the information on the Internet. There are scores of games, and each one offers a variety of gaming options. Many offer voice communication. Players wear headsets so that the entire team can communicate verbally while attempting to complete the mission. Voice communication during gaming is becoming increasingly sophisticated.

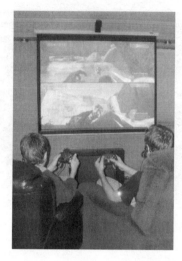

Figure 13-15 Halo 2 being played online via an Xbox on a home network

For example, some games enable proximity communication that limits the conversation to those gamers in the same area of gaming cyberspace. Most of the real-time talk involves strategizing, but the successful combatant will often engage in a little trash talking, too.

VoIP: Internet Telephone

Voice over IP (VoIP) refers to the ability to make telephone calls over the Internet. Yes, we can make Internet-based local and international calls using the same telephones that we have used for decades. And yes, VoIP offers the same features as traditional phones, such as caller ID, call waiting, and voice mail. Plus, VoIP's Internet connection gives us a host of new features, such as Locate Me (call other locations), Personal Conferencing (with up to nine other people), and Do Not Disturb. With most major providers of conventional telephone services, such as AT&T and SBC, offering or planning to offer VoIP services, it's apparent that the Voice over IP bandwagon is beginning to roll.

There are two primary differences between VoIP and conventional telephone services. First, VoIP uses broadband Internet to transmit calls rather than the world-wide telephone network. Second, VoIP service is less expensive, primarily because the rates for long distance and international calling are considerably less than for traditional landlines.

So, how does VoIP work? When you make a traditional telephone call, a switched network connects you to the dialed party over a dedicated voice-grade line. You hold that line until the call is completed. This approach wastes the phone network's transmission capabilities. A VoIP Internet call is transmitted like everything else on the Internet, as packets of information with IP addresses, thus making better use of the transmission media. Here's what you need to switch from a tradition telephone setup to VoIP:

- **Broadband Internet access**   Most VoIP uses DSL or cable modem Internet access.

- **A VoIP phone adapter**   The phone adapter in Figure 13-16 is an Ethernet device that is linked to the home network via a regular patch cable to any Ethernet port (usually in the home gateway or a switch). The adapter normally will have a couple of RJ-11 ports for connecting phones and fax machines. The ports can have different telephone numbers.

- **VoIP service**   You sign up for VoIP service just as you would conventional telephone service. Many telephone companies now offer both traditional switched telephone service and VoIP service.

Connect the VoIP phone adapter to a home network with broadband Internet access, connect the phone(s) to the adapter, set up the VoIP service, and you're ready to make calls over the Internet. When you talk into your telephone, an analog voice signal is sent to the phone adapter, where it is digitized and routed over the Internet to a destination phone adapter. That adapter converts the signal back to analog before transmitting it to the destination telephone.

Courtesy of Linksys

Figure 13-16   A VoIP phone adapter

> **NOTE** *The cellular phones of the future may have both GSM, the technology used for cellular telephones, and Wireless-G capabilities. This will enable them to switch seamlessly between the two wireless transmission technologies. When you're driving around town, your cell phone will use the GSM transmission towers, but back home, it will switch to VoIP using a Wireless-G link to your home network, thus relieving the pressure on the wireless telephone system and giving you a better connection and an expanded calling area.*

Video Monitoring and Surveillance

Put a new set of eyes in and around your house with a wireless network video camera. Video cameras like the one in Figure 13-17 can be placed anywhere within the range of your AP to send back video and sound to any PC on the home network. Connect the camera with Ethernet as well. Use the camera to monitor the baby in the crib and the kids in the playroom. Check out what's happening in the backyard or the pool area. The form factor of the video camera in Figure 13-17 lets you mount it on a wall or ceiling, or you can place it on a desktop.

You can see whatever the camera sees from any PC on the LAN. The image can be viewed full screen or in a window alongside your work. There's little chance that the audio/video feed could be intercepted, because it is shielded by the router's

Courtesy of Linksys

Figure 13-17 Wireless network video camera

security features. However, if you wish to view the video from any PC with Internet access, you can do that, too. You also have the option of sharing the video stream with friends and family.

Use it as a security camera to view and capture live images from one or more locations around the house. When placed in security mode, the Linksys camera in Figure 13-17 can send a message and a short video to several e-mail addresses whenever it detects motion. You can then log onto the live video stream, if needed. If you wish, you can record a continuous A/V stream to your hard disk, or you can do so according to a preset schedule.

As you see, a home network can be much more than a network of PCs. It can extend the reach of all forms of home digital entertainment to every corner of the house. It can enhance multiplayer gaming experience by extending it over the home network and into cyberspace. Voice over IP has emerged as a viable alternative to the conventional telephone system and its prices, further leveraging your investment in a home network. Relatively inexpensive video cameras give the network life as it transmits live imagery from in and around the house. These applications are just a peek at the ultimate potential of a home network. Over the next few years, it will be fun to watch innovators roll out exciting new home networking applications.

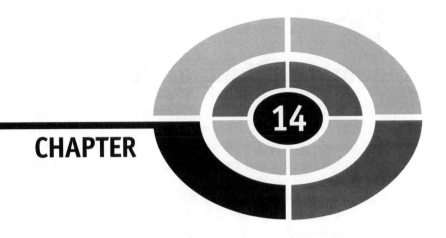

The Home Office and Home Networking

A home office is a small business office—it just happens to be at home. The ubiquitous use of *SOHO (small office/home office)* reminds us of their similarities. This chapter gives you insight into things you'll need to think about if at least one node on your home network is a home office. If you don't have a home office or are not interested in telework, you can skip this chapter.

Telework: Working at Home

One of the byproducts of the personal computing/home networking revolution is a clear trend toward more and more people working at home. Forty-five million or so people in America already work at least part time at home. Over 15 million *teleworkers* work at home full time. The umbrella term used for teleworkers and self-employed people who use the tools of personal computing, home networking, and the Internet to accomplish their jobs is *telework*. The trend to telework is changing the way we do business and having a dramatic affect on demographics. Telework frees people to spread out to small towns, the suburbs, the Caribbean Islands, or wherever they wish to live and work.

Today's networked environment is very accommodating for telework. A typical telework day for me involves communication and sharing with colleagues in at least three different locations in the United States and, often, with people in other countries. Most of my personal communication and all of the results of my work are electronic. This working scenario is possible in many professions.

Employers are beginning to encourage telework because studies consistently show increases in teleworker productivity of up to 20 percent. If the soothsayers are even half right, the telework movement is on course to turn office tradition upside down. Already, every other worker at IBM does telework, at least part time.

Creating an Environment for Telework

The home network is an integral part of any formula for successful telework. The home office PC is more than just another node on the home network because its business orientation presents a different set of challenges. I've been working out of my home for 25 years. The following sections present some of the home office maxims that evolved from that experience.

The Home Office Is a Place of Business

The office where you do your work is a place of business, whether at corporate headquarters or at home, and must be treated as such. My PC is dedicated to me and my applications. I've found that the best way to maintain a separation between the home office and the rest of the home is to ensure that the spouse and kids have everything they want on their PCs.

Choose a Good Location

Where you locate your home office can be the difference between a good and bad telework experience. These are the primary considerations for choosing a home office location: having a sufficient amount of space, having a separation between the office and the living areas, having a space that can be made physically secure, and having an ample number of electrical outlets and circuits. It's possible that a corner in the master bedroom might be preferable to an open bonus room or the extra bedroom just off the kitchen and next to the playroom.

A Good Workplace Design Yields Dividends

The beauty of having a home office is that it can be custom-designed to fit your personality and work habits. Remember, this is the place where you will spend about a third of every working day. I've been sensitive to the impact of good workplace design on productivity and health and have adopted many tools and concepts that can help me enjoy a better working environment. For example, I have a comfortable chair with a lot of flexibility in adjustment, wrist pads, a foot rest, directed lighting, a wireless mouse, dual monitors, a speakerphone, wraparound desks, and so on. You may not find having a window with a view featured in books on the ergonomic workplace, but I'm more productive when I take an occasional 15-second visual minibreak.

The Home Office Is Self-Contained

The home office PC or PCs will have a link to the home network and the Internet, and you probably will use one of the family PCs for backup. Mostly, however, the home office should be self-contained; that is, the home office PC(s) should be configured with needed peripheral devices, such as a dedicated all-in-one printer (fax, scan, and copy) and office software. Everything you need to do your job should be in the office, including the basic tools of business (stapler, telephone, file cabinet, and so on) and related supplies (paper, envelopes, and so on).

Give the Home Office Priority on the LAN

Network reliability and speed should be priorities for a home office. Because a wired Fast Ethernet connection is faster and more reliable than a Wireless-G link, I recommend that your home office PC be connected directly to the home gateway with Cat 5e/6 cabling. If wired cabling is not feasible, then you should do what you

can to ensure a strong wireless signal and the maximum data rate. If adjustments to wireless devices do not give you the desired data rate, then you may need to supplement your wireless network with a signal booster (see Chapter 6).

Security Must Be Maintained

At the top of the list of concerns for a company whose employees do telework is ensuring that company data is not at risk. A connected home office may have access to sensitive company information, making network and physical security important considerations. Security considerations are discussed in detail in Chapter 10.

File Management for the Networked Home Office

Practicing good file management can make life a little easier for the teleworker. The most important aspects of file management for the home office are organization, security, and backup.

File Organization

There are as many ways to organize files into folders and subfolders as there are teleworkers. Any file organization, especially in a home office, should facilitate backup of files. Backup can be made easier if you place your user files/folders in one of four folders within My Documents:

- **Active folder**   Create this active folder to house all active folders and files, except those containing disk space–eating images and video files. An active folder is one in which files/subfolders are added/deleted. An active file is one that you might at some time modify.

- **Static folder**   Create a static folder so that when you wrap up a project or end an association with an organization, you can move the associated files/folders to this folder for permanent backup. You would never modify the files/folders in the static folder.

- **My Pictures and My Videos folders**   I recommend you treat image and video files differently because of their large size and the fact that you do not modify them. A good organization for files in the standard Windows folders, My Pictures and My Videos, is by month within year.

By separating the static files/folders from active ones, you can substantially reduce the time and disk space required to perform a complete backup of volatile files/folders. Image folders are best organized by month within year so that only those files added since the last backup are backed up.

Securing Files from Unauthorized Access

The files on a networked home office PC can be vulnerable to unauthorized access from other PCs on the home network and, possibly, by family members and friends who might wander into the home office. Besides applying the security measures discussed in Chapter 10, there are several things you can do to minimize the possibility of your important work files being compromised.

- **Set up a password-protected user account**   Having a password-protected user account for the home office PC provides an important layer of security between access to this data and the overly curious child, guest, or intruder. To set up a user account, click Control Panel | User Accounts | Create A New Account. You will need to choose a password when you set up the account.

- **Set up a screen saver password**   Once you have logged on, whoever sits down at your office PC has access to your files—unless you password-protect your screen saver. To do this, right-click on the desktop to show the Display Properties dialog box. Check the "On resume, password-protect" box to require that the user account password must be entered to resume the desktop display.

- **Place sensitive files in a protected compressed (zipped) folder**   If you have created particularly sensitive files and you wish to give them another layer of protection, you can move them to a compressed folder. To create a compressed folder in Windows Explorer, right-click in the files area and then choose New | Compressed (Zipped) Folder. Drag the files you wish to compress into the compressed folder. To password-protect the compressed folder, double-click the folder and then choose File | Add A Password in the menu bar.

File Backup

The most critical component of any teleworker's PC is its hard disk, because it contains the files. You invest many hours, weeks, even years, in creating these files—so protect them! If you follow good backup procedures, these files can be restored in the wake of a disaster.

Anyone who has ever used a PC for any length of time has lost one or more critical files. It happens. It doesn't have to be something as exotic and chaotic as a disk crash (a scratched disk) or an attack from a malicious virus; sometimes it's the result of a couple of errant keystrokes. If you wish to survive and thrive as a teleworker, you will need to adhere to rigorous system backup and recovery procedures.

The frequency with which you back up user files depends on the level of risk you're willing to accept. Typically, teleworkers back up volatile work files (those you modify frequently) on a daily basis and do a full backup every week. Because the home office PC(s) is on a network, the most convenient way to back up files/folders is to copy them to the hard disk on another PC on the home network.

The typical home network will have plenty of hard disk capacity for active and backup files; however, if you feel you need more storage capacity, it's relatively easy to add another high-capacity hard disk to one of the PCs. The additional hard disk can be either an internal hard drive or an external USB 2.0 hard drive. USB 2.0 hard disks also can be linked directly to a home network via a network disk server device in the same way that a printer is connected via a print server. On the Longnet, Nancy's PC has two hard disks, one of which is a high-capacity *backup server* for all PCs on the Longnet.

The backup procedure shown in Figure 14-1 is one approach that teleworkers might use. A full backup is done every Monday to the backup server on the home network. Only *incremental backups* (files that are modified on a given day) are made for each of the other weekdays. If all files are lost on Friday, the full backup from Monday is restored to the hard disk, and then incremental backups are restored for Tuesday through Thursday. An alternative approach would be to perform a *differential backup* (files that have been modified since the last full backup) each day rather than an incremental backup. The restore process is easier and faster when you perform differential backups, incremental backups require less storage space.

Even though your daily/weekly backup is to a hard drive on the network's backup server, it's still a good idea to do monthly backups to rewritable CD or DVD discs that can be stored in off-site locations (see Figure 14-1). Always keep two sets of backup discs, a *first generation backup* (the most recent) and a *second generation backup,* and then alternate between the two each month. The backup discs should be taken to an offsite location, perhaps to your office or another secure location.

If you work for a company, you can upload backup files to your corporate server computer. Typically, server operators back up all files each day. If you are self-employed, you can take advantage of the personal storage space made available to you by your ISP, usually from 5MB to 30MB.

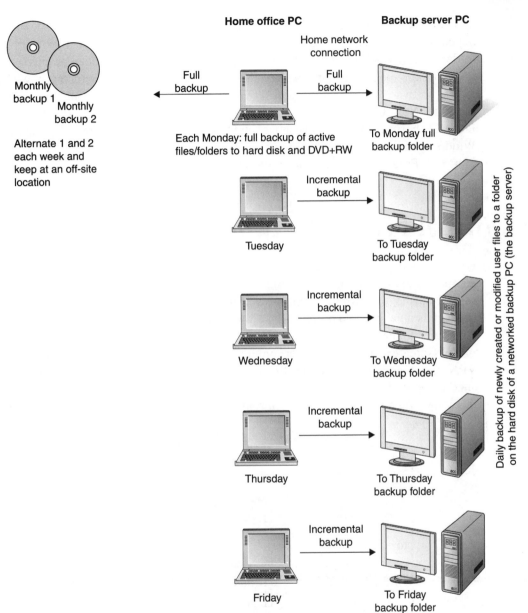

Figure 14-1 Daily/weekly/monthly backup procedure

The software that you would use to do full, incremental, and differential backups depends on what is available on your PC and the file/folder volatility. If your file/folder volatility is low, you can simply copy files that have been added or changed to the backup media via Windows Explorer. If file volatility is high, you might wish to use software with features that facilitate backing up and restoring files. For example, Nero 6 Ultra Edition has a BackItUp module (see Figure 14-2). Most DVD/CD burner programs have a backup feature that is more user friendly than the Windows XP backup utility. To back up files and folders using Windows XP, click Start | All Programs | Accessories | System Tools | Backup.

The Virtual Private Network

For decades, companies have leased communications lines from telecommunications companies to create their own private networks that link offices in remote locations, suppliers, and sometimes, employees who work at home. This type of private network is an expensive proposition. Now, there is a less expensive Internet-based alternative to the private network, called the *virtual private network,* or *VPN.*

VPNs create secure channels for communications over the Internet's infrastructure. VPN uses *tunneling* technology that enables one network to use the channels of another network to transmit information. In the case of VPNs, transmissions from the home office PC are "tunneled" through the Internet to the company LAN. The

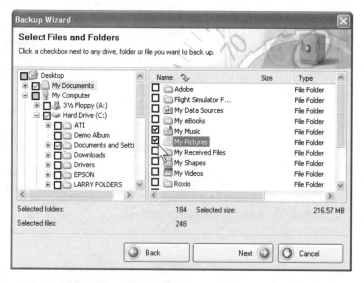

Figure 14-2   The Nero Backup Wizard guides you through the backup procedure.

flow of information over a VPN is secure because encryption and other measures are employed to ensure that communications are not intercepted and that only authorized users are allowed access to the LANs or home office PC. VPNs have been a boon to companies whose policies encourage telework and want mobile knowledge workers to stay connected.

Once the VPN link to the company network is established, the home office PC appears and acts like any other workstation on the LAN. This means that you, as a teleworker, have access to the same resources as those employees who commute to the office each day, including company files, databases, internal e-mail, printers, and the company *intranet* (an internal version of the Internet for employees). A home office PC with a VPN broadband link normally will operate at speeds similar to those of PCs at the company headquarters building.

The VPN link between the home office and the corporate office is illustrated in Figure 14-3. If you have a home network, you probably have the capability you need for a VPN link. Most modern home gateways support VPN and popular tunneling protocols, including *PPTP* (Point to Point Tunneling Protocol) and *L2TP* (Layer 2 Tunneling Protocol). Therefore, all you need to enable VPN is a VPN

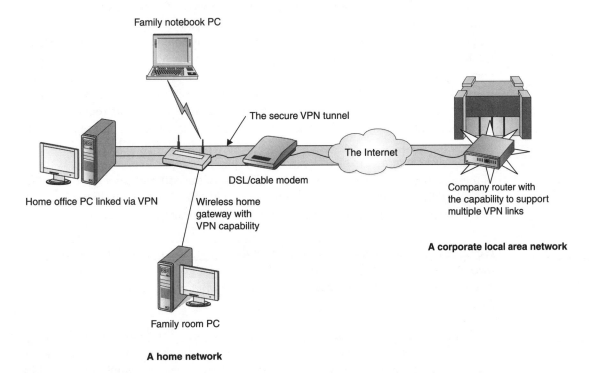

Figure 14-3 VPN transmissions are through a tunnel in the Internet.

home gateway and the connectivity settings provided by your company. The system administrator in your information technology department can give you the required settings and simple directions so that you can become a node on the company LAN from the comfort of your home office.

Home Office Productivity

Most of us who work at home enjoy a huge one-time boost in productivity when we recapture the time spent commuting to work, which is often an hour and as much as three hours each day. Improved productivity is always an objective for people who work at home because each minute saved in the office adds another minute to the time you spend with your family. This section contains several hints that have the potential to shift lots of minutes from work to family.

Virtually all of my online work is done in my office on my desktop PC. When I travel on business, I dump the files I need to a notebook PC via the home network. However, if I were traveling to client locations or commuting to a company office several days a week, my only PC would be a notebook. If your PC of preference is a notebook, I suggest that you purchase a *port replicator.*

The port replicator provides a quick and easy way to connect a notebook PC to the home network and other input/output devices in the home office. Also, with a port replicator you can enjoy the best of both worlds—portability plus the convenience of a desktop PC. Once "docked," the notebook PC has A/C power, is linked to the LAN, and can use whatever is connected to *ports* in the rear of the port replicator. Figure 14-4 shows a notebook PC that is inserted into a port replicator. If you would prefer to have a larger monitor, a full-size 104-key keyboard, quality speakers, and a mouse, then you may wish to purchase a port replicator and as many of these peripheral devices as you desire. The cost of the port replicator (around $200) and the additional input/output hardware is easily justified by the gains in productivity made possible by the improved ergonomics of the larger peripheral devices.

NOTE *An upscale variation on the port replicator is called a* docking station *(around $400). It may have additional functionality, such as a media bay for interchangeable notebook media modules (for example, a DVD+RW drive) or a PCI slot for an expansion card.*

The software that has made the greatest contribution to improving my productivity is speech recognition software. The home office is more conducive to the use of speech recognition than the company office, where colleagues would prefer not to listen to your unedited speech. I've been using speech recognition software since the

Figure 14-4   Notebook PC docked in a port replicator

mid-1990s, when the programs could only interpret discrete speech (slight separation between words). Today, I am able to enter text at the pace of speech, thus raising my productivity substantially and reducing the health risks associated with long-term keyboarding (primarily carpal tunnel syndrome). I use Dragon NaturalSpeaking, a ScanSoft, Inc. product, but the speech recognition feature built into modern versions of Microsoft Office suites works well, too. To set up the Microsoft Office version of speech recognition, click the Control Panel I Speech I Speech Recognition tab. Once you get used to the idiosyncrasies of speech recognition, you'll spend a lot less time answering e-mail, dictating reports, and entering data.

If you're looking for a quick way to improve your productivity by 10 percent to 20 percent and give yourself up to an hour and a half of extra time each day to work (or play), try going to a dual-monitor configuration. Until recently, most of us tacitly assumed that PCs have one monitor, one keyboard, and one mouse. Most modern PCs have video cards that support dual monitors, but if yours doesn't, you will need to upgrade the video card, which will cost from $50 to $200. If you are in a profession in which you routinely use three or more programs simultaneously, then you may realize dramatic improvements in productivity with dual monitors. On a dual-monitor system, the mouse pointer and application windows are moved seamlessly between the displays. A spreadsheet window can be stretched between the two viewing screens so that you can see the whole of an extra-wide spreadsheet.

NOTE *In the example in Figure 14-4, the notebook PC is closed and inserted into the port replicator. If you would prefer dual monitors, and your notebook PC supports dual monitors, you can open the notebook PC and use its monitor, too. Right-click on the desktop to open the Display Properties dialog box, and choose the Settings tab to arrange the dual-monitor configuration.*

I switched from a single 21-inch CRT display several years ago to two 19-inch flat panel monitors. Generally, I place my current work application on a primary display immediately in front of me and keep all online applications (e-mail, browser, and instant messaging), file management tools, and support documents on a secondary display positioned just to the right of the primary display (see Figure 2-6 in Chapter 2 for a photo of my dual-monitor setup). The extra viewing area has enabled me to work smarter, better, and a lot faster.

TIP *Typically, the graphics adapters with dual-monitor support have a standard VGA port and a DVI port. The DVI port, which supports both the analog VGA and digital DVI standards, is the next generation video interface. Most existing monitors have only a VGA connector. If your monitors are VGA, then you may need to purchase an inexpensive DVI-to-VGA adapter to connect both VGA monitors.*

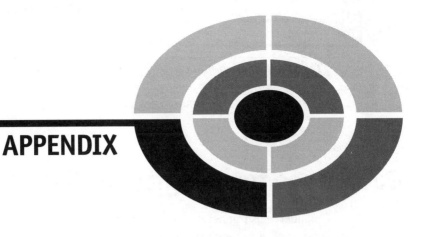

APPENDIX

Home Networking Buyer's Guide

Purchasing network devices is like purchasing any other consumer item: The more information you have, the more likely you are to buy the right products at a good price from a responsible retailer or e-tailer. This appendix includes guidelines, considerations, and recommendations to help you avoid purchasing pitfalls and get the network devices you need.

If you follow the network design process described in Chapter 6, the result is a graphic illustration of a home network and a shopping list. That list should identify all the hardware and software you need to implement the design. The focus in this appendix is the network devices on the list.

> ***TIP:*** *The companion book to this one,* Personal Computing Demystified *(Larry Long, McGraw-Hill/Osborne, 2004), devotes several chapters to buying personal computing equipment and related products.*

Guidelines for Purchasing Network Devices

Consider these general guidelines during your quest to buy the right devices in support of your network design.

- *Choose networking equipment that is compliant with established industry standards.* Having industry-standard net gear, such as IEEE 802.11g (Wireless-G) or Fast Ethernet, will ensure interoperability and, most likely, backward compatibility. On the other hand, choosing communications hardware based on a company's proprietary innovations, such as the enhanced Wireless-G products with 108 Mbps speeds, locks you into their equipment, which may or may not be supported in the next generation of communications hardware. Eventually, the next generation IEEE 802.11n (Wireless-N) standard for 108-plus Mbps wireless transmission will be approved and all vendors will begin building to that standard, thus enabling interoperability between all Wireless-N products, regardless of manufacturer.

- *Choose networking equipment that is current technology.* The relatively small extra amount you might pay to purchase current technology (for example, Wireless-G, or eventually, Wireless-N) versus older technology (for example, Wireless-B) is well worth it. Avoid buying heavily discounted net gear that is off the technology by a year or two.

- *Be consistent with your choice of vendors.* Purchase the same brand for all network devices other than the network adapters. This is especially true if you plan a wireless network. Network adapters, the exception to this guideline, are robust and seem to work well with network devices across all manufacturers. In theory, you should be able to mix and match industry-standard communications equipment from various manufacturers on a home network. In reality, however, each manufacturer devotes considerably more time to testing interoperability within its own line of products. Moreover, the manufacturer's technical support personnel are far more committed to solving your problem when they know that all of your network devices are their products.

- *Buy name brands.* A good rule of thumb for first-time buyers of communications gear is to go with name-brand products. The top home networking companies routinely offer specials and rebates that make their devices very competitive with off-brand products. The primary reason for this recommendation is that the name-brand vendors offer a complete line of networking products. When you decide to add a print server, you can be assured you can get one that is compatible with what you have. A secondary reason is that the name-brand company will be committed to comprehensive technical support. PC hardware is very reliable and can operate continuously without incident for years under harsh conditions, but occasionally, something can go wrong. When that happens, you'll appreciate having access to a major vendor's technical support resources.

Considerations for Purchasing Network Devices

Home networking is a very competitive marketplace, and good deals abound in your local stores and in cyberspace. Here are a few considerations, hints, and suggestions that might prove helpful when it comes time to make your selections:

- **Tremendous rate of return**   For most of us, the most difficult part of creating a home network is shelling out the money to purchase the equipment. Considering the impact that having a home network will have on your family's life and on domestic personal computing, you can take solace in the fact that your investment will be returned many times over.

- **Price as your guide**   All of the major manufacturers of networking devices offer quality hardware and service, so let price be your guide. If one of these companies has a promotion and can provide the equipment you need for your home network for $75 less than the others, I recommend that you go with this company and take your family out for a nice dinner with the savings. The major manufacturers are visually apparent in any big-box store, as they are allotted the lion's share of the shelf space.

- **Net gear with deep discounts**   You don't have to be on the bleeding edge of network technology, but you certainly don't want to buy hardware from the previous generation of network devices.

- **The full-function home gateway**   The typical multifunction home gateway will have a built-in router, an AP (if wireless), and a switch. However, home gateways come with a wide mix of built-in capabilities. If you know you want to convert to Voice over IP (VoIP) and your network design calls for an Ethernet print server, you can save $50 to $100 by purchasing a gateway that includes these features.

- **Home networking kits**   The typical home networking kit contains "everything you need" to set up a wireless home network with one wireless node. The kit normally will have a wireless home gateway with the basic router/AP functions, a CardBus network adapter, and possibly a PCI network adapter. These kits can cost as much or more than separately purchased devices. Generally, I would suggest that you avoid kits and retain the flexibility to purchase exactly what you want, device by device.

- **The stand-alone modem**   The broadband modem function can be built into the home gateway, but I would recommend that you use the stand-alone modem provided by your ISP. In this way, if you have connection problems, your ISP's technical support group is more willing and able to help you than they would if your modem is "unsupported." The rationale and exceptions to this rule are presented in Chapter 8.

- **Wireless network adapters**   I recommend you buy USB 2.0 wireless network adapters rather than the stationary PCI wireless adapters because the USB adapters can be physically positioned to give you the best possible signal.

- **Wireless at 108 Mbps**   At this writing, Wireless-N is yet to be approved and adopted as an industry standard by IEEE. Nevertheless, manufacturers are building and releasing "pre-N" devices that offer double the transmission speed of Wireless-G and a substantially expanded range. If you opt to step outside industry standards, be aware that the devices you purchase may not be compatible with true Wireless-N devices, should you wish to expand or upgrade your home network with the latest technologies at some time in the future. Also, understand that transmission speeds may drop to the lowest networking speed in a mixed-mode environment (for example, Wireless-G and pre-N products).

- **Ethernet cabling**   For wired home networks, I suggest you purchase and install either Cat 5e or Cat 6 cabling so that your infrastructure will be in place as we migrate to Gigabit Ethernet in the home. The cost of the better cabling (versus Cat 5) may add only a few dollars to the total cost of your network.

Which Network Device Manufacturer Is Best for You?

The networking industry is always changing with the technology and networking market demands. For example, media hubs capable of playing DVD-quality video are recent entries to the marketplace. Consequently, PC manufacturers are continually updating their product lines and adjusting their prices. Any decision about which network manufacturer is best must be made at a particular moment in time and for the circumstances of a particular buyer. All of these big-name manufacturers of home networking devices produce a complete line of quality devices that can be expected to last well beyond their useful life:

- Linksys (www.linksys.com)
- D-Link (www.dlink.com)
- NETGEAR (www.netgear.com)
- Belkin (www.belkin.com)
- SMC Networks (www.smc.com)

Other companies, including Network Everywhere, Blitzz, and electronics giant Motorola, produce and sell a full line of home networking equipment. Some companies produce specialty home network devices. For example, Hewlett-Packard manufactures the Media Center Extender, the media hub for Media Center PCs.

Ultimately, the answer to the question "Which networking manufacturer is best for you?" is the manufacturer that offers systems that provide the best match for your home networking needs and your bank account. Not surprisingly, that manufacturer could change from day to day. One day I went to Best Buy and the prices on the right side of the aisle were the most inviting. A few days later, a vendor on the other side of the aisle had declared a substantial rebate on every device in their extensive line, thus making their line of products the choice for the day.

Where to Buy Network Devices

Even into the late 1990s, network gear was designed for, priced for, and sold to the business world. Installing a home network in this era was cost-prohibitive and/or not technically feasible for most homes. For the most part, communications equipment was sold by traveling technical representatives who called on communications-savvy customers.

Today, home networking devices have emerged as popular consumer items that can be purchased at thousands of convenient bricks-and-mortar locations and from hundreds of retail sites on the Internet—electronic retailers or e-tailers. The various types of net gear retailers are discussed in this section and summarized in Table A-1.

I would like to think retailers have your best interest in mind when they make recommendations, but this may not always be the case. To be sure, they can be helpful, but keep in mind that they want to sell you something—anything. I visited a half dozen big-box electronics stores in several cities. In each, I described a mythical home scenario and asked for a "knowledgeable" salesperson's advice. Their advice ranged from flawed but helpful to self-serving. The best strategy is to understand home networking before you go in so that you will be a knowledgeable consumer.

Bricks-and-Mortar Retailers with Comprehensive Service Centers

There are thousands of independent computer and/or networking stores with no chain affiliation; several national retail chains; and many regional chains that specialize in the sale of PC hardware, software, and communications equipment. Most of these stores market and service a variety of PC systems and/or networking gear. Their authorized service centers are set up to address any personal computing or home networking concern. These dealers are easy to find; just look under "Computer and Equipment Dealers" or "Computer Networking" in the yellow pages.

Where to Buy Network Gear	Considerations
Bricks-and-mortar retailers with *comprehensive* service centers	Expert service and help; can provide on-site network installation, upgrade, and troubleshooting assistance
Bricks-and-mortar retailers with *basic* service centers	Can offer basic, but not comprehensive, service
Bricks-and-mortar retailers without service centers	Network devices sold as a consumer items with little or no in-store technical support
Direct marketers	Manufacturers provide support
Online e-tailers and telephone-order retailers	Wide variety of home networking devices at good prices
Online auctions	Hundreds of low-cost, high-risk "working" network devices (available 24/7)

Table A-1 Where to Buy Hardware and Software

Computer/networking retailers have their advantages, the big one being that they provide readily available personal "expert" service. Computer and networking retailers will help you design and install your network. Plus, these retailers typically are authorized service centers for the products they sell.

Bricks-and-Mortar Retailers with Basic Service Centers

Most audio/video/computer chains, college bookstores, and other specialty retailers sell PCs and net gear and provide basic services. Some will provide more extensive services than others. Mostly they sell prepackaged PC systems, but they will make minor changes to off-the-shelf PCs. A growing number of these stores are providing home networking design and installation services, too. The service charges for installing a home network are comparable to those of full-service companies.

Bricks-and-Mortar PC Retailers Without Service Centers

Computer/electronics departments of most department stores, "big box" discount stores, and office supply stores sell networking devices. These stores treat net gear and PCs as they do any consumer item. When you walk out the door, you are covered by the manufacturer's warranty, unless for some reason the system is obviously defective when you first attempt to use it. When this happens, a responsible merchandiser will exchange the device for one that works. Any support or advice from these types of establishments pretty much ends when the sales clerk hands you a receipt.

Direct Marketers

At this writing, only a few manufacturers of home network devices, such as D-Link and NETGEAR, sell directly to the customer. However, I expect these net gear manufacturers to follow the lead of PC and I/O device manufacturers who are experiencing success with direct sales. Major PC manufacturers who do direct marketing of their PCs, such as Dell and Gateway, will sell networking equipment as well. The direct marketer's "store window" is a web site on the Internet. Most orders are placed online via the Internet, but orders can also be submitted by telephone and fax. Usually, orders are shipped within a day or two, and deliveries are two to four days later.

Buying directly from the manufacturer via the Internet has many advantages. The manufacturers' web sites are comprehensive in that they present and sell their entire product line and they provide enough easily accessible information to answer most questions you might have. If you are looking for a home gateway with a unique mix of built-in functions, perhaps one with VoIP and a print server, you might find it more quickly by canvassing the online "shops" at the manufacturers' sites.

Online and Telephone-Order Retailers

The online/telephone order retailers provide an alternative to buying personal computing and home networking products at a bricks-and-mortar retail outlet. Most major bricks-and-mortar department stores, discount warehouses, electronics stores, and so on also have a presence on the Internet. You can buy a PC at any Wal-Mart or Best Buy store, or you can go to WalMart.com or BestBuy.com and get it there, too.

A number of online retailers specialize in the sale of PCs and electronics. E-tailers such as CDW, TigerDirect.com, Newegg.com, PC Mall, and many others have large online catalogs with literally thousands of items. Amazon.com (www.amazon.com), a general online retailer, offers a comprehensive line of networking devices. You can easily search their online catalogs to find what you need. I've ordered online computing and networking equipment scores of times over the years from many different e-tailers, and my experiences have been uniformly positive. I always get what I ordered, usually within two to four days. Online retailers are like bricks-and-mortar retailers in that when you click "buy," any further problems are between you and the manufacturer and are conducted within the restrictions of the warranty.

One of the beauties of Internet shopping is that comparison shopping is automated. Several Internet sites let you search dozens of online retailers to find the best price for a given item. In the example of Figure A-1, I requested prices for a Linksys Wireless-G Print Server and the CNET Shopper site (shopper.cnet.com). It returned pricing from 36 stores with a range of $106 to $149. It's a dream scenario for the smart shopper.

Many e-tailers offer customers the opportunity to post evaluations and reviews of products once they have had an opportunity to install and use them. Amazon.com and CNET Shopper do a good job with these online reviews. Customer reviews can be helpful as long as you keep them in perspective and remember that they come from individuals with widely varying backgrounds and biases.

The Internet is also a good source of information about customer satisfaction for various vendors. One of the best sources for information on online stores is ResellerRatings.com (www.resellerratings.com), where you can enter the e-tailer's name and then view cumulative ratings and read what customers have to say about the vendor. Comparison shopping sites such as CNET Shopper and PriceGrabber (www.pricegrabber.com) provide detailed merchant information as well.

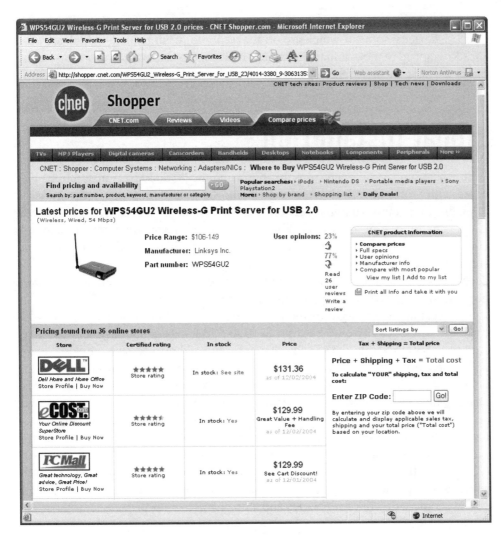

Figure A-1   Comparison shopping on the Internet

Online Auctions

A great source for anything is an online auction. PCs and networking equipment rank among the most popular items up for auction on the Internet. Online auctions go on 24 hours a day, with people all over the world registering bids on thousands of items. Each item has its own bidding period, and as in any auction, the item goes to the highest bidder.

At any given time, eBay, the most popular online auction site, lists hundreds of network devices, some of which are off the technology but many of which are new, shrink-wrapped in the original packaging. It's been my experience that the winning bid is less than the best retail or e-tail price.

Professional Installation

With what you have learned from this book and the "QuickStart" instructions that come with your network devices, you should be able to earn the satisfaction of implementing your own home network. As I indicated in Chapter 1, the tough part is the network design, not the installation. However, if you are computer/network challenged or don't have the time, professional help is readily available. Any specialty computer/networking retailer, any big-box electronics store with a service department, or any home technical support service, such as the Geek Squad (www. geeksquad.com), will be happy to install your home network—for a fee, of course.

A typical service charge for the professional installation of a wireless network with one wireless PC would be from $150 to $300, depending on where you live. Add from $30 to $60 to the service charge for the addition of each wireless device on the network. The service charge normally would include the installation of the broadband modem, the home gateway, and the network adapters, if needed. The charge would also include network testing. Of course, the cost of all hardware is over and above the service charge. The installation of Ethernet cabling for wired or mixed-mode networks is billed at an hourly rate that can range from $50 to $100 an hour.

There is a less professional and less costly solution. If your neighborhood is typical, you'll have at least one teenage technical wizard on your block who has experience with home networking and would be happy to help. Typically, these young people will work for cookies and a tip.

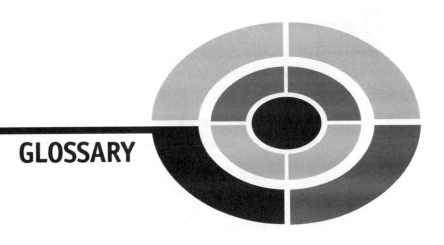

GLOSSARY

10/100 Ethernet   Reference to network devices and media that are compatible with 10 Mbps and 100 Mbps Ethernet.

10Base-T, 100Base-T, 1000Base-T   IEEE standards for 10 Mbps, 100 Mbps, 1000 Mbps Ethernet networks using UTP cabling.

1394 port   Enables connection to the IEEE 1394 (FireWire) bus, a standard that supports data transfer rates of up to 800 Mbps.

Access point (AP)   A base station for a wireless LAN that functions as a transceiver to connect one or many wireless devices to a wired LAN.

Ad hoc mode   An approach to creating a wireless peer-to-peer network where PCs communicate directly with no access point (AP) required. (Contrast with infrastructure mode.)

Address   A unique identifier for a specific LAN connection or network device. (See also IP address.)

Adware   Software that prompts targeted pop-up ads to display when you surf the Web and may gather and report personal information.

All-in-one multifunction printer   A multifunction device that can handle the paper-related tasks of printing, facsimile, scanning, and copying.

Antispyware software   A utility program that protects a PC from spyware programs.

Antivirus program   A utility program that protects a PC from computer viruses.

Applet   A small program sent over the Internet or an intranet that is interpreted and executed by Internet browser software.

ASCII file   A generic text file that is stripped of program-specific control characters.

Asynchronous transmission   A protocol in which data are transmitted at irregular intervals on an as-needed basis. (See also synchronous transmission.)

Attached file   A file that is appended to and sent with an e-mail message.

Backbone   A system of routers and the associated transmission media that facilitates the interconnection of computer networks.

Backup   Pertaining to equipment, procedures, or databases that can be used to restart the system in the event of system failure.

Backup file   Duplicate of an existing file.

Backup server   A PC or stand-alone file server (one or more hard disks) that provides storage space that other PCs can use to back up their files.

Bandwidth   Generally, the range of frequencies in a communications channel or, specifically, the number of bits the channel can transmit per second.

BIOS (Basic Input Output System)   Flash memory–based software that contains the instructions needed to boot a PC and load the operating system.

Bit A binary digit (0 or 1).

Bits per second (bps) The number of bits that can be transmitted per second over a communications channel.

Blog (web log) An online journal that includes the writings of some person or people.

Blogger A person who maintains and writes a blog.

Bluetooth A short-range wireless communications technology. (Contrast with Wi-Fi.)

Boot The procedure for loading the operating system to RAM and readying a computer system for use.

Bridge A device that connects any Ethernet device to a wireless home network.

Broadband Typically, a reference to a high-speed Internet link via cable, satellite, or DSL.

Browser A program that lets you navigate to, view, and interact with the various Internet resources.

Byte A group of adjacent bits configured to represent a character or symbol.

Cable modem A device that enables broadband Internet access via cable TV service.

CardBus An updated interface standard for the PC card. (See PC card.)

Cat 5, 5e, and 6 cabling Grades of LAN cabling that use twisted-pair wire with RJ-45 connectors to transmit data at speeds up to 1000 Mbps.

Channel The facility by which data are transmitted between locations in a computer network.

Channel capacity The number of bits that can be transmitted over a communications channel per second.

Chat   An Internet application that allows people on the Internet to converse in real time via text or audio.

Client PC   Typically, a PC or a workstation that requests processing support or another type of service from one or more server computers. (See also server PC.)

Client/server network   A networking environment in which processing capabilities are distributed throughout a network such that a client computer requests processing or some other type of service from a server computer.

Communications protocol   Rules established to govern the way data in a computer network are transmitted.

Computer virus   A man-made program or portion of a program that causes an unexpected event, usually a negative one, to occur within a computer system.

Cookie   A text file containing user preference information that is sent to a web server when its site is accessed.

Cracker   An overzealous hacker who "cracks" through network security to gain unauthorized access to the network. (Contrast with hacker.)

Crossover cable   A normal Ethernet cable except that the transmit data pair at one end is connected to the receive data pair at the other end to enable connectivity between two PCs or two switches. (See patch cable.)

CSMA/CA protocol   A IEEE 802.11 network access method that uses a collision avoidance technique requiring the network adapters to get permission to send information before actually transmitting it.

CSMA/CD protocol   An Ethernet network access method in which nodes on the LAN must contend for the right to send a message.

Data/voice/fax modem   A modem that permits data communication with remote computers via a telephone-line link and enables telephone calls and fax machine simulation via a PC.

Denial of service virus   A computer virus that places such heavy demands on e-mail server resources that the server is unable to handle the volume.

DHCP (Dynamic Host Configuration Protocol)   A communications protocol that works with TCP/IP to assign dynamic IP addresses.

DHCP server   A utility program that enables a server computer, including a multifunction home gateway/router, to dynamically assign IP addresses to PCs and network devices.

Dial-up connection   Temporary modem-based communications link with another computer.

Digital   A reference to any system based on discrete data, such as the binary nature of computers.

Digital home entertainment   An umbrella term that is used to describe the ability to manipulate and play digital media over a home network.

Digital signal   Electronic signals that are transmitted as in strings of 1's and 0's.

Digital Subscriber Line   See DSL.

Digitize   To translate data or an image into a discrete format that can be interpreted by computers.

Docking station   A device into which a notebook PC is inserted to give it expanded capabilities that might include a high-capacity disk, a large monitor, and a network connection.

Domain name   That portion of the Internet URL following the double forward slashes (//) that identifies an Internet host site.

Download   The transmission of data from a remote computer to a local computer.

Downstream rate   The data communications rate from server computer to client computer.

Drive mapping   A Windows feature that enables a disk drive or a folder on a networked PC to be assigned a drive letter so that it becomes a virtual disk that can be accessed directly through My Computer.

Driver   Software that enables interaction between the operating system and a specific peripheral I/O device or a network device.

DSL (Digital Subscriber Line)   A broadband digital communications standard for data delivery over twisted-pair lines with downstream transmission speeds up to 9 Mbps.

DSL modem   A device that enables broadband Internet access via a telephone service.

DSLAM (Digital Subscriber Line Access Multiplexer)   A device that communications companies use to multiplex DSL signals to/from the Internet.

DVR (digital video recorder)   A device that is capable of recording television programming in digital format on a hard drive (also called personal video recorder, or PVR).

Dynamic IP address   A temporary IP address that is assigned automatically to a PC or network device on an as-needed basis. (Contrast to static IP address.)

E-home   A home in which intelligent electronic devices communicate and cooperate through a home network to make our lives easier, safer, less expensive, and more enjoyable.

E-mail   A computer application whereby messages are transmitted via data communications to "electronic mailboxes" (also called electronic mail).

E-mail server   A host computer that services e-mail.

Encryption   The encoding of data for security purposes. Encoded data must be decoded or deciphered to be used.

Encryption key   An alphanumeric series that is used to scramble and unscramble the encrypted information sent over a network's communications links for the purpose of securing data transmissions.

E-tailing   Online retailing.

Ethernet   A LAN protocol for wired network implementations.

Ethernet card   An Ethernet network adapter for a PCI or notebook expansion slot.

EV-DO (Evolution-Data Optimized)   A wireless broadband capability based on a cell phone technology.

Fallback   A wireless communications feature that lets the transmission speed fall back or switch to a slower connection speed to maintain a reliable connection.

Fast Ethernet   An Ethernet standard that permits data transfer rates up to 100 Mbps.

Fiber optic cable   A data transmission medium consisting of very thin transparent fibers that carries data in the form of light impulses.

File server   A dedicated computer system with a high-capacity disk for storing the data and programs shared by the users on a LAN.

File Transfer Protocol (FTP)   A communications protocol used to transmit files over the Internet or any TCP/IP network.

Firewall   Software that is designed to protect a network from unauthorized Internet traffic.

FireWire   The Apple Computer Company name for the 1394 bus standard.

Firmware   Software or data stored in rewritable flash memory.

Full-duplex line   A communications channel that transmits data in both directions at the same time. (Contrast with half-duplex line.)

Gateway   See home gateway.

Gigabit Ethernet   An Ethernet standard that permits data transfer rates up to 1000 Mbps.

Hacker   A computer enthusiast who uses the computer as a source of mischievous recreation. (Contrast with cracker.)

Half-duplex line   A communications channel that transmits data in only one direction at a time. (Contrast with full-duplex line.)

Hexadecimal   A base-16 numbering system that uses 0 through 9 plus A through F for its numbers.

Home gateway   A multifunction device that can serve as a router to bridge the home network to the Internet, a wireless access point (AP), and a switch for wired connections; plus, it can provide other functions such as firewall, DHCP server, and NAT (also called residential gateway).

Home network   A network of PCs and other network devices in a home.

HomePlug   A standard that allows the elements of the network to communicate over a home's existing AC electrical power lines.

HomePNA (HPNA)   A Home Phoneline Networking Alliance standard that allows the elements of the network to communicate over a home's existing telephone wiring.

Hotspot   An area where wireless broadband service is made available to the public via one or more access points (may be called a coolspot in some parts of the world).

Hub   A multiport network device that enables transmissions from several Ethernet devices to be combined and transmitted over a single cable. (Contrast with switch.) Also, a common point of connection for computers and devices in a network.

IEEE 802.11a   See Wireless-A.

IEEE 802.11b   See Wireless-B.

IEEE 802.11g   See Wireless-G.

IEEE 802.11n   See Wireless-N.

Infrastructure mode   An approach to creating a wireless LAN such that connectivity is through an access point (AP). (Contrast with ad hoc mode.)

Instant messaging   An Internet application in which personal communications are sent and displayed in real time.

Internet (the Net)   A global network that connects millions of computers and networks.

Internet backbone   The major communications lines and nodes for the Internet to which thousands of Internet host computers are connected.

Internet Connection Sharing (ICS)   A capability built into Windows that permits a host PC to handle Internet sharing and other communications duties for networked PCs.

Internet Protocol address   See IP address.

Internet service provider (ISP)   Any company that provides individuals and organizations with access to or presence on the Internet.

Intranet   An Internet-like network whose scope is restricted to the networks within a particular organization.

IP (Internet Protocol)   An address-level set of rules than enables the sending and receiving of Internet messages. (See also TCP.)

IP address (Internet protocol address)   A four-number point-of-presence (POP) Internet address (for example, 206.28.104.10).

Ipconfig   A command that can be entered at the Windows command prompt to display the IP address of the current PC and its home gateway/router.

ISP   See Internet service provider.

Local area network (LAN or local net)   A system of hardware, software, and communications channels that connects PCs and network devices on the local premises. (Contrast with wide area network.)

Logoff   The procedure by which a user terminates a communications link with a remote computer. (Contrast with logon.)

Logon   The procedure by which a user establishes a communications link with a remote computer. (Contrast with logoff.)

Mailing list   An Internet-based capability that lets people discuss issues of common interest via common e-mail.

Malware   Malicious software that is designed to damage your PC, disrupt its operation, or in some way violate its security.

Media Access Control (MAC) address   A six-byte hardware address, which usually is displayed as 12 hexadecimal digits, that uniquely identifies each node on a LAN.

Media Center Extender   The media hub that is designed to work in conjunction with Media Center PCs.

Media Center PC   A PC especially configured to work with Windows XP Media Center Edition and run all forms of home digital entertainment.

Media hub   A network device that serves as an interface between the PCs on a home network, the Internet, and audio/visual equipment.

Media server   A PC that stores the images, music, and video files that are shared throughout a network.

Modem (modulator-demodulator)   A device used to convert computer-compatible signals to signals that can be transmitted over the telephone or cable lines and then turned back to computer signals at the other end of the line.

MP3   A sound file format that enables CD-quality music to be compressed to about 8 percent of its original size while retaining CD sound quality.

MPEG   A video file format with the extension MPG or MPEG.

Network   Any group of PCs or network devices linked via wired and/or wireless media.

Network adapter   A PCI card, PC card module, CardBus module, or equivalent external USB device that facilitates and controls the exchange of data between the PC and its network (also called a network interface card, or NIC).

Network Address Translation (NAT)   A networking capability that permits multiple PCs to dynamically share an incoming IP address from a broadband Internet.

Network interface card (NIC)   A network adapter in the form of a PCI expansion card or a notebook PC expansion module.

Network topology   The configuration of the interconnections between the nodes in a communications network.

Node   An endpoint on the network that has a unique network address.

Offline   Pertaining to data and/or hardware devices that are not connected to a computer system and/or network. (Contrast with online.)

Online   Pertaining to data and/or hardware devices accessible to and under the control of a computer system and/or network. (Contrast with offline.)

Operating system   The software that controls the execution of all applications and system software programs.

Packet   Part of a message sent over a packet-switching network that contains strings of bits that represent information and a network address.

Packet switching   A reference to a communications protocol that separates messages into packets for transmission and recompiles them at the destination.

Password   A word or phrase, known only to the user, that when entered permits the user to gain access to the system.

Patch cable   A preassembled Ethernet cable used to connect devices in a LAN.

Path   The hierarchy of LAN PCs, disks, and folders that leads to the location of a particular file.

PC card   A credit-card-sized module that is inserted into the PCMCIA-compliant interface of a notebook PC to offer add-on capabilities such as expanded memory, fax modem, network adapter, and so on.

Peer-to-peer network   A network in which all computers are capable of functioning as a client or a server (called a workgroup in Windows terminology).

Ping   A command that can be entered at the command prompt to determine how long it takes for an echo message to make a round-trip to a particular IP address on the Internet or a network.

Plenum cable   Ethernet cable with a fire-retardant sheath.

POP (point of presence)   A telephone line access point to the Internet.

Port   An access point in a PC or network device that permits communication between other PCs or network devices on a LAN.

Port filtering   A firewall feature that serves to insulate home gateways and their networks from cracker/hacker attacks by blocking entry to certain ports.

Port scanner software   Programs used by crackers and hackers to search the Internet for unprotected networks and PCs.

Print server   A stand-alone network device or feature built into a printer that enables a printer to be connected directly to a LAN.

Private IP address   An IP address that is used only within the confines of a LAN to route information to the appropriate PC (also called internal address).

Protocol   See communications protocol.

Proxy server computer   A computer between the client PC and the actual server computer that handles many client requests before they reach the server computer.

PVR (personal video recorder)   Same as DVR.

Radio frequency (RF) signals   Line-of-sight wireless data communications between radio transmitters and receivers.

Residential gateway   See home gateway.

RJ-11   The standard four-pin connector used for telephones and for HomePNA networks.

RJ-45   The standard eight-pin connector used for Ethernet networks.

Router   A device that connects two networks.

Secure Sockets Layer (SSL)   A protocol for transmitting sensitive information via the Internet.

Server   Any computer or device on a network that provides some service for other PCs and network devices on the LAN.

Server PC   A PC that provides some type of service or resources for the other PCs and devices on the network.

Shielded twisted pair (STP)   Cabling used for LANs that contains pairs of copper wires that are insulated with a protective coating and twisted to reduce external signal interference. The protective covering minimizes the impact of electromagnetic interference while protecting the wires from the elements. (Contrast with unshielded twisted pair.)

Smart home   Same as e-home.

Socket   The unique IP address and port number embedded in an Internet packet that directs communication on the Internet.

Spyware   Any clandestine program that gathers and reports personal information via an Internet link without the knowledge of the user.

SSID (service set identifier)   A unique 32-character identifier, sometimes called a network name, that is embedded within wireless LAN packets.

Star topology   A network design in which devices are connected to a central hub (for example, a home gateway), creating the appearance of a star.

Static IP address   An IP address that is permanently assigned to an Internet node. (Contrast to dynamic IP address.)

Streaming audio   Internet-based audio that is received and played in a steady, continuous stream.

Streaming video   Internet-based video that is received and played in a steady, continuous stream.

Structured wiring   A reference to the integration of all household communications, entertainment, and security wiring within a single wiring system.

Switch   An intelligent hub that facilitates the transmission of network traffic between connected Ethernet devices (also called a network switch or Ethernet switch).

Synchronous transmission   A communications protocol in which the source and destination points operate in timed alignment to enable high-speed data transfer. (See also asynchronous transmission.)

TCP   A communications protocol used with the Internet Protocol (IP) to transmit data in packets between computers on the Internet and in networks. (See also IP.)

TCP/IP (Transmission Control Protocol/Internet Protocol)   The foundation communications technology for the Internet and home networks.

Telework   An umbrella term used to describe work done at home via personal computing, home networking, and the Internet.

Tunneling   The technology where one network uses the channels of another network to send its data.

Twisted-pair wire   A pair of insulated copper wires twisted around each other for use in transmission of telephone conversations and for cabling in local area networks.

Unshielded twisted pair (UTP)   Cabling used for LANs and telephone lines that contains pairs of copper wires that are twisted to reduce external signal interference. (Contrast with shielded twisted pair.)

Upload   The transmission of data from a local computer to a remote computer.

Upstream rate   The data communications rate from client computer to server computer.

Virtual private network (VPN)   A secure, private network that is based on tunneling technology and uses the Internet as a medium for communications.

VoIP (Voice over IP) A technology that enables telephone calls to be made over the Internet.

VPN See virtual private network.

WAN See wide area network.

Webcam A digital video camera that sends still and video imagery over the Internet or a LAN.

WEP See Wired Equivalent Privacy.

Wide area network (WAN) A computer network that connects nodes in widely dispersed geographic areas. (Contrast with local area network.)

Wi-Fi A generic reference to the IEEE 802.11 communications standard.

Wi-Fi Protected Access (WPA) An enhanced Wi-Fi encryption technique that employs authentication via user ID and password.

Windows XP Media Center Edition 2005 This newest version of Windows that includes support for sophisticated digital home entertainment applications.

Wired Equivalent Privacy (WEP) A basic Wi-Fi security feature that uses data encryption techniques to scramble information passed between wireless devices.

Wireless access point (WAP) Same as access point (AP).

Wireless network bridge A network device used to link the wired Ethernet segment of a network to the wireless portions of a network (also called a wireless Ethernet bridge.)

Wireless signal booster A network device that can extend the coverage area of a wireless access point.

Wireless Zero Configuration (WZC) A Windows feature that enables auto configuration for wireless network devices.

Wireless-A An IEEE standard (802.11a) for wireless networks that operates up to 50 feet at a transfer rate of 54 Mbps.

Wireless-B An IEEE standard (802.11b) for wireless networks that operates up to 300 feet at a transfer rate of 11 Mbps.

Wireless-G An IEEE standard (802.11g) for wireless networks that operates up to 300 feet at a transfer rate of 54 Mbps.

Wireless-N A proposed IEEE standard (802.11n) for wireless networks that operates up to 1000 feet at a transfer rate of 200 Mbps.

WPA See Wi-Fi Protected Access.

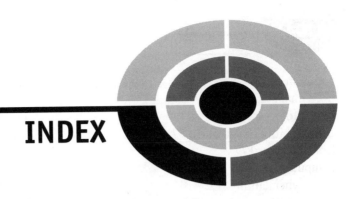

INDEX

CHANGE PRINTER
right click on Printer in
Control Panel

INTERNATIONAL CONTACT INFORMATION

AUSTRALIA
McGraw-Hill Book Company
Australia Pty. Ltd.
TEL +61-2-9900-1800
FAX +61-2-9878-8881
http://www.mcgraw-hill.com.au
books-it_sydney@mcgraw-hill.com

CANADA
McGraw-Hill Ryerson Ltd.
TEL +905-430-5000
FAX +905-430-5020
http://www.mcgraw-hill.ca

GREECE, MIDDLE EAST, & AFRICA
(Excluding South Africa)
McGraw-Hill Hellas
TEL +30-210-6560-990
TEL +30-210-6560-993
TEL +30-210-6560-994
FAX +30-210-6545-525

MEXICO (Also serving Latin America)
McGraw-Hill Interamericana Editores
S.A. de C.V.
TEL +525-1500-5108
FAX +525-117-1589
http://www.mcgraw-hill.com.mx
carlos_ruiz@mcgraw-hill.com

SINGAPORE (Serving Asia)
McGraw-Hill Book Company
TEL +65-6863-1580
FAX +65-6862-3354
http://www.mcgraw-hill.com.sg
mghasia@mcgraw-hill.com

SOUTH AFRICA
McGraw-Hill South Africa
TEL +27-11-622-7512
FAX +27-11-622-9045
robyn_swanepoel@mcgraw-hill.com

SPAIN
McGraw-Hill/
Interamericana de España, S.A.U.
TEL +34-91-180-3000
FAX +34-91-372-8513
http://www.mcgraw-hill.es
professional@mcgraw-hill.es

UNITED KINGDOM, NORTHERN,
EASTERN, & CENTRAL EUROPE
McGraw-Hill Education Europe
TEL +44-1-628-502500
FAX +44-1-628-770224
http://www.mcgraw-hill.co.uk
emea_queries@mcgraw-hill.com

ALL OTHER INQUIRIES Contact:
McGraw-Hill/Osborne
TEL +1-510-420-7700
FAX +1-510-420-7703
http://www.osborne.com
omg_international@mcgraw-hill.com

Sound Off!

Visit us at **www.osborne.com/bookregistration** and let us know what you thought of this book. While you're online you'll have the opportunity to register for newsletters and special offers from McGraw-Hill/Osborne.

We want to hear from you!

Sneak Peek

Visit us today at **www.betabooks.com** and see what's coming from McGraw-Hill/Osborne tomorrow!

Based on the successful software paradigm, Bet@Books™ allows computing professionals to view partial and sometimes complete text versions of selected titles online. Bet@Books™ viewing is free, invites comments and feedback, and allows you to "test drive" books in progress on the subjects that interest you the most.